NORMAN PERRIN

THE KINGDOM OF GOD
IN THE TEACHING OF JESUS

NORMAN PERRIN

THE KINGDOM OF GOD
IN THE TEACHING
OF JESUS

SCM PRESS LTD

334 00838 7
First published 1963 by
SCM Press Ltd,
26–30 Tottenham Road, London N1 4BZ
Fourth impression 1984

Printed in Great Britain by
Richard Clay (The Chaucer Press) Ltd,
Bungay, Suffolk

To those two great
New Testament scholars with whom it has been
the author's privilege to study:
T. W. Manson of Manchester
J. Jeremias of Göttingen

CONTENTS

PREFACE

THE FOLLOWING work is a revised version of a Dr. Theol. dissertation originally submitted to the University of Göttingen in 1959. It is my hope that the theological faculty of that University will accept this book as fulfilling the requirements for publication of the dissertation.

It is now my pleasant duty to express my deep sense of gratitude for the help that I have received at the various stages of this work. It was Professor T. W. Manson who first awakened my interest in the study of the teaching of Jesus during my student days at Manchester University, and it was Professor J. Jeremias, my *Doktorvater*, who guided and helped me at every stage of my work in Göttingen. All students of the teaching of Jesus are immeasurably indebted to these two great scholars, and any merit that this present work possesses is due in large measure to the privilege that the author has enjoyed in working closely with them. Then to a lesser, but none the less real extent I am indebted to Professor James M. Robinson, who read the original dissertation while he was a visiting professor in Göttingen and made detailed comments upon it which have helped me greatly, especially in the work of revision.

At the practical level I am indebted to the World Council of Churches for the scholarship which enabled me to spend a year at the *Kirchliche Hochschule* in Berlin, to Dr Williams's Trust for a travelling exhibition, and above all to the Alexander von Humboldt Foundation for the fellowship that made possible my two years of doctoral work in Göttingen. The original impulse towards the publication of this work I owe to Professor Jeremias, but the translation of this impulse into actuality would not have been possible without the help and encouragement of the editor of the SCM Press, the Rev. D. L. Edwards, nor could the manuscript have reached its present form without the skill of his editorial assistant, Miss Jean Cunningham. My two assistants, John B. Sheppard and John D. Thompson, have helped me greatly in the task of checking references, reading proofs and preparing indices.

Last but by no means least, my thanks are due to my wife, Rosemary, for without her constant encouragement and glad preparedness to sacrifice herself and her interests to its demands no part of this work could have been accomplished.

Emory University, Atlanta   NORMAN PERRIN
January, 1963

ABBREVIATIONS

BJRL	*Bulletin of the John Rylands Library*
DJD	Barthélemy and Milik, *Discoveries in the Judaean Desert*, 1955 ff.
ET	English translation
EVV	English versions
ExpT	*Expository Times*
JBL	*Journal of Biblical Literature*
JBR	*Journal of Bible and Religion*
JEH	*Journal of Ecclesiastical History*
JR	*Journal of Religion*
LXX	Septuagint
MT	Massoretic Text
NEB	New English Bible
NT	*Novum Testamentum*
NTS	*New Testament Studies*
PEQ	*Palestine Exploration Quarterly*
PL	Migne, Patrologia Latina
RGG	*Religion in Geschichte und Gegenwart*
RSV	Revised Standard Version
SJT	*Scottish Journal of Theology*
TLZ	*Theologische Literaturzeitung*
TR	*Theologische Rundschau*
TWNT	*Theologisches Wörterbuch zum Neuen Testament*, ed. G. Kittel, 1932 ff.
VT	*Vetus Testamentum*
ZNW	*Zeitschrift für die neutestamentliche Wissenschaft*
ZTK	*Zeitschrift für Theologie und Kirche*
	For abbreviations of Qumran scrolls, see *DJD* I

I

THE DISCUSSION BEGINS

THE COMING OF *KONSEQUENTE ESCHATOLOGIE*

THE MODERN DISCUSSION of the Kingdom of God in the teaching of Jesus may be said to begin with Schleiermacher. Not that he was particularly concerned with the concept as it is used in the teaching of Jesus—far from it!—but he did give the concept itself a central place in his theology and so brought it into focus for modern theological discussion. Following him Ritschl also gave a central place to the Kingdom of God and did make some attempt to relate his use of the concept to the teaching of Jesus. Then came Johannes Weiss, who protested that justice was not being done to the teaching of Jesus in this regard and who offered an interpretation of that teaching radically different from anything that had gone before him. Finally Albert Schweitzer took up Weiss's interpretation of the teaching of Jesus and used it as the basis for a challenging interpretation of the life of Christ which attracted wide attention, and as a result of which the modern discussion really got under way.

SCHLEIERMACHER

In his great work *The Christian Faith*[1] Schleiermacher understands the Kingdom of God as all-important and indeed all-inclusive for Christianity (§ 9.2). It is the corporate life of Christians in fellowship with God made possible and indeed founded by Christ (§ 87.3; 90.1) within which men become truly conscious of God (§ 90.2). This consciousness of God within the corporate life which is the Kingdom of God is possible only because of Christ's God-consciousness in which alone there is an existence of God in any proper sense. Christ's God-consciousness is the impulse and dynamic through which the human

---

[1] *Der Christliche Glaube* [1]1821, [2]1830. ET of the second edition, edited by H. R. Mackintosh and J. S. Stewart, *The Christian Faith*, 1928.

God-consciousness becomes an existence of God in human nature (§ 94.2).

For Schleiermacher therefore the Kingdom of God is the corporate human God-consciousness which is the existence of God in human nature and which comes into being as a result of Christ's God-consciousness (§ 164.1). This Kingdom of God is the sole object of the divine world government, and individual believers are the objects of the divine care in that the divine care is bent on furthering their activity in the Kingdom, i.e. their manifestation of God in the world through their corporate God-consciousness (§ 164 f.).

The corporate God-consciousness that is the Kingdom has come into being as a result of the redemptive work of Christ in that the God-consciousness that was already present in human nature, although enfeebled and oppressed, is stimulated and made dominant by the entrance into human nature of the living influence of Christ and of his dynamic God-consciousness (§ 106.1). Within the Kingdom there is a communication by Christ of his sinless perfection to others, and all developing blessedness known and to be known will be within this corporate life and through the communication of the absolutely potent God-consciousness of Christ to others (§ 87 f.). All that comes to exist in the world as a result of redemption is embraced in the fellowship of believers that is the Kingdom (§ 113).

It has been well said of Schleiermacher that what we find in his thought is only too often 'but the attenuated creed of idealistic Monism',[1] and certainly there seems to be more of Monism than there is of biblicism in his understanding of the Kingdom of God. But his work is important not because of the interpretation he offers but simply because he did give such a central place in his thought to the Kingdom of God. His work was tremendously influential[2] and the importance he gave to the Kingdom of God led others to turn their attention to this concept, and especially it led Albrecht Ritschl to do so.

RITSCHL

'The concept of the Kingdom of God has been brought to the centre

---

[1] H. R. Mackintosh, *Types of Modern Theology*, 1937, p. 100.
[2] Not for nothing does Karl Barth, himself no follower of Schleiermacher, devote four times as much space to Schleiermacher as to anyone else except that strange and stormy petrel, D. F. Strauss, in his *Die Protestantische Theologie im 19. Jahrhundert*, ²1952 (ET, abridged, *From Rousseau to Ritschl*, 1959).

of current theological interest through Albrecht Ritschl.'[1] Thus
Johannes Weiss in tribute to one whose understanding of the concept
he was to criticize very severely. Ritschl begins with the work of
Schleiermacher and agrees with him that the concept of the Kingdom
of God is all-important for Christianity and is the embodiment of the
divine final end, the redemption that has come through Christ being
the means to that end. But he criticizes Schleiermacher for not having
done justice to the teleological nature of the Kingdom of God as the
divine end, and for not having made clear the mutual relationship
between this final end and the function of the Mediator.[2] These
essential weaknesses in Schleiermacher's view Ritschl proposes to
remedy by describing Christianity, not as a circle described from a
single focal point, but as an ellipse determined by two focal points.[3]

The first of these two focal points is the redemption wrought by
Christ, which is that freedom from guilt and over the world to be won
through the realized Fatherhood of God. It is the divine operation
whereby through the redeemer this is established for each individual
Christian; it is freedom in God, the freedom of the children of God,
and it is the personal end of the individual Christian. The second
focal point is the Kingdom of God. This is the specifically teleological
aspect of Christianity; arising out of redemption it is the moral
organization of humanity through action inspired by love; it is the
common end of God and of Christians as a community—and it is the
goal to which the believer directs his spiritual and ethical activity.
Redemption is therefore the function of the redeemer; activity
directed toward the establishment of the Kingdom of God is the
function of the redeemed.[4]

In order to express the relationship between redemption and the
Kingdom of God in Ritschl's thought we might characterize it in
three ways, putting the emphasis respectively upon God, upon Christ
and upon the individual Christian. Putting the emphasis upon God
we may say that the revelation of God is directed to the first goal of
redemption, and also to the final end of the Kingdom which he

[1] Johannes Weiss, *Die Idee des Reiches Gottes in der Theologie*, 1901, p. 1. The
translation is by the present writer, as will always be the case in this work when
a quotation is given in English and the book quoted is referred to by its German
title.

[2] A. Ritschl, *Rechtfertigung und Versöhnung*, 3 vols., [1]1870–74, [2]1883, [3](Vol. III)
1888. English translation of vol. III edited by H. R. Mackintosh and A. B.
Macaulay, *The Christian Doctrine of Justification and Reconciliation*, [2]1902, p. 9.

[3] *Ibid.*, p. 11.

[4] *Ibid.*, pp. 11–13.

realizes in fellowship with the redeemed. With the emphasis upon Christ we may say that the life and activity of Jesus, the Founder of Christianity, issued at once in redemption and in the foundation of the Kingdom of God, the expansion of which he entrusts to his disciples as a moral task. With the emphasis upon the individual Christian we may say that he is redeemed and enabled to dedicate himself to the work of establishing the Kingdom of God.

In all of this the Kingdom of God is conceived by Ritschl in purely ethical terms. Jesus saw in the Kingdom of God the moral task to be carried out by the human race, and, as we have already said, it is the organization of humanity through action inspired by love.[1] Christianity itself is therefore both completely spiritual and thoroughly ethical. It is completely spiritual in the freedom given to the children of God through redemption, which involves the impulse to conduct through the motive of love—and it is thoroughly ethical in that this conduct is directed towards the moral organization of mankind, the establishment of the Kingdom of God.[2] Karl Barth has summed up Ritschl's thought very well by saying that at its heart lies the concept of a completed reconciliation in which God confronts the believer as Father, gives him spiritual dominion over the world and sets him to work in the Kingdom of God![3]

JOHANNES WEISS

The most important criticism of Ritschl's interpretation of the Kingdom of God is that by Johannes Weiss. He began his contribution to the discussion with a short work of some sixty-seven pages[4] in which he welcomed the growing interest in and emphasis upon the concept in the current theological discussion, and pointed out that in using what was admittedly the central concept in the teaching of Jesus theologians ought to begin by making a conscious attempt to interpret that teaching in its original and historical form, being careful not to read into it modern ideas foreign to the world in which Jesus taught.[5] This sounds obvious and innocuous enough and Weiss must have felt that the matter would not be too difficult, since he did it in sixty-

[1] *Ibid.*, p. 12. Cf. Vol. II, p. 28.
[2] *Ibid.*, p. 13.
[3] K. Barth, *Die Protestantische Theologie in 19. Jahrhundert*, [2]1952, p. 601 (ET, p. 393).
[4] *Die Predigt Jesu vom Reiche Gottes*, 1892 (= *Predigt*[1]).
[5] *Predigt*[1], p. 7.

seven pages. But Weiss's historical interpretation of the Kingdom of God in the teaching of Jesus proved to be so radically different from anything that had gone before that a veritable storm broke around his head and to defend himself he wrote two further works: a full-scale' critical study of the concept of the Kingdom of God as it had been used in systematic theology[1] and a second edition of his book on the Preaching of Jesus concerning the Kingdom of God.[2] This second edition was, in fact, a completely new book; it had grown to 214 pages and included a thorough and detailed criticism of the views of some of his contemporaries, and especially of the views of Ritschl, his own teacher and father-in-law.

In the foreword to *Predigt*[2] he writes that as a student with Ritschl he had been troubled by the feeling that Ritschl's understanding of the Kingdom of God and the concept of that same name in the teaching of Jesus were two very different things, and in the course of his work he develops three major criticisms of Ritschl. In the first place Ritschl does not do justice to the antithesis between the Kingdom of God and the Kingdom of Satan to be found in such apocalyptic passages as Assumption of Moses 10.1 ff., and in the teaching of Jesus at Matt. 12.25–9.[3] Secondly, he puts the emphasis upon the activity of men in building the Kingdom, whereas in the teaching of Jesus the emphasis is upon the Kingdom of God as the activity of God as king. Far from being built or furthered by the work of men it is the irruption of God as king into history which has its nearest previous parallel in the Flood.[4] Thirdly, Ritschl sees the intention of Jesus as being to make a beginning of something that would develop into a moral organization of humanity. This assumes a continuity of human history in which the coming of Jesus marks the beginning of a new epoch. But Jesus himself took an absolutely opposite view; he is conscious that he stands at the end of the world and at the end of history. The one thing remaining is the Judgment, and what will come after the Judgment is not a development in human affairs but the absolute opposite of any development: the consummation of all things in which God will be All in All.[5]

Weiss's criticism of Ritschl is simply that he is not building his understanding of Kingdom of God on the basis of the understanding

[1] *Die Idee des Reiches Gottes in der Theologie*, 1900 (= *Idee*).
[2] *Die Predigt Jesu vom Reiche Gottes*, [2]1900 (= *Predigt*[2]).
[3] *Idee*, p. 111; *Predigt*[2], pp. 26–35.
[4] Referring to Luke 17.26. *Idee*, pp. 111 f; *Predigt*[2], pp. 2–11, 105 ff.
[5] *Idee*, pp. 112 f; *Predigt*[2], pp. 40–48.

which we find in the teaching of Jesus[1] and in his own work Weiss is, as we said above, solely concerned to offer an historically accurate interpretation of the teaching of Jesus in this regard. He begins by pointing out that the concept of the Kingdom of God can be viewed in two ways, depending upon whether the emphasis is put upon God as ruler or upon man as subject of that rule. In Jewish thought both of these emphases are to be found and the second emphasis tends to concentrate attention upon those moments or experiences in which men come to know the rule of God. The high point of this develop-ment is the rabbinical conception of an act of obedience whereby a man or a people take upon themselves the yoke of the Kingdom of God.[2] Involved in this conception is the idea of the rule of God as something that is eternal; a continuous and lasting ordering of things which a man may deny or reject but which he ought to accept in an act of obedience whereby the Kingdom becomes manifest in his experience. In the teaching of Jesus, however, the Kingdom of God is conceived quite differently from this; it is the breaking out of an overpowering divine storm which erupts into history to destroy and to renew, and which a man can neither further nor influence.[3]

The true background to Jesus' teaching is to be found in that aspect of Jewish thought concerning the Kingdom of God where the emphasis is put upon God as ruler, and upon his Kingdom as the manifestation of his kingly activity.[4] Weiss claims that this is the dominant emphasis in the Old Testament, and he shows that such

---

[1] In the preface to *Predigt*[2] he writes: 'I am still of the opinion that his (Ritschl's) theological system, and especially this central concept (of the Kingdom of God), presents that form of teaching concerning the Christian faith which is most effectively designed to bring our generation nearer to the Christian religion; and, properly understood and rightly used, to awaken and further a sound and strong religious life such as we need today' (p.v). This is an interesting example of the gulf that has existed in Germany between the academic study of theology and the practical work of the Church; or perhaps it is simply that Weiss is being respectful to his teacher and father-in-law!

[2] This was used as the key to understanding the teaching of Jesus by Dalman, see below pp. 23–25, and later by T. W. Manson, following Paul Billerbeck, below pp. 92 f.

[3] *Predigt*[2], p. 5. It is impossible to reproduce in English the vividness of Weiss's German here. He writes that the Kingdom of God in the teaching of Jesus is '*das Losbrechen eines überwältigenden Gottessturms, der vernichtend und erneuernd einherbraust . . . den der Mensch weder herbeiführen noch beeinflüssen kann*'.

[4] This is wholly in keeping with Dalman's findings concerning the actual meaning of the phrases translated 'Kingdom of God', reported below, pp. 23 f. Weiss does not, in fact, discuss the meaning of the Hebrew and Aramaic terms, not even in *Predigt*[2] when the work of Dalman was available to him.

an emphasis carries with itself the thought of conflict with a worldly or human kingship. The conception is that God will demonstrate his kingship by an act of judgment against the worldly kingship.[1] Against this background we can see that it was natural for the prophets and apocalyptists, when they proclaimed the great crisis that was to come, to do so in the form of a proclamation of the coming of a mighty act of God as king. Such proclamations we find in Isa. 40.10; 52.7; 52.9 f. (the coming of an eschatological act of redemption of which the Exodus events will have been the prototype); Zech. 14.9, 16–21 (the eschatological victory of monotheism over all the peoples); and Obadiah (the Day of the Lord will bring the destruction of Edom and the Jewish reconquest of Palestine) in all of which we find either the verb or the noun from the Hebrew root *m-l-k* (to rule) used in reference to God. The hope expressed in these proclamations is for the coming of a mighty kingly activity of God whereby his people would be redeemed, his enemies and theirs destroyed, and the present evil state of things totally and for ever reversed. This hope is the foundation stone upon which all apocalyptic is built, and it is this hope which is expressed in the ancient Kaddish prayer of the Synagogue, almost certainly contemporary with Christ: 'Magnified and sanctified be his great name in the world which he has created according to his will. May he establish his kingdom in your lifetime and in your days and in the lifetime of all the house of Israel ever speedily and at a near time.'[2] It is this hope which lies behind Jesus' usage of the term Kingdom of God. 'The greatness of Jesus is . . . that he lived, fought and suffered for the conviction that the sovereignty of God was now about to be manifest and to achieve for ever the victory. What in late Judaism was a longing and a hope for the distant future is for Jesus an immediate certainty: God is indeed the single Lord and King of the World. The time has now come when he will demonstrate this and destroy all his enemies. Jesus is the herald of this new epoch; his words are not instruction but gospel; his work is a battle for the things of God, and its starting-point is the assurance of God's victory. He left behind for the community of his followers not a new teaching concerning the Kingdom of God but the certainty that Satan was fallen and the world in God's hand.'[3]

[1] *Predigt*[2], pp. 9–11.

[2] *Predigt*[2], p. 15. We owe the recognition of the antiquity of this Aramaic prayer, and the establishment of the text of it translated above, to Dalman who however, interpreted it differently. See below, pp. 26 f.

[3] *Predigt*[2], p. 35.

This is Johannes Weiss's great contribution to the discussion; his brilliantly and decisively argued claim that there is an essential relationship between the teaching of Jesus and the teaching of prophetic and apocalyptic Judaism concerning the Kingdom of God, and that the teaching of Jesus must be interpreted against the background of this relationship. Popularized by Albert Schweitzer, this view was at first to be vehemently rejected, especially in Britain and America but eventually it was to prove irresistible, as we shall see.

On the basis of this insight Johannes Weiss proceeds to an interpretation of the teaching of Jesus, and the first main point he makes is that the coming of the Kingdom of God is expected by Jesus in the immediate future. Sayings which speak of the Kingdom as 'at hand' (*ēggiken*) i.e. Matt. 4.17; 10.7; Luke 10.9; 10.11; 21.31 (*eggus estin*); Mark 1.15; are used to control the interpretation of Matt. 12.28 = Luke 11.20, which says that it 'has come' (*ephthasen*).[1] The teaching of Jesus is primarily concerned with the hope of the coming Kingdom. He is not different from his contemporaries in that he proclaims as present that which they hoped for in the future, but in that he proclaimed the nearness and the absolute certainty of the coming fulfilment of that hope.[2] But this coming Kingdom is not something that can be built, furthered or developed by the work of men; it is something that God will give and for which men can only pray.[3] It is not a fellowship into which men enter, nor something that grows gradually in the world, *pace* the parables of growth which are not parables of growth at all, but of contrast.[4] All modern ethical interpretations of the Kingdom of God fall to the ground before the saying Matt. 12.28 = Luke 11.20 in which the Kingdom of God is manifested in demon-exorcism. For those with eyes to see it, and faith to respond, the Kingdom is already breaking into history in a destruction of the power of Satan.[5] At the Last Supper Jesus is still expecting

---

[1] Weiss, *Predigt²*, pp. 70 f., argues that both Greek verbs go back to a common Aramaic *mᵉtā'*, pointing to the parallelism in meaning between Luke 10.9 and 11.20 in proof of this. Thirty-five years later Dodd was to revive this argument and to draw from it the opposite conclusion, namely that since *mᵉtā'* certainly means 'has come' all of these sayings should be so interpreted. See below, pp. 60 f.

[2] *Predigt²*, pp. 69–73, cf. *Predigt¹*, pp. 12 f.

[3] *Predigt²*, pp. 73–78, where Weiss discusses and discards the views of Ritschl and others.

[4] *Predigt²*, pp. 78–85. This is now generally accepted as the true interpretation of these parables, above all perhaps because of the decisive work of Professor Jeremias of Göttingen. For details of this work see below, pp. 81 f.

[5] *Predigt²*, pp. 88 ff. As we shall see, a great deal of the subsequent discussion was to revolve around the point as to whether or not this saying indicates the

the Kingdom and promising his disciples a part in this glorious future; elements in his teaching which seem to speak of the Kingdom as present are references to the sign that God is about to fulfil the promises of old in the immediate future.[1] The glorious hope, when it is fulfilled, will bring to men all these elements which the Jews later included in the concept of the 'age to come'[2] and so the coming of the Kingdom of necessity involves a complete break in history; the new will not be an organic development out of the old, but something completely different. It will involve a new and different world, a new and different kind of human nature. Jesus gives no systematic account of the state of things in this glorious future, he uses 'Kingdom of God' in reference to all that was hoped for and understood by his contemporaries under the concept of Messianic salvation. The very fact that he gives no systematic account of the blessedness of the Kingdom of God shows that he shares the views of his contemporaries and felt no need to correct their expectations.[3] One particular aspect of this salvation which Jesus does stress is the destruction of Satan and all evil, which is already beginning for the disciples, and the end of Death. This emphasis makes it impossible for us to suppose that Jesus was concerned at all with political activity. The changed world, the changed human nature, the destruction of Satan and his minions, the end of Death; being concerned with these things Jesus is not concerned with practical politics. Not only so but the Kingdom of God is something that only God can bring; any implied political restoration or reform is quite outside Jesus' calling and interest.[4]

---

actual presence of the Kingdom of God in the ministry of Jesus. Weiss is mainly concerned to argue that this saying indicates the conflict element in the teaching of Jesus, conflict between the Kingdom of God and the Kingdom of Satan. So far as the presence of the Kingdom is concerned he argues that it is still actually future; what this saying, and related sayings, teach is that for the disciples the power of Satan is already broken and so they may truly hope for an inheritance in the Kingdom when it is finally manifested (*Predigt*[2], p. 95).

[1] *Predigt*[2], p. 101.

[2] *Predigt*[2], pp. 107 f., following Dalman. See below, p. 28.

[3] *Predigt*[2], p. 115. Here Weiss is allowing his enthusiasm for the insight that Jesus used Kingdom of God in the prophetic apocalyptic sense to run away with him. In fact, as was to be pointed out in the subsequent discussion, there are many and grave differences between Jesus and his contemporaries here. See below pp. 41, 176 ff.

[4] *Predigt*[2], pp. 117–25. So Weiss replies in advance to the many who were to claim that the Kingdom of God was related to political activity. See below, pp. 51 f., 84.

If the Kingdom of God is for Jesus wholly a future expectation, what then is the relationship of his ethical teaching to this expectation? It cannot be that the ethical teaching is designed to illustrate what must be done in order that the Kingdom may come, for the Kingdom comes from God alone and not as a result of anything that man does. It must therefore be concerned with the conditions of entry for men into the Kingdom when it comes; the ethical teaching is designed to explicate what is involved in the repentance which the imminence of the Kingdom demands.[1] After the publication of *Predigt*[1] Weiss was attacked at this point on the grounds that he had brought the ethical teaching of Jesus into too close a connection with the proclamation of the imminence of the Kingdom. In *Predigt*[2] he admits this up to a point, and agrees that there are aspects of the ethical teaching that are not related directly to the eschatology, especially the command to love God and one's neighbour, but these are only one side of the picture, and they make up a comparatively minor aspect of the teaching.[2] In the main the ethical teaching is designed to explicate the demand of repentance before the imminence of the Kingdom. In the short time left before the Kingdom comes Jesus demands a great and, in fact, superhuman effort, which under normal circumstances would be simply impossible, of those who would fulfil the conditions for entry into the Kingdom. When the Kingdom came all this would be ended, for in the Kingdom there would be no more commandments, no more obedience, only the complete reign of the will of God with no further opposition to it.[3] Schweitzer was to characterize this understanding of the ethical teaching of Jesus as *Interimsethik*[4] and a great deal of the subsequent discussion revolves around the question that is raised by it of the relationship between eschatology and ethics in the teaching of Jesus.

Finally Weiss turns to the question of the Messianic consciousness of Jesus, which is certainly involved in the understanding of his eschatological teaching. Conscious of his mission to proclaim the imminence of the Kingdom of God, conscious of the power within him to destroy the power of Satan, Jesus must have known himself to be the Chosen of God. But this does not solve the problem of his Messianic consciousness; just as the hope for the coming of the

---

[1] Weiss, *Predigt*[1], pp. 42–49.
[2] *Predigt*[2], pp. 134–8.
[3] *Predigt*[2], pp. 138 f.
[4] See below, p. 30.

Kingdom is a future hope, so also the claim of Jesus to Messiahship is something that is directed towards the future. It is for this reason that he chose to designate himself 'Son of Man'; this is no generally accepted Messianic title, but is connected with the establishment of the Kingdom in Dan. 7.13, in the Ezra Apocalypse and in Ethiopian Enoch; and in his use of it Jesus reveals his own uncertainty about the future in that he does not clearly identify himself fully with this figure. The fact is that although in the present he could be Teacher, Prophet, Envoy of God, Chosen of God, Son of David, even Son of God, the Son of Man he could only *become* with the final coming of the Kingdom, and this it lay entirely in the hand of God to determine. So Jesus believed in the imminence of the Kingdom, and in the possibility that with its coming he would be manifest as Son of Man.[1]

Before we turn to the development and popularization of the views of Weiss by Albert Schweitzer we must consider the work of Gustaf Dalman, who settled once and for all certain linguistic questions, and whose interpretation of the Jewish material was different from that of Weiss and therefore helps us to see clearly the points at issue in the question as to whether or not the teaching of Jesus did owe a great deal to apocalyptic Judaism, as Weiss maintained.

DALMAN

The world of New Testament scholarship is immeasurably indebted to Gustaf Dalman: in a series of works he demonstrated that Jesus had spoken and taught in Galilean Aramaic; he provided us with a grammar of this language, and a lexicon to it; he published in a convenient form a series of texts by means of which the language could be studied and its importance for New Testament studies readily appreciated; and finally he crowned the long years of linguistic studies by publishing two books in which he interpreted the teaching of Jesus in accordance with the insights developed out of the study of the language in which this teaching was given.[2]

Dalman begins his interpretation of Kingdom of God in the

---

[1] Weiss, *Predigt*[2], pp. 156–75.

[2] *Grammatik des jüdisch-palästinischen Aramäisch*, 1894, [2]1905.
   Aramäisch-Neuhebräisches Handwörterbuch, [1]1887–1901, [2]1922, [3]1938.
   Aramäische Dialektproben, 1896.
   Die Worte Jesu, [1]1898, [2]1930 (ET by D. M. Kay of a revision of the first edition, *The Words of Jesus*, 1902 = *Words*).
   Jesus-Jeschua, 1922 (ET by Paul P. Levertoff, *Jesus-Jeshua*, 1929).

teaching of Jesus by examining carefully the Hebrew and Aramaic expressions that are translated 'Kingdom of God' or 'Kingdom of Heaven'[1] and shows that 'heaven' is here simply a circumlocution for 'God'; the two expressions are absolutely synonymous and there is no justification whatever for reading into the expression 'Kingdom of Heaven' any reference to the especially transcendental nature of the object so designated.[2] With regard to the word translated 'Kingdom', *malkuth*, Dalman demonstrates that in the Jewish literature, when the word is applied to God, it means always 'kingly rule', never 'Kingdom'; it describes the sovereignty of the King, not the territory ruled by him.[3] So in the teaching of Jesus the synonyms Kingdom of God/Kingdom of Heaven must always be understood in the sense of the kingly rule of God; they refer to the sovereignty of God, to his activity in ruling.

Thus far the work of Dalman is epoch-making; there can be no going back from his conclusions in regard to the meaning of this phrase. But in interpreting the whole teaching of Jesus concerning the Kingdom of God he moves less surely, for here two factors come into play which militate against the validity of his conclusions. In the first place he views the Jewish literature as a unity and does not give sufficient attention to the fact that there is a very considerable difference between the usage of Kingdom of God in the prophetic and apocalyptic writings on the one hand and in the later rabbinical literature on the other. In the second place he is unduly influenced by the older ideas of the liberal theologians who envisaged the Kingdom

---

[1] Greek *basileia tou theou* or *basileia tōn ouranōn*; Hebrew *malkuth shamayim*; Aramaic *malkuthā dishmayā*.

[2] *Words*, pp. 91–93. Dalman has recently been quite misunderstood on this point by William Strawson, *Jesus and the Future Life*, 1959, p. 64, who quotes him 'the *basileia tōn ouranōn* is the sovereignty of a transcendent God' and goes on to argue that Dalman is here suggesting that there is a distinctive quality about 'Kingdom of Heaven' which arises out of the idea that it is the rule of the transcendent God. But in this interpretation of Dalman Strawson is wholly in error; Dalman is only saying that the idea of 'heaven' does not have any transcendental significance, it is simply a circumlocution for God, and although God is certainly transcendent he is equally so whether designated directly or by circumlocution. The two expressions are absolutely synonymous, anything that can be read into the one must also be read into the other, and any attempt to differentiate between the two or to give a more transcendental significance to 'Kingdom of Heaven' is doomed to shipwreck on the rock of Dalman's argument.

[3] *Words*, pp. 93–96. We might add at this point that the meaning of *malkuth shamayim* can very clearly be seen in Ps. 145.11 f., where we have 'thy (God's) kingdom' paralleled by 'thy power', and 'thy mighty deeds' paralleled by 'thy kingdom'.

of God as something that comes in the hearts of men and is concerned
with the renovation of human society.

Dalman begins his interpretation of the teaching of Jesus with a
consideration of the use of *malkuth shamayim/malkuthā dishmayā* in the
Jewish literature, and argues that here the concept of the sovereignty
of God[1] is primarily an eternal one, quoting the Onkelos Targum at
Ex. 15.18: 'God . . . his kingly sovereignty (*malkuthēh*) endures
forever and ever.' The earthly manifestation of this sovereignty begins
with Abraham, Siphre Deut. 113: 'Before our father Abraham came
into the world, God was, as it were, only the king of heaven: but
when Abraham came, he made Him king over heaven and earth',
and also with the allegiance which Israel gave to this sovereignty at
both the Red Sea and at Sinai. So the eternal sovereignty of God is
manifested in the world through the confession of allegiance by an
individual or people, and thus an individual can 'take upon himself
the sovereignty of heaven' by separating himself from transgression,[2]
by adopting the law,[3] by reciting the Shema.[4] This last becomes
particularly important among the rabbis; to recite the Shema is to take
upon oneself 'the yoke of the sovereignty of God', e.g. j. Ber. 4a; 7b.[5]

In these rabbinical sayings there is undoubtedly a relationship
between the manifestation of the sovereignty of God and the human
confession of allegiance, and Dalman allows this to control his interpretation of the remainder of the Jewish literature to which he refers.[6]
He quotes the Sibylline Oracles 3.47 f.: 'the mightiest Kingdom of
the immortal King shall appear over men', and 3.767: 'He will raise
up his Kingdom for all ages over men', interpreting both of these
references in terms of the future recognition of God as King throughout
the whole world.[7] In this he is surely wrong. Sibylline Oracles 3.47 ff.

---

[1] Following upon his discussion of the meaning of the term, Dalman is careful
to use the German translation *Gottesherrschaft*. The English translator uses
'sovereignty of God' and 'theocracy', but the use of the latter term was unfortunate
since it does not represent the Jewish concept at all well. We shall use 'sovereignty
of God' uniformly in presenting and discussing Dalman's views.

[2] Siphra, ed. Weiss, 93d.

[3] A saying attributed to Simeon ben Hakish (c. AD 260).

[4] So Gamaliel II (c. AD 110), Ber. 2.5.

[5] Dalman, *Words*, pp. 96–98.

[6] In contrast to this Johannes Weiss had argued that·there were two emphases
in the Jewish conception of Kingdom of God; that this rabbinical conception was
the high point of one of these emphases; and further that this was the minor
emphasis in comparison with the other which dominates the Old Testament,
and reaches its high point in prophetic and apocalyptic writings. See above pp. 18 ff.

[7] *Words*, p. 99.

continues with a description of the coming of the Messiah and of the eschatological conflict which will then ensue, a conflict which will bring 'inexorable wrath on Latin men', 'ruin on Rome', 'a cataract of fire' from heaven, and the judgment of God. Here the emphasis is certainly upon the kingly activity of God and not upon any human confession of allegiance to him. Similarly in Sibylline Oracles 3.767 ff.: although this includes a possible reference to a confession of allegiance in the description of a world-wide pilgrimage to Zion (772 f.) the main emphasis is upon the everlasting blessings which God will bring to his people as he manifests his sovereignty (769–71). Both of these references therefore belong to the category described rightly by Weiss as being the major element in the Jewish conception of the Kingdom of God, that in which the emphasis is upon God as ruler and upon his activity in ruling,[1] and Dalman's interpretation of them is therefore incorrect.

Dalman refers also to the Kaddish prayer: 'May he (God) establish his sovereignty in your lifetime and in your days and in the lifetime of all the house of Israel even speedily and at a near time'; to Psalm of Solomon 17.3 f.: 'The might of our God is for ever (upon us) with mercy, and the sovereignty of our God is upon the peoples for ever in judgment'; and to the Assumption of Moses 10.1: 'His sovereignty shall appear'. The first two references are interpreted as referring to the process by which God establishes his sovereignty and men submit themselves to his yoke, and since this is both a present opportunity and a future hope it can, as a future hope, be spoken of as 'appearing' as in the third reference.[2]

Again, Dalman is here allowing the later and different rabbinical usage to influence him unduly. The Assumption of Moses passage goes on to detail the way in which God will arise from his throne to punish the Gentiles, destroy their idols and to make Israel happy.[3] The reference is clearly to an intervention of God in history whereby the present unhappy state of things is totally reversed, and the Jews made happy by the complete destruction of their enemies. Psalm of Solomon 17 refers to the same hope for a dramatic intervention of God in history. Verses 3 f. and 46 refer to the eternal sovereignty of

---

[1] See above, pp. 18 f., and Weiss, *Predigt*[2], pp. 8–29. Weiss does not, in fact, discuss these passages from the Sibylline Oracles at all, but that does not alter the fact that they do belong with the passages he does discuss.

[2] Dalman, *Words*, pp. 99 f.

[3] Ass. Mos. 10.3, 7–8.

God, but this is the basis for the major message of the Psalm: the proclamation of the coming of God's intervention in history in the form of the coming of the Messianic King and the dramatic changes that he will initiate (vv. 21–46). In both of these references the emphasis is all upon the kingly activity of God; in Ass. Mos. 10 God himself acts, in Ps. Sol. 17 he acts through his Messiah, but in neither passage is there any emphasis upon the allegiance of men as a means whereby the sovereignty of God is manifested. We are here in a different world from that of the rabbinical concept of taking upon oneself the yoke of the sovereignty of heaven. Similarly in the Kaddish prayer: in the light of the emphasis in Ass. Mos. 10 and Ps. Sol. 17 it is natural to interpret the Kaddish prayer as a petition for the coming of that moment when God will erupt into history to change dramatically, drastically and permanently the circumstances of his people.[1]

In his discussion of the Jewish usage of *malkuth shamayim* and its equivalents Dalman therefore gives too much weight to the rabbinic usage and underestimates the more characteristic prophetic-apocalyptic emphasis and its importance. In his discussion of the teaching of Jesus all this is reinforced by the undue influence of views such as those of Ritschl. So Dalman interprets the teaching of Jesus concerning the Kingdom of God in terms of the manifestation of the divine sovereignty wherein men were to find their salvation in the most intimate relationship to God, and in full obedience to his will, and goes on to claim that for Jesus 'the sovereignty of God meant the divine power which from the present onwards with continuous progress, effectuates the renovation of the world'.[2] In contrast with Ritschl we have here the use of sovereignty of God in referring to the divine power rather than Kingdom of God referring to the completed state of things which this power will effect, and this is a step in the right direction, but the 'renovation of the world' which is effectuated 'from the present onwards with continuous progress' is pure Ritschlianism; it has no basis in the teaching of Jesus, as Weiss was to show, and it is possible only for Dalman because of the weight he gives to the rabbinic usage in discussing the Jewish usage of *malkuth shamayim*.

There is, however, one further element in Dalman's interpretation of the teaching of Jesus in this regard that is worthy of serious

---

[1] For Weiss on the Kaddish prayer see above, p. 19. On the passages from Sib. Orac., Ass. Mos. and Ps. Sol., see further below, pp. 168 ff.

[2] *Words*, p. 137.

attention. He is able to show that in some respects there is an affinity between the teaching of Jesus concerning the 'age to come' (*ha'ōlām habā*) or the 'life of the age to come' (*hayē ha'ōlām habō*). These expressions came to be for the Jews comprehensive terms for the blessings of salvation, and although the expressions themselves are not an important element in the vocabulary of Jesus, if indeed he used them at all,[1] ideas which the Jews later associated with them are to be found in the teaching of Jesus associated with the sovereignty of God. Jesus used the term 'sovereignty of God' in a distinctively eschatological manner, and he preferred to use this term rather than any other, because it puts the emphasis upon 'the honour of God',[2] and also because it can be used to imply the salvation, blessing and absolute happiness which are involved for men in the establishment of God as sovereign.[3] Here is a truly valid insight; in the teaching of Jesus the salvation of men is very much involved in the coming of the sovereignty of God.

We can see then that the views of Dalman and Weiss reinforce one another concerning the actual meaning of the expression Kingdom of God, and concerning the fact that the salvation of men is involved in the coming of that Kingdom. Where the two differ as to the emphasis to be seen in the immediate background to the usage of Jesus and in that usage itself it is Weiss rather than Dalman who is to be followed, since Dalman depends excessively upon the rabbinical usage and is too heavily influenced by the liberal ideas that really have no basis either in first-century Judaism or in the teaching of Jesus.

ALBERT SCHWEITZER

We come now to a consideration of the work of Albert Schweitzer, who developed and popularized the views first presented by Johannes Weiss. To Schweitzer must be given the honour that is his due; he forced the world of New Testament scholarship to consider seriously the problem of the Kingdom of God in the teaching of Jesus. He was concerned with a major theme of nineteenth-century theology, the many and varied attempts to write a life of Christ, and he set forth

---

[1] Dalman, *Words*, p. 148. Weiss followed Dalman at this point. See above, p. 21.

[2] So near and yet so far! Had it not been for his excessive dependence upon the rabbinical usage Dalman would surely have followed the logic of the results of his own linguistic research and have said 'the activity of God' rather than 'the honour of God'.

[3] *Words*, p. 136.

his own basic understanding of the correct approach to problems involved in a book *The Secret of the Messiahship and the Passion: A Sketch of the Life of Christ* in 1901,[1] and he followed this with a full-scale review of nineteenth-century work in *Vom Reimarus zu Wrede* in 1906.[2] This was so written as to give the reader the impression that he is travelling down a long and difficult road with Albert Schweitzer as his guide. The traveller is continually faced with forks in the road, either-or alternatives, until he comes to the last and final fork: either the thorough-going scepticism of Wilhelm Wrede or the thorough-going eschatology of Albert Schweitzer. In no case does the guide fail to point out the fork that is to be taken, least of all in the case of the last one!

Now there can be no doubt but that the work was brilliantly written and that at all points the arguments were most persuasively stated. Schweitzer remorselessly exposed the weaknesses of the attempts to write a life of Christ within the context of the liberal theology of the nineteenth century; indeed so remorselessly and so successfully did he expose these weaknesses that it was fifty years before there was another serious attempt to write a Life of Christ in German New Testament theology, and when the attempt was made again it was made in a context very different from that of the liberal theology of the nineteenth century.[3]

Having swept his reader through, and past, the previous attempts to write a Life of Christ, Schweitzer confronts him with his own understanding of that life, the key to which is a development of Johannes Weiss's interpretation of the Kingdom of God in the

---

[1] *Das Messianitäts-und Leidensgeheimnis. Eine Skizze des Lebens Jesu*, 1901. Originally this was the second part of a treatise *Das Abendmahl*, but it is really independent of the first part and it was translated into English by Walter Lowrie and published as a separate work under the title *The Mystery of the Kingdom of God* (= *Mystery*) in 1925.

[2] Subsequent German editions were entitled *Geschichte der Leben-Jesu-Forschung*. An English translation of the first edition by W. Montgomery was published under the title *The Quest of the Historical Jesus* (= *Quest*) [1]1910, [2]1911, [3]1954. All our quotations are from the third edition.

[3] Günther Bornkamm, to whose *Jesus von Nazareth*, 1956, we are referring, says that Schweitzer's work was at one and the same time a memorial to the liberal quest of the historical Jesus and its funeral oration! (p. 11; ET [see p. 120, n. 1, below], p. 13). A similar, if less pregnantly expressed, judgment from the English point of view is that of C. J. Cadoux: 'The real death blow to the liberal, spiritualizing solution of the problem was dealt by Albert Schweitzer. . . . When once his views had become known to English students . . . the conviction rapidly gained ground that things could never be the same again' ('The Historical Jesus: a study of Schweitzer and after', *ExpT* 46, 1934–5, p. 406).

teaching of Jesus. The essence of Schweitzer's approach is the assumption that the whole life, work and teaching of Jesus was dominated by a fixed eschatological expectation, an expectation which must be interpreted in terms of what we find in the Jewish apocalyptic literature.[1] This expectation can, and must, be reconstructed by bringing together elements from the apocalypses and from the New Testament,[2] and its central feature is the coming, eschatological Kingdom of God.

The Kingdom of God in the teaching of Jesus is an apocalyptic conception and its coming is expected in the immediate future. He summarizes with approval the view of Johannes Weiss: 'The general conception of the Kingdom was first rightly grasped by Johannes Weiss . . . a Kingdom of God which is wholly future; as is indeed implied in the petition of the Lord's Prayer, "Thy Kingdom come". . . . It is present only as a cloud may be said to be present which throws its shadow upon the earth; its nearness, that is to say, is recognized by the paralysis of the kingdom of Satan. In the fact Jesus casts out the demons, the Pharisees are bidden to recognize, according to Matt. 12.25–28, that the Kingdom of God is already come upon them.'[3]

This future eschatological expectation has particularly influenced the ethical teaching of Jesus. According to this theory the ethical teaching is concerned only to show what is involved in true repentance, and is valid only for the short time that will remain between the proclamation of the coming of the Kingdom with the consequent call for repentance, and the actual coming of the Kingdom. It is, in Schweitzer's phrase, an *Interimsethik*.[4]

---

[1] 'The eschatology of Jesus can only be interpreted by the aid of the curiously intermittent Jewish apocalyptic literature of the period between Daniel and the Barcochba rising' (*Quest*, p. 365, following Weiss).

[2] It must be noted that Schweitzer does not first examine the expectation of the apocalypses and then compare with this the expectation of Jesus. He mixes together elements taken from the apocalypses and from the New Testament, calls this mixture 'Jewish eschatology of the time of Jesus', and then uses it as the basis for his theory. (See *Quest*, p. 366.) In this respect his work is inferior to that of Weiss.

[3] *Quest*, p. 238. We have given this quotation at length because it is Schweitzer's only mention of those elements in the teaching of Jesus which deal with the Kingdom as, in some sense, a present experience.

[4] *Quest*, p. 352. Cf. *Mystery of the Kingdom of God*: 'Jesus' whole theory of ethics must come under the conception of repentance as a preparation for the coming of the Kingdom' (p. 53). 'As repentance unto the Kingdom of God the ethics also of the Sermon on the Mount is interim-ethics' (p. 55). For Weiss on this, see above, pp. 22 f.

Not only the ethical teaching of Jesus, but the whole of his work, what in English we call his 'ministry', is dominated by the eschatological expectation. According to Schweitzer, Jesus knew himself to be the designated Messiah, the one who would be revealed as the Son of Man when the Kingdom came. In the confident knowledge that he was the Messiah, Jesus proclaimed the coming of the Kingdom, and he sent out his disciples with the same message. He expected the Kingdom to come at harvest-time that same year (this is the significance of the teaching of the parables in Mark 4), and when he sent out the disciples on the mission recorded in Matt. 10, he did not expect to see them back before the Kingdom should have come.[1]

The failure of the Parousia to take place on this occasion was the turning-point in Jesus' ministry, and from this point onwards his plans were altered.[2] Not only the prediction of the Parousia but also the prediction of the sufferings in Matt. 10 remained unfulfilled. According to Schweitzer's interpretation these sufferings were the Messianic woes, which, in Jewish apocalyptic expectation, precede or accompany the coming of the Kingdom.[3] The Son of Man was to share these Messianic woes and the Kingdom could not come until they had taken place. Since they did not take place when he expected them, Jesus determined to force their coming, to go up to his death in Jerusalem so as to fulfil them in himself, and so bring in the Kingdom.[4] In this way he would fulfil his Messianic vocation, the Kingdom would come, and with it his manifestation as the Son of Man.

[1] *Quest*, p. 357. The acceptance of the charge to the disciples as we find it in Matt. 10-11, as an authentic record of the teaching of Jesus on this occasion, and especially 10.23, is the keystone of Schweitzer's theory. See below, pp. 33 ff.

[2] *Quest*, p. 358. W. G. Kümmel, *Promise and Fulfilment*, 1957 (=*Promise*) (ET by D. M. Barton of *Verheissung und Erfüllung*, ³1956), pp. 62 f., points out that in this part of his work Schweitzer is tacitly combining the circumstances of Matt. 10 with those of Mark 6. Thus he sets the Matthaean charge to the disciples in the context of Mark 6.6 ff., so that the return of the disciples and Jesus' endeavour to separate himself from the crowd (Mark 6.30 f.) appears as the sequel to the Mission, although, in fact, the Matthaean account omits the return of the disciples. 'This combination produces therefore an *artificial* connection between the missionary discourse and the disciples' return; and to this it must be added that nothing in the sources affords grounds for the assertion that Jesus was disappointed that the disciples came back without the end of the world having appeared.'

[3] *Quest*, pp. 359–63.

[4] 'In the secret of his passion which Jesus reveals to the disciples at Caesarea Philippi the pre-Messianic tribulation is for others set aside, abolished, concentrated upon himself alone, and that in the form that they [*sic*] are fulfilled in his own passion and death at Jerusalem. That was the new conviction that had dawned upon him. He must suffer for others . . . that the Kingdom might come.' *Quest*, pp. 386 f.

These are the main points of Schweitzer's '*konsequente Eschatologie*'.[1] Equally as interesting as the theory itself is the story of how he came to it, which he has told in his *Selbstdarstellung*, 1929.

In the spring of 1894 he began a year's military service and it was his intention, at the end of that time, to apply for a scholarship as a theological student. In order to do this he would have to take an examination in the Greek New Testament, and he had chosen to offer himself for examination in the Synoptic Gospels. To prepare himself for this he took his Greek New Testament with him on manoeuvres in the autumn of that year, intending to study in such spare time as he had, and having previously worked through Holtzmann's Commentary on the Synoptics. On a rest day in the village of Guggenheim he was reading Matthew 10 and 11. The remainder of the story we tell in an English translation of his own words:

> Matthew 10 contains the account of the Sending out of the Twelve. In the address with which he sent them out Jesus promised them that they would undergo persecution. This however did not happen.
>
> He proclaimed to them also that the Son of Man would come before they had completed their journey through the cities of Israel, which could only mean that with his coming the supernatural Messianic Kingdom would be established. He therefore did not expect them to return.
>
> How came it that Jesus proclaimed things to the disciples which did not in fact come to pass?
>
> The explanation of Holtzmann, that this address was not from the historical Jesus but was a composition made up of words of Jesus brought together after his death, was for me unsatisfactory. Later, words would not have been put into his mouth that were unfulfilled in the course of the narrative.
>
> The text itself forced me to the conclusion that Jesus has in fact expected persecution for the disciples and the coming of the Son of Man, but in the event had been proved wrong. But how did he come to have such an expectation, and what consequences did it have for him that events proved to be other than he had expected?[2]

The whole of Schweitzer's subsequent theory stems from this experience, the question which it led him to ask, and the way in which it prepared him for a glad acceptance of the work of Weiss. It is because of this that we can understand at once the strength and the weakness of his work. His basic insight came to him at the very

---

[1] 'Thoroughgoing eschatology.' This is the term by which he designates Weiss's interpretation of the teaching of Jesus and his own interpretation of the Life of Christ. We shall use it as a technical term referring to the Weiss-Schweitzer views.

[2] Schweitzer, *Selbstdarstellung*, p. 4.

beginning of his studies and all his subsequent work is dominated by it, for the experience out of which it grew gave it for him almost the force of a revelation. Because it came to him with such force he was able to present it forcefully to others, and therein lies its strength. But because it came to him at the very beginning of his studies his later studies of the New Testament and of the apocalyptic literature were dominated by it, and therein lies its weakness. Adolf Jülicher wrote of Schweitzer's theory that it 'sprang out of his own head, already full grown, before he entered into detailed work on the sources'.[1] That is exactly what had happened.

How much the theory came to dominate the study of the New Testament narratives can be seen from Schweitzer's treatment of the New Testament text, which seems to follow the needs of his theory rather than the weight of the evidence on any of the questions involved. As we have already said, his theory is built upon a literal acceptance of the account of the Mission of the Twelve in Matt. 10. He defends this, as we have seen, by arguing that such an unfulfilled prediction as Matt. 10.23 would not have been put into the mouth of Jesus by the later community. In this he has probably a good deal of right on his side, but this does not adequately defend the authenticity of the Matthaean account as it stands. A glance at a synopsis of the Gospels in Greek shows that we are dealing here with an account that has a complex textual history. Also, as we followed Kümmel in pointing out above, Schweitzer's conception of the mission of the disciples and its consequences depends upon a tacit, unacknowledged combination of the charge in Matt. 10, with the circumstances of Mark 6.6 ff. The impression is unavoidable that the preconceived theory is determining the treatment of the texts.

Another instance of the preconceived theory dominating the treatment of the text is in the treatment of the narrative of the Transfiguration and the confession of Peter. Schweitzer argues that the section of Mark 7.31–9.30, is composite, and that it consists of two sets of narratives, now in such disorder that we 'cannot fully reconstruct each of the separate sets of narratives'. The section 8.34–9.30, which includes the Transfiguration and is centred on the northern shore of the lake, after the confession at Caesarea Philippi, does not, he claims, belong there at all. It should be placed around Bethsaida, after the feeding of the multitude and before the confession of Peter. In this way he is able to place the Transfiguration before

[1] *Neue Linien in der Kritik der evangelischen Überlieferung*, 1906, p. 5.

Caesarea Philippi and to argue that it 'had, in fact, been the revelation of the secret of the Messiahship to the three who constituted the inner circle of the disciples'.[1] The three disciples, having involuntarily stumbled upon the secret of the Messiahship, are commanded to silence, but Peter disobeyed this command. At Caesarea Philippi he betrayed to the Twelve Jesus' consciousness of his Messiahship and so Jesus is forced 'to take a different line of action in regard to the Twelve from what he had intended . . . Jesus did not voluntarily give up his Messianic secret, it was wrung from him by the force of events.'[2] All this is strictly in accordance with Schweitzer's version of the Messianic secret, but it cannot be said that there is any real evidence for it in the sources. Many critical scholars are agreed that there are two sets of narratives to be traced in Mark 7.31–8.26.[3] But they are also agreed that the relevant section is Mark 7.31–8.26; Schweitzer is alone in wanting to extend the relevant section of the Gospel to include 8.27–9.30, and it is a fair conclusion therefore that he is being led by the needs of his theory rather than by the actual evidence for duplication in the text of Mark's Gospel.

But for all the weaknesses of Schweitzer's theory it has one great strength: it is a thoroughgoing presentation of an interpretation of the life of Jesus wherein the concept of the Kingdom of God in his teaching is conceived wholly in terms of Jewish apocalyptic. As an interpretation of the Kingdom of God in the teaching of Jesus it is inferior to the work of Johannes Weiss, to which it owes so much, but because it interprets the *life* of Christ in these terms it has had an impact far greater than that of Johannes Weiss, who restricts himself with true academic sobriety to the teaching of Jesus and to the implications of his interpretation of this for systematic theology. Not so Schweitzer! He plunges into the whole life of Christ and thus strikes a note of tremendous interest and import to all Christians, whether they be academically interested in New Testament theology or not. A work so brilliantly written as is Schweitzer's *Quest*, and on a subject of such general interest, could not fail to reach a wide

---

[1] *Quest*, p. 383.

[2] *Quest*, p. 384.

[3] So, for example: J. Wellhausen, *Einleitung in die Drei Ersten Evangelien*, 1905, pp. 48 f.; J. Weiss, *Die Schriften des Neuen Testaments* I, 1906, *ad loc.* (p. 133); E. Meyer, *Ursprung und Anfänge des Christentums*, I, 1921, pp. 130–32; E. Klostermann, *Das Markusevangelium* (Handbuch zum Neuen Testament 3), 1950, p. 78; A. E. J. Rawlinson, *The Gospel According to St Mark*, [7]1949, pp. 103 ff.; V. Taylor, *The Gospel According to St Mark*, 1952, pp. 628–32.

public and so arouse a general interest to which New Testament scholars must respond. And so thoroughgoing a presentation of an interpretation of Kingdom of God in the teaching of Jesus in terms of Jewish apocalyptic could not fail to provoke a debate in which the pros and cons would be thoroughly, and sometimes heatedly, argued. So it was, and we turn now to a delineation and a discussion of the major aspects of this debate.

Before we move to this, however, it must be pointed out that this debate has taken place much more in Britain and America than in Germany. The reasons for this are manifold, and not without their interest. One reason is that of the very different circumstances which surround theological discussion in Germany on the one hand and Britain and America on the other. For Germany theological discussion has been, and up to a point still is, the province of the academic-ally trained theologian rather than that of the general lay member of the Church.[1] In the English-speaking world, however, theological issues are much more widely discussed, even if at a lower academic level, and lay interest in them is proportionately greater. Under these circumstances Schweitzer's work, in which the general interest is greater than the purely academic merit, was bound to arouse more interest in Britain and America than it would in Germany. Another reason is that the discontinuity between the periods before and after the First World War was very much greater in Germany than it was in either Britain or America. The consequences of this war were much more catastrophic for the German-speaking world than for the English, and when theological discussion was resumed again it was under very different circumstances. The changing circumstances found their prophet in Karl Barth, and the more purely New Testament scholarship moved to a new interest: *Formgeschichte*.[2] The

[1] This situation is now changing. The role of the 'bekennende Kirche' in the struggle against Hitler; the post-war movements such as the 'Evangelische Akademien' and the 'Kirchentag' movement; the great interest among non-theological students in the work of Dietrich Bonhoeffer, all this and much more is helping to make the situation after the Second World War very different from that before it. In 1956, for example, Günther Bornkamm's *Jesus von Nazareth* was published in a paper-back edition with a printing of 20,000 copies in the first two years of publication, and recent issues in the *Calver Hefte*, a series of small paper-backed volumes published 'to further Biblical Faith and Christian Life', include Joachim Jeremias on the Sermon on the Mount (No. 27, *Die Bergpredigt*) and on the Problem of the Historical Jesus (No. 32, *Das Problem des historischen Jesus*).

[2] On the consequences for New Testament theology of the break created by the First World War in Germany see the discussion by W. G. Kümmel, *Das Neue Testament. Geschichte der Erforschung seiner Probleme*, 1958, especially pp. 417–20.

discussion of *konsequente Eschatologie* did not therefore continue in the same way in Germany as it did in Britain and America, where there was not the same drastic break.

In what follows therefore we shall be more concerned with the discussion in English than with that in German, since it is in English that the discussion has been carried on continuously. There have been German contributions to it, and very important ones, but these can be best fitted into the over-all picture of the continuous discussion in English, and this is the procedure that we shall follow.

II

THE SUBSEQUENT DISCUSSION

1. THE ANGLO-AMERICAN LIBERAL RESPONSE TO THE CHALLENGE OF WEISS & SCHWEITZER

SANDAY

THE IMPACT of *konsequente Eschatologie* upon the English-speaking theological world begins with the work of William Sanday, and especially with his book *The Life of Christ in Recent Research*, 1907.

Sanday had been deeply interested in life of Christ research for some time, and had written the article 'Jesus Christ' for the Hasting's *Dictionary of the Bible*.[1] As this is a good example of a typical Anglo-American liberal approach to the subject before the coming of Schweitzer's influence, it is worth while indicating its views on some of the questions which Schweitzer was to raise afresh. The true meaning of the Kingdom of God for Jesus was that of God exercising his rule and working out his purpose in the world of men. It is something that is gradually and inevitably growing in the world of men, beginning in the ministry of Jesus and continuing under the influence of his Spirit, totally independent of all eschatological or catastrophic expectations. It is both present and future, since it began in the present of Jesus' ministry and continued, and continues, to grow in the future. Jesus was indifferent to the precise degree of extension it was to receive during his life on earth, because he was confident of the inevitable growth of the seed he was planting. The question of the influence of the eschatology upon the ethics does not arise

---

[1] Hasting's *Dictionary of the Bible*, Vol. II, 1899, pp. 603–53. This article was later published separately as a book, *Outlines of the Life of Christ*, 1907, and had a very wide influence. A. M. Hunter, *Interpreting the New Testament 1900–1950*, 1951, ranks the book as one of the ten most important contributions to the study of the life of Christ in the first half of the twentieth century.

because eschatology plays no significant part in the teaching of Jesus. Jesus envisaged himself as the chief Founder and permanent Vice-regent of the Kingdom of God, and when he expressed his office in the term Son of Man he meant that he was the ideal of humanity, the representative of the human race.

Schweitzer's book made a great impression upon Sanday. In *The Life of Christ in Recent Research*, 1907, he praised it very highly and admitted that its impact upon him had been to make him rethink some of his previous positions. It had brought him to the realization of 'how far the centre of gravity of our Lord's ministry and mission, even as they might have been seen and followed by a contemporary, lay beyond the grave', and also to the realization 'to what an extent he (Jesus) conceived of the Kingdom of heaven, that central term in his teaching, as essentially supernatural'. As a consequence of reading Schweitzer Sanday now doubted 'if we have appreciated the extent to which our Lord, while transcending the Jewish notions of the time, yet in almost every instance starts from them'.[1]

Here we see exemplified in one scholar the general and immediate impact which Schweitzer's theory made; the eschatological-apocalyptic element involved in the concept of the Kingdom of God which had previously been disregarded must now be taken into account. As time went on Sanday thought the problems through more carefully and in 1911 he published his second thoughts on the subject.[2] He now admitted that there was a real element of apocalyptic in the Gospels and that many of the leading terms employed by Jesus were apocalyptic terms. But he argued that Jesus, in using these terms, had introduced profound changes into their meaning. For example, the Kingdom of God is now accepted as an apocalyptic term, but it is argued that the Kingdom which Jesus came to found was of an essentially inward and spiritual nature, and that he therefore infuses the term with this new meaning. Jesus uses the imagery of apocalyptic but gives it a new and non-apocalyptic meaning. In this way Sanday is able to bow before the force of Schweitzer's theory, but at the same time to maintain the essentials of his old position. In this he is typical of many scholars who, at this period, were speaking of Jesus' 'transformation of apocalyptic'.[3]

---

[1] *Life*, pp. 121 f.
[2] 'The Apocalyptic Element in the Gospels', *Hibbert Journal* 10, 1911, pp. 83–109.
[3] For a detailed consideration of the views of these scholars, see below, pp. 41–45.

THE OXFORD CONGRESS ON THE HISTORY OF RELIGIONS

The immediate impact of Schweitzer is to be seen not only in the work of Sanday, but also at the Third International Congress for the History of Religions, held at Oxford in 1908. In Section VIII of the Congress, 'The Christian Religion', a number of papers were read on the subject of eschatology.[1] In these papers various aspects of Schweitzer's theory were discussed. E. von Dobschütz argued that the Kingdom of God in the teaching of Jesus is only partly an eschatological conception, because the main emphasis is upon the Kingdom as a present experience of unbroken communion with God, and not upon the Kingdom as a purely future hope. F. C. Burkitt discussed the significance of the parable of the Wicked Husbandmen as an aid to our understanding of Jesus' conception of the significance of his death. He accepted Schweitzer's contention that Jesus, after the failure of the End to come at the time of the Mission of the Twelve, saw his death as 'instrumental in bringing on the great catastrophe'.[2] F. G. Peabody raised the question of the relationship between eschatology and ethics in the teaching of Jesus, arguing that the emphasis is to be put not upon the eschatology but upon the ethics, in which 'the conscience of the world has found its Counsellor and Guide'.[3]

In the work of William Sanday, and in the papers read to the Third International Congress for the History or Religions, we see the beginnings of the Anglo-American discussion of *konsequente Eschatologie*. The discussion was carried on vigorously during the next decade, in a series of publications.[4]

[1] E. von Dobschütz, 'The Significance of Early Christian Eschatology'; F. C. Burkitt, 'The Parable of the Wicked Husbandmen'; F. G. Peabody, 'New Testament Eschatology and New Testament Ethics'; all were reprinted in *Transactions of the Third International Congress for the History of Religions*, Vol. II, 1908.

[2] *Transactions*, II, p. 326. Of all British scholars F. C. Burkitt was the one most influenced by Schweitzer's views. His main publications fall within the next period of our review, and they show the result of a considerable period of reflection rather than of an immediate impact, so we shall deal with them in their chronological place.

[3] *Transactions*, II, p. 308.

[4] F. C. Burkitt, 'The Eschatological Idea in the Gospel' in *Some Biblical Questions of the Day* edited by H. B. Swete, 1909; E. F. Scott, *The Kingdom and the Messiah*, 1911 (=*Kingdom*); C. W. Emmett, *The Eschatological Question in the Gospels*, 1911 (=*Question*); E. C. Dewick, *Primitive Christian Eschatology*, 1912 (=*Eschatology*); J. Moffatt, *The Theology of the Gospels*, 1912 (=*Theology*); J. H. Leckie, *The World to Come and Final Destiny*, 1918 (=*Final Destiny*); William Manson, *Christ's View of the Kingdom of God*, 1918 (=*Christ's View*).

EMMETT

Of these contributions only one is a complete rejection of *konsequente Eschatologie*, that from C. W. Emmett. He regards it simply as the latest theological mode, and a mode to be resisted strenuously because of the false picture of Jesus which it gives us. He compares the Christ pictured by the eschatologists and the Christ pictured by the liberals and concludes: 'They (the liberals) portray for us a Christ whom we can unreservedly admire and love, even if it is a little doubtful whether logically we ought to worship him. The Jesus of eschatology it is difficult either to admire or to love; worship him we certainly cannot.'[1] For Emmett the subjective factor of our being able to admire, love or worship the Jesus we portray was more important than the objective consideration of whether this picture is historically accurate. Schweitzer had demonstrated that one of the weaknesses of the liberal quest of the historical Jesus was that each individual created his own picture of Jesus in accordance with his own character or ideals;[2] Emmett's argument is more interesting as an illustration of the tenacity of this tendency than it is decisive as an argument against *konsequente Eschatologie*.

BURKITT

F. C. Burkitt accepted the contention that the Kingdom is a conception taken by Jesus from current Jewish apocalyptic but argued that Jesus' use of the term is 'almost as much a criticism of the popular ideals as a preaching of them. . . . If the Kingdom of God was at hand, then above all things was a call for God's chosen nation to repent. . . . But as our Lord's ministry went on, other elements gradually came to the front, elements of which the Old Testament analogue is found in the process by which the old national State changed under Jeremiah and Ezekiel into a religious community. The Jewish nation as a whole, both rulers and people, did not obey the call of Jesus.'[3] The final act of obedience was part of the essential preparation for the coming of the Kingdom.

[1] C. W. Emmett, *Question*, p. 77.
[2] Cf. *Quest*, p. 4.
[3] F. C. Burkitt, *op. cit.*, pp. 204 f. This emphasis upon the Remnant idea, upon Jesus' private teaching to his disciples, and upon the element of obedience as preparation for the coming of the Kingdom was to play a large part in the work of T. W. Manson twenty years later. See below, pp. 90–95, and especially p. 93.

THE TRANSFORMATION OF APOCALYPTIC

The remainder of the contributors to this stage of the discussion can be considered as a group because there is a considerable unity of opinion among them. Their main criticism of Schweitzer is that he excessively underrates the ethical aspects of the teaching of Jesus. He does not take into account the purely ethical and religious teaching of Jesus, finding no place in his theory for Jesus' teaching of simple piety.[1] It is assumed as self-evident that Jesus did teach a simple piety.

A second criticism is that there are such fundamental differences between Jesus and the apocalyptic writers that we may not interpret the eschatology of Jesus in terms of Jewish apocalyptic.[2]

Again, it is argued that Schweitzer's treatment of the apocalyptic literature itself leaves very much to be desired. He 'takes astonishing liberties with the historical evidence. For instance, he says that John the Baptist appeared at a time when apocalyptic prophecy had fallen into silence, in face of the fact that the most vivid predictions of the Parousia in the whole of Jewish literature were written by a contemporary of John and Jesus (the Assumption of Moses). Also he speaks as if there had only been one Jewish doctrine of the Kingdom; whereas there were several. And, further, he denies that there was any political colour in the Messianic expectation as expressed in

---

[1] See e.g. E. C. Dewick, *Eschatology*, p. 137; J. Moffatt, *Theology*, pp. 59–61; Wm. Manson, *Christ's View*, pp. 100, 116 f.

[2] E.g. J. H. Leckie (*Final Destiny*, pp. 46 f.), who stresses the pessimism of the apocalyptists in regard to the world and contrasts this with the optimism which he finds in the teaching of Jesus. This is too superficial an approach; a much better statement of the differences between Jesus and the apocalyptists, which are very real, is that by A. Schlatter, *Die Geschichte des Christus*, ²1923, p. 210. Schlatter points out that Jesus does not attempt to present an elaborate and unified picture of the future, as did the apocalyptists, and that there is not one single instance in his teaching of any direct reference to one of the apocalypses. Things which are referred to frequently in the apocalypses, such as the Fall of the Angels in Genesis 6 or the figure of Enoch, are not referred to at all in the teaching of Jesus. The special experiences which the apocalyptists claim as their authority and as a sign of the coming of the End are completely absent from the teaching of Jesus. The apocalyptic writers constantly look back over the history of their own times and look forward into the future as they expect it to be, building up one total picture which they present under various symbols; there is nothing of this in the teaching of Jesus.

All this is true, and much more could be added to it, but it does not alter the fact that there is still the one crucial thing in common between Jesus and the apocalyptic writers: the use of 'Kingdom of God' in connection with the future hope.

Apocalypse, although there is clear evidence to the contrary in the Psalms of Solomon.'[1]

For the writers we are at present considering, the key to the understanding of Jesus' eschatological teaching is the conception that Jesus has taken over certain elements from contemporary Jewish apocalyptic, but that in so doing he has transformed them.[2] They use this conception of Jesus' transformation of apocalyptic to maintain an essentially non-apocalyptic interpretation of the Kingdom of God in the teaching of Jesus. E. F. Scott claims that the main element in Jesus' conception of the Kingdom, to which all else is subsidiary, is 'that man will be conformed to the will of God and enter into fellowship with him'.[3] E. C. Dewick says that 'there were higher spiritual truths lying behind our Lord's eschatological language—above all, the call to a holy life, and to spiritual fellowship with a Heavenly Father'.[4]

These writers used the conception of Jesus' transformation of apocalyptic far too readily. It is not sufficient to say, in effect, that while the language of Jesus may have been apocalyptic, his essential ideas were not. In order to be able to say this one would have to offer a detailed study of the teaching of Jesus against the background of apocalyptic, with a careful and detailed exposition of the similarities and differences. This we do not find here; instead we have generalizations that assume as self-evident propositions about the essential nature of the teaching of Jesus that were, in the light of *konsequente Eschatologie*, no longer self-evident.

There is also unanimity among these writers in that all were agreed that Schweitzer was wrong in seeing the Kingdom of God as, for Jesus, a purely future expectation. From E. F. Scott to William Manson all maintain that Jesus did teach the Kingdom of God as, in some sense, a reality in the present. Scott and Leckie content themselves with general statements of this; Moffatt, Dewick and Manson all argue the point in detail.[5] They argue, for example, that *ephthasen* in Matt. 12.28 and Luke 11.20 indicates that the Kingdom is present

---

[1] J. H. Leckie, *Final Destiny*, p. 42. Similarly, E. C. Dewick, *Eschatology*, pp. 131 f.

[2] In our discussion of Sanday's 'second thoughts' on eschatology we called attention to this tendency in the work of this period. See above, p. 38.

[3] *Kingdom*, p. 99.

[4] E. C. Dewick, *Eschatology*, p. 202. Similarly, J. Moffatt, *Theology*, pp. 67–69; J. H. Leckie, *Final Destiny*, p. 46; Wm. Manson, *Christ's View*, pp. 72, 78.

[5] E. F. Scott, *Kingdom*, pp. 111 f.; J. H. Leckie, *Final Destiny*, p. 61; J. Moffatt, *Theology*, pp. 49–57; E. C. Dewick, *Eschatology*, pp. 133–5; Wm. Manson, *Christ's View*, pp. 81 ff.

in Jesus' work;[1] that *entos hymōn* in Luke 17.21 means 'the Kingdom of God is within you', i.e. present in the moral and spiritual order.[2] They point to the Baptist's question and Jesus' answer, Matt. 11.2 ff.; Luke 7.18 ff., and argue that here Jesus is claiming to have fulfilled in his own ministry prophecies of the Messianic times; they turn to the saying concerning the blessedness of the disciples in Luke 10.23; Matt. 13.16 and claim that this implies that the disciples have experienced the Kingdom. The very difficult saying Matt. 11.12 f. (cf. Luke 16.16) is interpreted as indicating that the time of Jesus is set in opposition to the time of the Baptist, the present to the past, and that it is to this present that the Kingdom of God belongs.[3]

There is no doubt but that at this point a real contribution is being made to the discussion. Schweitzer's dismissal of this whole aspect of the teaching of Jesus, by maintaining that the Kingdom can only be said to be present in the sense that a cloud is present which casts its shadow upon the earth,[4] is totally inadequate. A major part of the future discussion was to revolve around this point, and it is in this context that C. H. Dodd was to make his contribution. But we must emphasize that at the stage of the discussion which we are now reviewing, this aspect of Jesus' conception of the Kingdom was not being interpreted as Dodd was to interpret it. At this stage the present aspect of the Kingdom is being used as a means of maintaining the liberal interpretation of the Kingdom as essentially concerned with the 'moral and religious sphere of life', as 'present in the moral and spiritual order', as 'some experience of happiness which men try to get', and the like. All this is a far cry from Dodd's 'realized eschatology'. The scholars whom we are discussing at this point called attention to an aspect of the New Testament evidence which did not fit into Schweitzer's interpretation of the Kingdom, but they were still too near the liberal and psychologizing interpretations of their own immediate past to be able to offer an adequate interpretation of it.

With regard to the question of the relationship between eschatology and ethics, there is also unanimity among these scholars in

---

[1] For Weiss' argument at this point see above, pp. 20 f.

[2] Weiss had rejected this on the grounds that such an interpretation of a saying addressed to the Pharisaic opponents of Jesus is quite out of order (*Predigt²*, pp. 85 f.).

[3] Weiss had interpreted this saying as referring to Messianic movements of the Zealot type which at the time of Christ were attempting to establish the Kingdom of God by force of arms (*Predigt²*, pp. 192–7).

[4] See above, p. 30.

rejecting Schweitzer's *Interimsethik*, but by no means unanimity in regard to what should be given in its place as the true interpretation of the relationship. Dewick is still under the influence of the conception of the Kingdom as coming as a result of Christ-inspired moral activity within the world, and he argues that the teaching of Jesus was not so much the prediction of a coming event, but rather the proclamation of a great opportunity, the good news of God's willingness to inaugurate the Kingdom. By repentance and moral effort the goal of the inauguration of the Kingdom could be reached.[1] Moffatt sees the ethical teaching as essentially a preparation for the Kingdom: 'Jesus lays down the qualities and characteristics which belong to the Kingdom itself, and endeavours to prepare men for it by inducing repentance or a change of heart and life'.[2]

The weakness of this view is that there is in it no adequate recognition of the significance of the fact that the Kingdom was in some sense already present for Jesus. Here Wm. Manson is a much surer guide, for he recognizes that Jesus envisaged true righteousness as 'something flowing from the Kingdom', a life issuing from the new stream of divine redemptive forces liberated in the Kingdom. The ethical teaching of Jesus is 'the new Law of the Kingdom of God, and needs to be envisaged in that new context of grace, resource and power'.[3] It will be argued below that this is a wholly valid insight, vastly superior to the *Interimsethik* of Weiss and Schweitzer, and it is important to note that Wm. Manson could only attain it because he sees clearly that element in the teaching of Jesus in which the Kingdom is a fact of present experience.

The discussion of Jesus' conception of his own role in the Kingdom is characterized, among the scholars whose work we are reviewing at this point, by a readiness to speak of the inner psychology of Jesus,[4] and by a simple reiteration of the view that Jesus knew himself

---

[1] E. C. Dewick, *Eschatology*, pp. 142 ff.

[2] J. Moffat, *Theology*, p. 61. Similarly, E. F. Scott: 'The aim of Jesus was not to prescribe values for a mere interval of waiting, but to declare the moral law as it would hold good for the Kingdom. He taught men how they might strive already after the new righteousness, and thus bring themselves into inner harmony with the Kingdom' (*Kingdom*, p. 127).

[3] Wm. Manson, *Christ's View*, pp. 116.

[4] For example: '. . . as he proclaimed the Kingdom he could not but reflect on his own relationship to it. His belief that he represented the new order assumed an even more definite form, till he was compelled to recognize himself as the Messiah' (E. F. Scott, *Kingdom*, p. 173). Similarly, Wm. Manson, *Christ's View*, p. 126; E. C. Dewick, *Eschatology*, pp. 60 f.

to be the Messiah and that he re-interpreted the traditional views of Messiahship in terms of the Isaianic Servant. To the scepticism of Wrede concerning the Messianic texts in the Gospels,[1] and to the difficulties in the narratives to which Schweitzer had called attention, it seemed sufficient to reply with a general statement of confidence, such as: 'That Jesus claimed to be the Messiah admits on critical grounds of no reasonable doubt.'[2] But it was, in fact, already too late in the day for such an easy shrugging-off of German scepticism, as it was already too late for such confident statements about Jesus' inner convictions concerning himself. The Anglo-American discussion of these questions does not become important until the scepticism had been taken more seriously, and the grounds for it more thoroughly investigated.

[1] W. Wrede, *Das Messiasgeheimnis in den Evangelien*, [1]1901, [2]1913, unfortunately never translated into English.

[2] Wm. Manson, *Christ's View*, p. 125.

III

THE SUBSEQUENT DISCUSSION

2. THE DENIAL AND TRIUMPH OF APOCALYPTIC

THIS SECOND PERIOD, roughly the decade 1920–30, is of
interest in three ways: it was the period in which the American
social gospel movement came into contact with *konsequente
Eschatologie*; it saw the last widespread attempts to deny the influence
of apocalyptic in the teaching of Jesus concerning the Kingdom of
God; and it witnessed the failure of these attempts and the general
triumph of the view that Kingdom of God is an apocalyptic term
and must be interpreted as such.[1]

RAUSCHENBUSCH AND THE SOCIAL GOSPEL

The American social gospel movement had found its theologian in
Walter Rauschenbusch, whose most important work *A Theology for
the Social Gospel* had been published in 1919. Rauschenbusch had
shown that a theology for this movement must be built upon the
foundation of a particular interpretation of the Kingdom of God in
the teaching of Jesus. Indeed, he had claimed that this movement
was rediscovering the essential nature of the teaching of Jesus
concerning the Kingdom of God, and the essential dynamic of his
concern for its establishment, after the long centuries in which these
things had been neglected in favour of a concern for the Church.
Jesus himself always spoke of the Kingdom of God and was not
concerned with founding the kind of institution, the Church, which
afterward claimed to be acting for him. The Kingdom of God was
for Jesus an ideal concerned with the transformation of society. It
was an ideal that would become effective by a movement concerned
with ethical teaching, with social reform, with political action. It
was and is a movement, divine in origin, progress and consummation.

---

[1] With certain exceptions, see below, p. 57.

This movement was initiated by Jesus, in whom the prophetic spirit came to its consummation, it is sustained by the Holy Spirit, and it will be brought to its fulfilment by the power of God in his own good time. The Kingdom of God is concerned with the establishment of a community of righteousness in mankind, it is the energy of God realizing itself in human life, it is humanity organized according to the will of God, it is the Christian transfiguration of the social order.[1]

Rauschenbusch attributes this understanding of the Kingdom of God to the teaching of Jesus, but he makes no attempt to offer any exegesis of Jesus' teaching in support of this understanding. In discussing eschatology he simply says that the earlier parables show us that Jesus 'took his illustrations from organic life to express the idea of the gradual growth of the Kingdom' and that although apocalypticism was part of the environment in which he began his teaching it was not his personal product, he was emancipating himself from it.[2]

As an interpretation of the teaching of Jesus the Social Gospel movement's understanding of the Kingdom of God is unacceptable for the simple reason that it is not an interpretation of the teaching of Jesus at all. It uses a mosaic of ideas drawn together from many different places and then reads these back into such aspects of the teaching of Jesus as can be made to bear them. We find in this movement an emphasis upon the ethical aspects of Christianity, an ethical social concept of salvation, moral teachings taken from the Gospels and the Old Testament, an evolutionary concept of inevitable progress,[3] but no adequate or detailed exegesis of the teaching of Jesus. The reason for this is clear: such an understanding breaks down as soon as it is made the basis for detailed exegesis of the sayings recorded in the Gospels.

A good example of this fundamental and total weakness in the work of the Social Gospel school is to be found in the article 'Kingdom of God' by Shailer Mathews in *A Dictionary of Religion and Ethics*.[4] Here Kingdom of God is defined as 'the reign of God over an ideal social order conceived of both temporally and transcendentally'

---

[1] Rauschenbusch, *Theology*, pp. 131–45.

[2] *Ibid.*, p. 220.

[3] All this has been demonstrated by the historian of the early stages of this movement, C. W. Hopkins, in his work *The Rise of the Social Gospel in American Protestantism, 1865–1915*, 1940. See especially pp. 99, 109, 121 ff., 127.

[4] *A Dictionary of Religion and Ethics*, edited by Shailer Mathews and Gerald Birney Smith, New York, 1921, pp. 245 f.

and it is immediately admitted that 'certain exegetical questions present themselves'. But the answers to these questions 'can best be reached by a study of the group of ideas centring about the conception as held by the Jews rather than by philology or lexicography'. This enables Mathews to claim that Jesus 'uses the term Kingdom of God as a conventional symbol of the supreme good to be enjoyed by humanity' without having to face the unanswerable question of how such an interpretation can be justified in face of the actual meaning and use of *malkuth shamayim* among the Jews at the time of Christ.[1] Similarly the total neglect of exegesis in the article[2] enables him to avoid the difficulty of reconciling this understanding of Kingdom of God in the teaching of Jesus with the irruption of a divine activity presupposed in such Kingdom sayings as Mark 1.15 par. and Matt. 12.28.

That the Social Gospel movement has made a tremendously significant contribution to American church life and work, and to American society at large, is not to be denied. In this respect its understanding of Kingdom of God is important. But concerning the interpretation of the Kingdom of God in the teaching of Jesus, the fact that its insights were not derived from an exegesis of the teaching of Jesus really precluded it from making any significant contribution to the discussion.

But the tendency that we saw in Rauschenbusch to deny any apocalyptic influence in the teaching of Jesus did come to be a widespread tendency in both America and Britain in the 1920s. This period in the discussion is further removed in time from the impact of *konsequente Eschatologie*, and it had been preceded by the work of the previous decade, which we reviewed in Chapter II above. One would expect therefore that the discussion would now be carried further by a building upon the foundation already laid. For example, the fact that Kingdom of God is a term taken from Jewish apocalyptic might have been accepted and the discussion taken further by an examination of Jesus' use of the term against the background of its use in apocalyptic, with a view to determining the truly distinctive element in Jesus' usage. Or, again, since the previous discussion had called attention to an element in the teaching of Jesus concerning the

---

[1] For Dalman's decisive work on this see above, pp. 25 ff.

[2] A parenthesis '(although some scholars find a present Kingdom in Luke 17. 20–22 and a few other passages)' on p. 246 is the only reference to the actual text of the New Testament at any point in the article!

Kingdom of God which Schweitzer had ignored and Johannes Weiss denied—that it is in some sense a present experience—it might be expected that this avenue should be explored further. In fact, these things were not done at this period at all; instead there is a return to the question as to whether or not Jesus' use of the terms Kingdom of God and Son of Man does, in fact, owe anything to apocalyptic, a question that one would have thought already settled. But in Britain and America there were serious attempts to deny altogether that Jesus' use of these terms did owe anything to their use in apocalyptic. It was not denied that these terms were in use in Jewish apocalyptic; what was denied was that their usage there was of any significance for their usage by Jesus. There is a subtle difference here between what was being said now and what had been said before. Before it had been argued that Jesus used these terms and, in using them, transformed them; now it is being argued that Jesus used them in a totally non-apocalyptic sense. We have moved from the transformation of apocalyptic to the denial of apocalyptic.

THE DENIAL OF APOCALYPTIC

The definitive American attempt to demonstrate that Jesus used apocalyptic forms and language to express and enforce a non-apocalyptic teaching is the 'Symposium on Eschatology', written by a representative group of scholars.[1] The way is prepared by going back to Old Testament prophecy and arguing that 'that interpretation (of the Old Testament prophets) which emphasizes the ethical and spiritual in them rather than the supernatural and apocalyptic is not an attempt to modernize them, but is a hard-won recognition of their real character'.[2] To L. Ginzberg is entrusted the task of arguing that apocalyptic itself never played an important role in Judaism. 'The Apocalyptics cut loose from life, the Rabbis were the guardians and leaders of a nation and they did not fail to see in the wild and vague visions of these dreamers a true menace to the physical and spiritual welfare of Israel.'[3]

[1] Kemper Fullerton of the Oberlin Graduate School of Theology, Nathaniel Schmidt of Cornell University, Louis Ginzberg of the Jewish Theological Seminary of America, E. F. Scott, at this time at Union Theological Seminary, New York, and B. W. Bacon of Yale University. The 'Symposium' was published in *JBL* 41, 1922, pp. 1–204.
[2] K. Fullerton, 'Symposium', p. 101.
[3] L. Ginzberg, 'Symposium', p. 134. In fact, the relationship between the

The stage having been set for him in this way, E. F. Scott argues that underlying the apocalyptic element in the teaching of Jesus there was a 'practical religious purpose, which meant more to him than the forms in which he expressed it'. The function of the apocalyptic teaching 'is to enforce a message that is not apocalyptic . . . His demand was for a new kind of life, a new relation to God, and while he looked for the Kingdom his interest was in the moral requirements which it involved.'[1] In the same spirit B. W. Bacon approaches the problem of the Son of Man sayings in the Gospels and argues that they were used by Jesus in two ways. During the Galilean ministry the reference is to the Son of Man as the coming Judge, a concept taken from apocalyptic and used by Jesus to emphasize his call to repentance; during the period from Caesarea Philippi onwards the reference is to Daniel 7, and this figure is used by Jesus to indicate the assurance of ultimate victory.[2] Thus we have again the use of apocalyptic concepts to enforce elements that are non-apocalyptic.

The fatal weakness of this particular attempt to explain away the apocalyptic element in the teaching of Jesus is that there is a fundamental contradiction between the outer apocalyptic forms and the inner meaning of the message which these forms are supposedly expressing and enforcing. E. F. Scott admits this in connection with the central concept, that of the Kingdom of God, and is thereby driven to a position in which he must accuse Jesus of, in the very least, extremely clumsy thinking. 'We have to deal with a contradiction between the forms employed by Jesus and the inner drift and purport of his message. He declared that the Kingdom was future, as the apocalyptists had taught; and yet he never wavers in his belief that God is reigning, God is silently working now. Was he himself aware of the contradiction? Probably not. He took over the apocalyptic ideas as they were current in his time, without reflecting on their origin or on the philosophy that lay behind them.'[3] [*Sic*!]

Rabbis and the apocalyptic literature was an intimate one, since the apocalyptic literature most probably represents the esoteric teaching of the scribes. Cf. J. Jeremias, *Jerusalem zur Zeit Jesu*, IIb, 1937, pp. 106–11. For further comments on Ginzberg's argument see the work of B. S. Easton, below, pp. 54 f.

[1] E. F. Scott, 'Symposium', pp. 138 f.
[2] B. W. Bacon, 'Symposium', pp. 145–7.
[3] E. F. Scott, 'Symposium', p. 141. Undeterred by this consequence of his estimate of the relationship between the apocalyptic form and the essential content of the teaching of Jesus, he went on to repeat the thesis in two later works: *The*

We may fairly refuse to follow an approach that demands such an estimate of the abilities of the historical Jesus as a thinker, and especially as a thinker in the realm of religious ideas.

B. W. Bacon went on to give a complete, and completely non-apocalyptic, picture of the life and ministry of Jesus in his book *The Story of Jesus and the Beginning of the Christian Church*, 1928. Here he repeats the liberal view of the Kingdom as an inward spiritual reality gradually growing in the world, and rejects *konsequente Eschatologie* on the grounds that we must refuse the notion that Jesus was a mere fanatic.[1] His conception of the ultimate purpose of Jesus in his work is as follows: 'He planned wisely and fought bravely for the cause to which he had dedicated himself from the very beginning: to bring Israel back into loyal obedience to its national calling as Servant and Witness for Jehovah.' He cherished 'national aspirations and designs'; he worked at the level of practical politics, appealing to the common people for support, seeking to organize a popular move-ment. His aim was to reform the State and people of Israel; by means of a national act of repentance and an acceptance of his leadership to establish a reformed people of Israel, with a purified Temple worship and with political institutions reflecting a true theocracy.[2] But the eschatological nature of the Kingdom in the teaching of Jesus is not so lightly to be dismissed. Like the members of the Social Gospel school, Bacon had not considered sufficiently the essential meaning of *malkuth shamayim* on the lips of Jesus and his contemporaries, he had not recognized the reference to the inception into history of a divine activity which destroys and renews, he had not met the arguments of Johannes Weiss, who showed that political

---

Ethical Teaching of Jesus, 1924, especially pp. 140–2, and *The Kingdom of God in the New Testament*, 1932, especially pp. 57, 69, 115 f.

[1] This is a note that has been sounded in American studies right down to the present time. For the latest examples see our chapter on the American 'Jesus as a prophet' school, below, pp. 148-57.

[2] *Op. cit.*, pp. 208–24. Bacon had given a similar interpretation of the aims of Jesus in his article 'Jesus Christ' in the *Schaff-Herzog Encyclopedia*, Vol. VI, 1908, pp. 160–7. Similar views were part of the stock in trade of the Social Gospel school, e.g. Rauschenbusch, *Christianity and the Social Crisis*, 1907, p. 66: 'No one will understand the life of Jesus truly unless he has asked himself the question, what would have happened if the people as a whole had accepted the spiritual leadership of Jesus? The rejection of his reign involved the political doom of the Galilean cities and of Jerusalem; would the acceptance of his reign have involved no political consequences?' They have continued to find expression both in Britain and America right down to the present. The most recent example is from England: R. Dunkerley, *The Hope of Jesus*, 1953.

restoration or reform was quite outside Jesus' calling and interest.[1]

Turning again to England, C. W. Emmett returns to the discussion to argue once more that *konsequente Eschatologie* must be rejected. He argues now that the distribution of apocalyptic matter in the Gospel sources shows that much of it was erroneously ascribed to Jesus by the early Christian writers, and that the remainder ought to be interpreted figuratively. The apocalyptic teaching, particularly that part of it which deals with the future punishment of the wicked, is so inconsistent with the doctrine of the fatherly love of God that one of them must be rejected as not having emanated from Jesus, and the apocalyptic teaching is rejected as being the less original of the two. Jesus looked forward, not to an apocalyptic kingdom, but to a slow and patient process of regeneration of the individual and to the building up of a society by the creation and development of independent spirits capable of fellowship and co-operation.[2]

The weakness of these arguments is obvious. There is no attempt to explain how a community of disciples founded by a non-eschatological ethical teacher came to have an intense interest in apocalyptic expectation, and then to attribute such an expectation to their Master.[3] There is an obvious dependence upon a liberal sentimentalism about God, and a liberal optimism about man, that is completely non-biblical. It is still assumed that Jesus must have shared the ideals of a nineteenth-century liberalism, and that he therefore could have had nothing in common with a first-century apocalypticism.

A. C. Headlam[4] rejects *konsequente Eschatologie* as an interpretation dominated by one overpowering idea and therefore untrue to the source-texts. For him it is self-evident that apocalyptic language is 'a pictorial representation of spiritual truths'[5] and the spiritual truth represented in the apocalyptic picture of the Kingdom of God is the fact of Christianity and the growth of the Christian Church.

TWO CHAMPIONS OF *konsequente Eschatologie*

These rejections of an apocalyptic element in the teaching of Jesus

---

[1] For these arguments of Weiss see above, pp. 18 ff.

[2] C. W. Emmett (with L. C. Macdougall), *The Lord of Thought*, 1922, pp. 268 ff.

[3] Cf. the comment by H. A. Guy, *The New Testament Doctrine of the Last Things*, 1948, p. 84.

[4] A. C. Headlam, *The Life and Teaching of Jesus Christ*, 1923, and *Jesus Christ in History and Faith*, 1925.

[5] *Life and Teaching*, p. 249.

concerning the Kingdom of God produced a reaction on both sides of the Atlantic. In England F. C. Burkitt[1] arose to defend the views of Johannes Weiss and Schweitzer, and in America B. S. Easton performed the same service to the continuing discussion.

In one respect the work of Burkitt[2] is an advance on that of Schweitzer. He had made a thorough study of Jewish apocalyptic and he handles this material more responsibly than Schweitzer had done. In respect of command of this material, and facility in the languages involved, Burkitt fully matches the standards set by Johannes Weiss, something that could not be said of all Anglo-American contributors to this discussion.

Out of the study of the apocalyptic material Burkitt had developed a high regard for the apocalypses, regarding them as a product of what he called the heroic age of the Jewish nation, the period between the Maccabaean rising and the destruction of Jerusalem.[3] He showed that in this literature the concept of the Kingdom of God developed to express the fundamental hope of the Jews during this period; the hope that the succession of world powers, Babylonian, Median, Persian, Seleucid Greek, would be brought to an end by an act of God in history whereby God himself will take the dominion into his own hands. 'The Kingdom of God himself will be inaugurated, and he will reign forever, protecting his faithful people and rewarding them for all the trials they have undergone at the hands of the heathen.'[4] On the basis of this sympathetic presentation of the apocalyptic concept of the Kingdom of God Burkitt moves to the Gospel story showing how, on the assumption that this is the background to the teaching of Jesus, 'sentence after sentence of the Gospels, saying after saying, parable after parable, falls into its place'.[5]

In his general picture of the ministry of Jesus Burkitt follows

---

[1] We remarked above, p. 39, that of all British scholars Burkitt was the one most influenced by Schweitzer's views, and we have already dealt with his two earlier contributions to the discussion. See above, pp. 39 f.

[2] His contributions to this stage of the discussion are: *Jewish and Christian Apocalypses*, 1914 (= *Apocalypses*); *Earliest Sources for the Life of Jesus*, 1910, 2nd, greatly revised edition, 1922 (= *Earliest Sources*); *Christian Beginnings*, 1924; *Jesus Christ, an Historical Outline*, originally published as the first part of a larger work by a number of authors, *History of Christianity in the Light of Modern Knowledge*, 1929, and then published separately, with an epilogue, 1932 (= *Outline*).

[3] *Apocalypses*, p. 15.

[4] *Earliest Sources*, p. 61.

[5] *Ibid.*, p. 66.

Schweitzer closely. He sets the ministry in the context of the Jewish apocalyptic hope, as that hope was spread among the people, and he characterizes this hope as a belief in 'the Good Time Coming'.[1] He accepts Schweitzer's contention that the message with which Jesus began his ministry, and which he committed to his disciples, was simply: 'The Kingdom of God is at hand'; he regards the teaching of Jesus as *Interimsethik*; he accepts the delay in the coming of the Kingdom as the major problem for Jesus, and the fact that it did not come at the time of the mission of the Twelve as the turning-point of his ministry. From this point onwards the ministry of Jesus is dominated by his determination to bring things to a crisis, and there is a new element in his teaching, that of his own sufferings and their significance.[2]

In his presentation of the ministry of Jesus, Burkitt does not therefore add anything significantly new; he restates the view of Schweitzer, reinforcing it with the authority of his own scholarship. His own significant contribution to the discussion lies in the fact that he delineated carefully the essential apocalyptic understanding of the Kingdom of God and showed the relationship between this understanding and that to be found in the teaching of Jesus. In this regard his influence was decisive, at any rate in England, and his work therefore makes an effective end to the denial of this apocalyptic element in the teaching of Jesus concerning the Kingdom of God among English scholars.

In America Burton Scott Easton was the champion of the eschatological approach to the ministry of Jesus.[3] He wrote in full knowledge of the 'Symposium on Eschatology' published in the *Journal of Biblical Literature* in 1922[4] and he set out to refute the minimization of the apocalyptic element in first-century Judaism that is to be found in this work. He demonstrated the difficulty of using rabbinical sources as direct evidence for conditions at the time of Christ, and showed that 'the Talmudists often have no hesitation in revising the past in any matter that does not seem right to the mind of a later

---

[1] *Outline*, p. 6. This characterization used to occur frequently in the lectures of T. W. Manson in Manchester, testifying to the influence of Burkitt upon a pupil who in turn was to make an outstanding contribution to this discussion.

[2] *Outline*, pp. 32–38. In his later works, as earlier, Burkitt still uses the parable of the Wicked Husbandmen as the key to the understanding of the significance of Jesus' death. See above, p. 39, and *Earliest Sources*, ²1922, pp. 70 f.

[3] B. S. Easton, *Christ in the Gospels*, 1930 (= *Christ*).

[4] On this Symposium see above, pp. 49 ff.

age'. In regard to apocalyptic, the mood of the rabbis is set by the calamitous experiences of AD 66–70 and 130–135, and so their indifference to apocalyptic is not to be read back into the former period. In fact a Pharisee, Saddouk, certainly supported the apocalyptic militarist, Judas of Galilee, and the greatest rabbi of them all, Akiba, went to his death in support of an apocalyptic Messianic pretender, Bar-Cochba. All our evidence indicates that the atmosphere in which Jesus began his ministry was electric with the apocalyptic hope, and, in this kind of atmosphere, when Jesus used a technical apocalyptic term such as 'Kingdom of God', he must have used it in the generally accepted sense. 'If his own tenets were non-apocalyptic, he failed signally in impressing them on his disciples.'[1]

This aspect of Easton's work is convincing enough, but he goes further and discusses the question of the relationship between eschatology and ethics, and here he shows a surprising weakness. He not only rejects Schweitzer's *Interimsethik*; he also continues to maintain the liberal view of the ethical teaching of Jesus as a means of salvation. So he is in the strange, and probably unique, position that he is convinced of the reality of the apocalyptic element in the teaching of Jesus, and also of the reality of the ethical element, and he sees them both as a means of salvation. Finding no solution to the problem of the relationship between the two he can do no other than hold them both together, and maintain that Jesus taught a double soteriology. On the one hand, 'Men, children of God by the fact of their creation, win salvation by accepting the fact and the responsibilities of sonship—and by trusting the Father to supply what they cannot supply themselves.' On the other hand, men can also win salvation by responding in the right way to the challenge of Jesus' message about the Kingdom, and especially by sharing his work in connection with it. 'So we find in Jesus' words, as they stand in the synoptic sources, not one set of religious ideas, but two.'[2] One is tempted to describe this as *inkonsequente Eschatologie*; certainly it is nonsense. The fundamental conception of God in the teaching of Jesus is a unity, therefore the Kingdom of God—the absolute expression of the righteousness of God—and the ethical requirements of that righteousness, must also be capable of expression as a unity.

[1] Easton, *Christ*, pp. 95–99, 161.
[2] *Christ*, pp. 152–4.

THE TRIUMPH OF APOCALYPTIC

The true triumph of apocalyptic in the interpretation of the Kingdom of God in the teaching of Jesus can be seen in the papers presented to a conference of six English and six German theologians held at Canterbury, April 2–9, 1927. This conference was called to discuss the nature of the Kingdom of God and its relation to human society.[1] Four of the scholars concerned themselves particularly with the New Testament and the teaching of Jesus[2] and among these four there is absolute unanimity in regarding Kingdom of God as an apocalyptic concept and interpreting the teaching of Jesus in accordance with this insight. Gone are the older ideas of the Kingdom as an ethical concept, as something which evolves, as concerned with political or social reform; instead we find language and ideas reminiscent of Johannes Weiss. Hoskyns writes: 'Our New Testament is almost entirely controlled by the thought of God as active and powerful, and the writers show no tendency to regard his activity as an activity within the sphere of developing history, or as the energy which gives movement and life to the physical structure of the universe. The action of God is consistently regarded as catastrophic.'[3] Similarly Schmidt: 'Chiefly we have to deal with an eschatological conception which goes back to the prophets and is further developed by the apocalyptists . . . (this conception) cannot represent a kingdom which can be established by a natural development of worldly circumstances or by human exertions, but only by the interference of God from heaven.[4] Kittel speaks of 'an inrush of the "other time" and the "other world" into this time and this world', and of 'the act

---

[1] The papers presented to it were published in *Theology* 14, 1927, pp. 249–95.

[2] E. C. Hoskyns, Cambridge: 'The Other-Worldly Kingdom of God in the New Testament', pp. 249–55; K. L. Schmidt, Jena: 'The Other-Worldly Kingdom of God in Our Lord's Teaching', pp. 255–7; C. H. Dodd, Cambridge: 'The This-Worldly Kingdom of God in Our Lord's Teaching', pp. 258–60; G. Kittel, Tübingen, 'The This-Worldly Kingdom of God in Our Lord's Teaching', pp. 260–2.

[3] P. 253.

[4] P. 256. K. L. Schmidt also wrote the New Testament section of the article *basileus-basileia* in *TWNT*, I, pp. 576–95 (ET by H. P. Kingdon, *Basileia*, 1957). In this he follows Dalman in arguing that the essential meaning of *basileia* in the teaching of Jesus is not Kingdom but *Herrschaft* (Kingdon translates this as 'sway'), and he follows Weiss in arguing that the emphasis is upon an intervention of God in history. For all the differences between Jesus and the apocalyptic writers they are at one in understanding the Kingdom as a cosmic catastrophe which changes all things (*TWNT*, I, pp. 596 f.; *Basileia*, pp. 45 ff.).

of God, who out of this world makes his world'.[1] The position of
C. H. Dodd is more complex. He shares with his colleagues on this
occasion the belief that the apocalyptic conception has a real part
in the teaching of Jesus, but argues that the rabbinical conception of
'taking upon oneself the yoke of the Kingdom of Heaven' has also a
real part in that teaching. In addition he introduces the argument
that the Kingdom is present in the ministry of Jesus. In fact, Dodd's
paper is the first statement of his 'realized eschatology' and since
this is in itself a major contribution to the whole discussion we will
discuss this paper when we take up Dodd's total contribution in our
next chapter. For the moment it is sufficient to note that his paper is
in no way an attempt to deny the apocalyptic element in the teaching
of Jesus; rather, accepting this as proven, he goes on to introduce
important new factors into the discussion.

The future of the discussion lay in the hands of those who were
prepared to accept the Kingdom of God as an apocalyptic concept
in the teaching of Jesus and to go on from there to discuss the further
questions which then arose. Weiss and Schweitzer were right in
their first contention; were they also right in claiming that for Jesus
the Kingdom was wholly future? Was their estimate of the relationship between eschatology and ethics in the teaching of Jesus to be
accepted? If Kingdom of God is an apocalyptic concept, what then
of Son of Man? It is to these further questions that the discussion
now turns. True, there were in Britain and America[2] some scholars
who still sought to resist the force of the first conclusion, but these
became ever fewer in number and the main stream of the discussion
passed them by.

[1] P. 261.

[2] Three examples from Britain would be J. Mackinnon, C. J. Cadoux, and
A. H. Curtis. J. Mackinnon, *The Historic Jesus*, 1931, maintained that Jesus was
both a teacher of an inward spiritual religion and of eternal moral values, and also
a proclaimer of the imminent apocalyptic transformation of this present aeon;
the former aspect of his work has proved of abiding worth, the latter has been left
behind as the relic of a bygone mentality. Both C. J. Cadoux, *The Historic Mission
of Jesus*, 1943, and A. H. Curtis, *Jesus Christ the Teacher*, 1943, recognize 'Kingdom
of God' as an apocalyptic concept, but argue that in the teaching and work of
Jesus this is strictly secondary to the filial consciousness of God which he had and
sought to inculcate in others. The work of some representative American scholars
who sought to deny, minimize or modify the apocalyptic element in the teaching
of Jesus will be discussed in Chapter IX below. In Germany the older ideas never did
survive the onslaughts of *konsequente Eschatologie* and the effects of the First World
War and its aftermath.

IV

C. H. DODD AND 'REALIZED ESCHATOLOGY'

C. H. DODD

THE MOST IMPORTANT single contribution made to the Anglo-American discussion of 'Kingdom of God' in the teaching of Jesus is undoubtedly the 'realized eschatology' of C. H. Dodd. Following upon the general acceptance of 'Kingdom of God' as an apocalyptic concept Dodd raised the question of the time element in the coming of the Kingdom in the teaching of Jesus. He argued that for Jesus the Kingdom was present, that Jesus taught the reality of the Kingdom as realized in his own ministry, the eschatology of Jesus is 'realized eschatology'.

Dodd expounds, defends, and finally somewhat modifies this view in a series of contributions,[1] the first of which is his paper to the 1927 Canterbury Conference of German and British theologians.[2] In this paper he follows Dalman in seeing both the rabbinical and prophetic-apocalyptic usage of the Kingdom of God as the background to the teaching of Jesus. Unlike Dalman he does not interpret the latter in terms of the former,[3] but holds them apart, arguing that the two usages are both to be found in the teaching of Jesus. The rabbinical concept of the Kingdom as realized in human experience by submission to the divine will is to be found in the teaching of Jesus 'in such sayings as that about "receiving the Kingdom of God as a child".' It is here that the ethical teaching of Jesus has its place. 'Jesus certainly, no less than contemporary teachers, held that it is

---

[1] 'The This-Worldly Kingdom of God in our Lord's Teaching', *Theology*, 14, 1927, pp. 258–60 (see above, pp. 56 f.); 'The Gospel Parables', *BJRL* 16, 1932, pp. 396–412; *The Parables of the Kingdom*, [1]1935, [4]1948 (= *Parables*); 'The Kingdom of God has come', *ExpT* 48, 1936–7, pp. 138–42; *The Apostolic Preaching and Its Developments*, [1]1936, [2]1944; *The Kingdom of God and History* (with H. G. Wood and others), 1938 = (*Kingdom*); *The Interpretation of the Fourth Gospel*, 1953; *The Coming of Christ*, 1951 (= *Coming*); *Gospel and Law*, 1951.
[2] See above, pp. 56 f.
[3] See above, pp. 24 ff.

possible to realize God's sovereignty here and now. His ethical teaching tells us how.'[1] The prophetic-apocalyptic concept is also to be found in the teaching of Jesus where it is found not as a future hope but as a present reality. Dodd argues that the *ephthasen* in Matt. 12.28 = Luke 11.20 'means quite unequivocally that the future has become present', since *phthanō* in LXX = *naga'* and in the Theodotian text of Daniel = *m'tā*', both of which certainly mean 'has arrived'. He suggests the possibility that *ēggiken* has a similar meaning, but does not argue this further.[2] Turning to the parables of growth Dodd points out that growth is a property of this order of space and time, and so these parables speak of a progressive revelation of the Kingdom of God within this historical order. But this process is not limited to the present order; when it has reached a certain maturity 'life passes to a higher plane'.[3]

In this paper we have a complex mixture of ideas. The Kingdom is realizable through human obedience, to which end the ethical teaching is directed; it is also the dynamic inbreaking of God in the ministry of Jesus, the final outcome of which, however, will be manifest not in history but on a higher plane. During the next few years Dodd worked further on the parables, and he also came into contact with Rudolf Otto's *Reich Gottes und Menschensohn*, published in 1934.[4] In 1935 he published *The Parables of the Kingdom*, the definitive statement of 'realized eschatology', in which he brought together his work on the parables, the further work he had done on

---

[1] *Theology*, 14, 1927, p. 258.

[2] P. 259.

[3] P. 260.

[4] English translation by Floyd V. Filson and Bertram Lee-Woolf from a revision of the German edition, *The Kingdom of God and the Son of Man*, [1]1938, [2]1943.

Otto argued that there was an inherent irrationality in all apocalyptic and we therefore should not seek to be consistent (*konsequent*) in our depiction of the teaching of Jesus, as Weiss and Schweitzer had sought to be. At one and the same time Jesus could and did teach that the Kingdom was imminent in the future and operating redemptively as an in-breaking realm of salvation in the present. As an in-breaking realm of salvation the Kingdom is present in the exorcisms of Jesus, which destroy the kingdom of Satan, and men of determination may seize it for themselves (Matt. 11.12). The parables teach that the blessing of salvation is now present as God's seed, not man's deed, and Luke 17.20 reveals the salvation activity of God as 'in the midst' of Jesus' contemporaries (*Kingdom of God and Son of Man*, pp. 97–146). But this is not the whole of the matter. Although the Kingdom exercises its force in the present it only does this as a power 'effective in advance'; (Otto, *op. cit.*, pp. 109, 147–9. Cf. the German edition, p. 85: '*Es packt und ergreift. Es ist nicht schon fertig da, aber es wird wirkend spürbar. Es harrt noch nach seiner vollen Offenbarung. . . .*')

the Kingdom sayings, and those insights he had found in Otto to reinforce his own insights.

The point of departure for Dodd's work on the parables is the principle that they must be interpreted against the background of their setting in the life of Jesus. Although not an entirely new principle, this was the first really successful attempt to put it into practice, and in this respect Dodd's work was epoch-making.[1] Before beginning an interpretation of the parables in this light Dodd turns to a discussion of the meaning of the term Kingdom of God. Here he follows Dalman in arguing that the *malkuth* of God connotes the fact that God reigns as king, and repeats his earlier view that in the teaching of Jesus it is used both in a way parallel to the usage of the rabbis and also in a way parallel to the prophetic-apocalyptic usage.[2] But there are sayings which do not fall within this framework, sayings which reflect the prophetic-apocalyptic use of 'Kingdom of God' in an eschatological sense, but with this difference: 'the "eschatological" Kingdom of God is proclaimed as a present fact, which men must recognize, whether by their actions they accept or reject it'.[3]

At this point Dodd advances on his previous argument in that what he had suggested as a possibility in his earlier paper is now claimed as a fact. Both the *ephthasen* of Matt. 12.28 = Luke 11.20 and the *ēggiken* of Mark 1.15 go back to a common Semitic original like the Hebrew *nāgaʿ* or the Aramaic *mᵉtā'* and should be translated: 'the Kingdom of God has come'.[4] Dodd also refers to other sayings in which the same message is taught or implied. In the mission charge the Kingdom has come (Luke 10.9–11, *ēggiken*) whether men repent or not. The sayings about the blessedness of the disciples (Luke 10.23 f. par.) and the greater than Solomon or Jonah (Luke 11.31 f. par.) both imply that the Kingdom had come in the ministry of Jesus, as does the reply to the Baptist's question (Matt. 11.4–6 par.). The very difficult saying Matt. 11.12 (cf. Luke 16.16) certainly

---

[1] Jeremias, *Parables* (see p. 73, n. 4 below), p. 18, says of Dodd's *Parables*: 'In this extraordinarily significant book for the first time a really successful attempt was made to place the parables in the setting of the life of Jesus, thereby introducing a new era in the interpretation of the parables.'

[2] *Parables*, pp. 34–43.

[3] *Ibid.*, p. 44.

[4] *Parables*, p. 44. This is the exact reverse of the argument of Weiss that both of these verbs went back to a common original such as *mᵉtā'* and both should be translated 'at hand'. See above, p. 20.

implies a contrast between the past and the present; between the law and the prophets and the Kingdom of God.[1]

From his discussion of these sayings Dodd draws the conclusion: 'Whatever we may make of them, the sayings which declare the Kingdom of God to have come are explicit and unequivocal. They are moreover the most characteristic and distinctive of the Gospel sayings on the subject. They have no parallel in Jewish teaching or prayers of the period. If therefore we are seeking the differentia of the teaching of Jesus upon the Kingdom of God, it is here that it must be found.'[2]

Dodd now turns his attention to those sayings in which there seems to be implied a future coming of the Kingdom of God. He deals with Mark 9.1, which he translates: 'There are some of those standing here who will not taste of death until they have seen that the Kingdom of God has come with power', and which he is inclined to interpret as meaning 'that the Kingdom had already, in his ministry, come "with power", and that his hearers would afterwards recognize this fact'.[3]

He turns to Matt. 8.11 par. and argues that here 'it is not said that the Kingdom in which the patriarchs feast is yet to come. What has not yet happened, but will happen, is that many who are not yet "in the Kingdom of God" in its earthly manifestation, will enjoy its ultimate fulfilment in a world beyond this.'[4] This is the key to Dodd's understanding of those sayings which imply a future Kingdom of God. They do not refer to a future coming in this world, because the Kingdom has already fully come in this world in the ministry of Jesus; they refer to something beyond time and space. So with Mark 14.25, the reference is to 'the transcendent order beyond time and space'.[5]

Dodd now turns to a discussion of the parables of the Kingdom, interpreting them in accordance with their 'setting in life', and arguing that the burden of their message is that the great crisis, the coming of the Kingdom, is something present in the ministry of

---

[1] *Parables*, pp. 43–48.
[2] *Ibid.*, p. 49.
[3] *Parables*, p. 54. He later somewhat modifies his position on this point and interprets this saying in terms of the Resurrection, Pentecost, and the beginning of a new era: 'the Kingdom of Christ on earth!' *Coming*, pp. 13 f. See below, pp. 67 f.
[4] *Parables*, p. 55.
[5] *Ibid.*, p. 56.

Jesus. In the Hid Treasure and the Costly Pearl (Matt. 13.44–46) the possession of the highest good, the Kingdom of God, is a present opportunity. The Tower-builder and the King Going to War (Luke 14.28–33) challenge men to take great risks with open eyes, in view of the presence of the crisis. The Children in the Market-place calls attention to the egregious folly of childish behaviour in the presence of the supreme crisis of history. Mark 2.18–19, in which Jesus is the Bridegroom, equates the present time with the time of blessing which is the object of Jewish expectation. The Patched Garment and the Old Wine-skins implies that the ministry of Jesus cannot be accommodated to traditional Judaism. In the ministry of Jesus the Kingdom has come, and one of the features of its coming was an unprecedented concern for the lost. This is the theme of the Lost Sheep and the Lost Coin, and the background to such sayings as Mark 2.17. The Prodigal Son has reference to the same situation, the calling of the outcasts in the ministry of Jesus, a situation which finds more elaborate expression in the parable of the Great Feast. The generosity and compassion of the employer in the Labourers in the Vineyard has a similar reference.

The parables of crisis (the Faithful and Unfaithful Servants, the Waiting Servants, the Thief at Night and the Ten Virgins) 'as we have them are intended to be referred directly to the expected second advent of Christ', but in their original context in the ministry of Jesus they were intended to enforce the appeal to men to recognize that the Kingdom of God was present, and that by their conduct in the presence of this crisis they would 'judge themselves as faithful or unfaithful, wise or foolish'.[1]

The parables of growth (the Sower, Tares, Seed Growing secretly and Mustard Seed) are considered together with the parables of the Leaven and the Dragnet and are now interpreted as having reference to the harvest which is being reaped in the ministry of Jesus, the sowing having taken place before the beginning of that ministry.[2] This is a change from Dodd's earlier view of these parables as

---

[1] *Parables*, pp. 154, 174.

[2] *Ibid.*, pp. 175–84. Dodd dismisses as strained and artificial Schweitzer's interpretation of these parables. Schweitzer had pointed out that mustard is a quick-growing plant and suggested that the stages of sowing, growth and harvest were intended to correspond with the actual lapse of time between the beginning of the ministry of Jesus and the catastrophic irruption of the Kingdom, which Jesus expected at harvest-time in the year he taught these parables (*Quest*, pp. 353–6; Dodd, *Parables*, pp. 175 f.). For Weiss on these parables see above, p. 20.

teaching a progressive revelation of the Kingdom in this present order.

In regard to the ethical teaching of Jesus the insight that the Kingdom is present in the ministry of Jesus leads Dodd, as it had William Manson, to see the ethical teaching as the new Law of the Kingdom. 'From the ministry of Jesus onwards men would be living in a new age, in which the Kingdom of God, his grace and judgment, stood revealed.' 'Hence there is a place for ethical teaching, not as "interim ethics", but as a moral ideal for men who have accepted the Kingdom of God, and live their lives in the presence of his judgment and grace, now decisively revealed.'[1] But having said this his actual interpretation of the ethical teaching of Jesus seems to fall short of this insight. In *Gospel and Law* he speaks of the law of Christ as working 'by setting up a process within us which is itself ethical activity'; of precepts of Christ which 'stir the imagination, arouse the conscience, challenge thought and give an impetus to the will'. By reflection on the law of Christ there comes gradually to be built up in Christians 'a certain outlook on life, a bias of mind, a standard of moral judgment' which will then 'find expression in action appropriate to the changing situation in which we find ourselves'.[2] But what is there that is specifically concerned with the Kingdom of God in all this ? What is there here that is specifically Christian? Any follower of a moral philosophy, ancient or modern, could simply substitute here the name of his teacher for 'Christ' and then say all these things of his moral philosophy. Two things seem to have hindered Dodd's insight at this point. In the first place he never repudiated his earlier view that Jesus uses 'Kingdom of God' as did the rabbis and that the ethical teaching of Jesus is designed to show us how we manifest our obedience, how we 'take upon ourselves the yoke of the Kingdom'. A rabbi could have said of the yoke of the Kingdom what Dodd says of the ethical teaching of Jesus. But, in fact, the usage of Jesus is incompatible with the usage of the rabbis, and nowhere does this show itself more clearly than in the treatment of the ethical teaching of Jesus to which Dodd is led by his attempt to combine the two. In the second place Dodd has not sufficiently recognized the essential nature of Old Testament law as *response* to

[1] *Parables*, p. 109. Cf. *History*, p. 125; 'the absolute ethic of the Kingdom of God'; *Gospel and Law*, p. 64, 'the new law which supersedes the law of the Old Testament—the law of the Kingdom of God.'
[2] *Gospel and Law*, p. 77.

God's saving activity on behalf of his people, and the essential nature of the ethical teaching of Jesus as response to the saving activity of God manifest in Christ which is the Kingdom, a response by means of which men appropriate for themselves the dynamic of that Kingdom.[1]

CRITICISM OF 'REALIZED ESCHATOLOGY'

Dodd's 'realized eschatology' has been extensively discussed and this discussion can perhaps best be summarized under three headings: (1) the interpretation of Mark 1.15 and related sayings as 'the Kingdom of God has come'; (2) the interpretation of Mark 9.1 and other sayings relating to the Kingdom as future; (3) the interpretation of the parables of the Kingdom.

1. *The interpretation of Mark 1.15 and related sayings as 'The Kingdom of God has come'*

An intensive discussion of the sayings which speak of the coming of the Kingdom and use the Greek verbs *ēggiken* and *ephthasen* has followed upon the publication of Dodd's *Parables*, but it cannot be said that this discussion has produced any definite results. The fact is that the sayings must be parallel because of the parallelism in meaning between Luke 10.9 (*ēggiken*) and Luke 11.20 (*ephthasen*),[2] but at the same time *eggizo* and *phthanō* are not exactly parallel in meaning, nor do they usually represent the same Semitic verbs in the Septuagint, *eggizō* represents *q-r-b* often,[3] but *n-g-ʿ* and *m-t-ʾ* only rarely;[4] *phthanō* represents *n-g-ʿ* or *m-t-ʾ* almost uniformly[5] and *q-r-b* not at all. So if other things were equal we would expect *ēggiken* to represent an original *q-r-b* and to mean 'has drawn near', 'is at hand', and *ephthasen* to represent a verb like *n-g-ʿ* or *m-t-ʾ* meaning 'has come'. But the parallelism between Luke 10.9 and 11.20 render a distinction such as this extremely unlikely. So everything depends upon the individual interpreter, and whether he puts the emphasis upon *phthanō/m-t-ʾ* and interprets *eggizō/q-r-b* in the light of this, or *vice versa*.

---

[1] On this see below, pp. 201 ff.

[2] So Weiss, see above, p. 20 n. 1.

[3] Hatch and Redpath's *Concordance* gives 128 references to *eggizō*; of these seventy-two have *q-r-b* as the original.

[4] *n-g-ʿ* six times; *m-t-ʾ* twice.

[5] In eighteen of the twenty-one occurrences in LXX.

J. Y. Campbell[1] objected to Dodd's interpretation and chose the latter alternative, interpreting *phthanō* in the light of *eggizō*; Dodd replied to this[2] by resolutely arguing for the former alternative, interpreting *eggizō* in the light of *phthanō*, and pointing to cases in the LXX where *eggizō* can mean 'arrive', namely, Jonah 3.6; Jer. 28(51).9; Ps. 31(32).6; Ps. 87(88).4; Ps. 106(107).18; Sir. 51.6; Dan. 4.8(LXX); Dan. 4.19(LXX).

Other factors have been sought to solve the problem, without any conspicuous success. Matthew Black[3] agreed that the most natural equivalent for *ēggiken* in Hebrew or Aramaic would be *q-r-b* and revived a suggestion originally made by Paul Joüon[4] that *q-r-b* can be used in cases where 'nous disons, non plus "il est proche", mais "il est arrivé".' So Black argued, *q-r-b* could underlie *ēggiken* in Mark 1.15 and be translated 'has come'.

W. R. Hutton has argued[5] that there are at least fourteen places in the New Testament where *eggizō* must be translated 'come to', 'reach', 'arrive', a fact which seems to have escaped the attention of the lexicographers. The examples are, in Hutton's order: Acts 21.33 (the police officer came up); 23.15 (before he reaches you); Luke 15.1 (the folk were coming to Jesus to hear him, that implies arrival); 18.40 (when he came up); and, similarly, Luke 12.33; 22.47; 24.15; 24.28; 19.41; 18.35; 21.8; 21.20; Heb. 7.19; James 4.8; Matt. 26.45. In fact, these examples do not demand that we add a new meaning to *eggizō* in our lexica; they indicate only that the verb means 'coming near' and that it sometimes can be used loosely of a 'coming near' that passes over into the meaning of 'coming up to'.

A more important discussion of *eggizō* in the New Testament is that by R. H. Fuller.[6] He examines the instances of the use of the verb in the New Testament where it has a time reference, apart from Mark 1.15, coming to the conclusion that in all of them the reference is to 'events which have not yet occurred, but which lie in the proximate future'.[7] This creates a presupposition that the verb is

---

[1] 'The Kingdom of God has come', *ExpT* 48, 1936–7, pp. 91–94.
[2] In *ExpT* 48, 1936–7, pp. 139–42.
[3] 'The Kingdom of God has come', *ExpT* 63, 1951–2, pp. 289 f.
[4] 'Notes Philogiques sur les Évangiles' in *Recherches de Science Religieuse* 17, 1927, p. 538.
[5] *ExpT* 64, 1952–3, pp. 89–91.
[6] *Mission and Achievement of Jesus*, 1954 (= *Mission*), pp. 21–25.
[7] Fuller, *Mission*, p. 23. In this analysis he is following W. G. Kümmel, *Verheissung und Erfüllung*, ²1953.

similarly used in Mark 1.15, and this is supported by the fact that the use of *eggizō* in the Synoptic Gospels in connection with the Kingdom of God is related to the use of that word in the LXX version of Deutero-Isaiah in connection with the 'righteousness' or 'salvation' of God (Isa. 50.8; 51.5; 56.1). In Deutero-Isaiah the reference is to the impending act of God in the event of the return from captivity, and this decisive event is still in the future although it is already 'so near that it is operative in advance in the preliminary victories of Cyrus (Isa. 41.25, etc.)'. So with the Kingdom of God in Mark 1.15 par: 'The Kingdom of God has not yet come, but it is near, so near that it is already operative in advance.'[1]

These excerpts from the extensive discussion of Dodd's interpretation of Mark 1.15 and related sayings are sufficient to show that a case can be made out both for and against this interpretation.[2] In fact half a century of discussion since Johannes Weiss first raised the question of these sayings has not settled the problems in connection with them. Dodd's interpretation has not established itself, nor has it been driven from the field; the question of the Kingdom as present or as future in the teaching of Jesus has to be settled on grounds other than the interpretation of these sayings.

[1] Fuller, *Mission*, p. 25. Fuller's interpretation of the eschatology of Jesus, which is based on this concept of a Kingdom 'operative in advance' will be discussed in our next chapter. See below, pp. 86 f.

[2] In view of the extensive nature of discussion of Mark 1.15 par. a complete review is not possible. A few further examples may be given of the various suggestions that have been made: M. J. Lagrange, *Évangile selon Saint Marc*, [3]1928, 1947, pp. 16 f., translates Mark 1.15 '*le règne de Dieu est proche*', but in his discussion inclines towards '*est arrivé*'. H. Preisker, *TWNT* II, pp. 330 f., speaks of the promised coming of the Kingdom of God as having drawn near to the present (*es ist 'unmittelbar an die Gegenwart herangerückt'*). E. Lohmeyer, *Das Evangelium des Matthäus* (ed. Schmauch), [2]1958, (on Matt. 4.17), p. 69, argues that the usage of the verb is not such as to allow us to determine whether the Kingdom is present or future; it is both present and future and the use of *eggizō* allows this double meaning. H. V. Martin, 'The Messianic Age', *ExpT* 52, 1940–1, pp. 270–5, has a position similar to that taken later by R. H. Fuller; *eggizō* means 'to come near', 'to reach up to', but not actually 'to arrive', and the Kingdom has therefore come only 'proleptically' (p. 272) in the ministry of Jesus. Kenneth W. Clark, 'Realized Eschatology', *JBL* 59, 1940, pp. 367–83, argues that both *eggizō* and *phthanō* mean 'to draw near, even to the very point of contact', but not actually to arrive, since the experience which draws near is still sequential. V. Taylor, *The Gospel According to St Mark*, 1952, p. 167, inclines to the translation 'is at hand' in Mark 1.15. C. E. B. Cranfield, *St Mark* (Cambridge Greek Testament), 1959, pp. 67 f., argues that the reference is not primarily temporal but rather spatial, that the Kingdom has come close to man in the person of Jesus, and in his person actually confronts them.

2. *The interpretation of Mark 9.1 and other sayings relating to the Kingdom as future*

Dodd's interpretation of Mark 9.1 was rejected by J. Y. Campbell[1] and J. M. Creed,[2] who argued that the reference can only be to a future event in which the people become aware of something that has just happened, not of something that had long existed.[3] In the later *Coming of Christ*, 1951, Dodd modified his view on this point and now interprets the saying in terms of the Resurrection, Pentecost and the beginning of a new era, 'the Kingdom of Christ on earth'.[4] He now appears to differentiate between the coming of the Kingdom *in* history and the consummation *beyond* history, and actually seems to envisage three elements in the total process. First, there is the coming of the Kingdom in the ministry of Jesus; secondly, there is the coming 'in power', the Resurrection, Pentecost and the era of the Kingdom of Christ on earth. But these two 'comings' do not exhaust the matter, there is a third element. 'But that is not the whole truth about what Christ taught. There are some mysterious sayings about the coming of the Son of Man which I have passed over too lightly. There are passages where we are told that before he comes there will be a breakdown of the physical universe . . . it would be absurd to take literally the language about the darkened sun and the falling stars. All the same, we cannot easily dismiss the impression that the final scene is laid where the world of space, time and matter is no longer in the picture . . . the total impression is that the forecasts of the coming of Christ in history . . . are balanced by forecasts of a coming beyond history: definitely, I should say, *beyond* history, and not as a further event in history, not even the last event.'[5]

This interpretation of Mark 9.1 as referring to the Resurrection, Pentecost and the era of the Christian Church is decidedly popular in British scholarship,[6] but the decisive argument against it has been well stated by T. W. Manson: 'Against the identification of the coming of the Kingdom with the outpouring of the Spirit and the astonishing

---

[1] J. Y. Campbell, *ExpT* 48, 1936–7, pp. 93 f.
[2] J. M. Creed, *ibid.*, pp. 184 f.
[3] See also Kümmel (*Promise*, p. 27), who accepts this.
[4] *Coming*, pp. 13 f.
[5] *Coming*, pp. 15 f.
[6] We find it for example in H. B. Swete, *The Gospel According to St Mark*, ³1909, *ad loc.*; A. C. Headlam, *Life and Teaching of Jesus Christ*, 1923, pp. 260 f.; C. Gore, *Jesus of Nazareth*, 1929, p. 119; T. F. Glasson, *The Second Advent*, 1945, ²1947, p. 112; and A. M. Hunter, *The Words and Works of Jesus*, 1950, p. 75.

progress of Christianity in the first century is to be set the fact that the people who lived through these great events did not make the identification. Paul, who was at the head of the triumphant march of the Gospel through the Empire, still looked for some greater thing. According to the account in the Acts of the Apostles, Peter found in the descent of the Spirit the fulfilment, not of Mark 9.1, but of Joel 3.1 f. (EVV 2.28 ff.).'[1] We may add that the evangelists themselves also failed to see in the saying a reference to the Resurrection, Pentecost or the era of the Christian Church. Mark has placed the saying at 9.1 because he sees at least a partial fulfilment in the Transfiguration (9.2–8), in which he is followed by many patristic writers;[2] Matthew (16.28) reinterprets the saying so that it refers to the Parousia; Luke (9.27) simply omits the phrase *elēlythyian en dynamei* and so makes the reference a quite general one. All of this is very strong evidence against the interpretation which Dodd, and the scholars mentioned in the last note on the previous page, have sought to give to this saying.

An aspect of 'realized eschatology' that has been severely criticized is the interpretation of such sayings as Matt. 8.11 par. and Mark 14.25 as referring to 'the transcendent order beyond time and space', an interpretation, which, as we saw above, Dodd has maintained in his latest work. It has been pointed out that in this a concept is being introduced which is Greek rather than Hebraic and which has no place in first-century Judaism.[3] A lone voice has been raised in defence of Dodd at this point, that of one of his pupils, W. D. Davies, who calls attention to the fact that there is an element in late Judaism in which the age to come is conceived of as existing eternally in the heavens, and the souls of the righteous as entering into it after death.[4] So 'such a conception . . . as is advocated by Dr Dodd . . . would be familiar to Palestinian Judaism'.[5]

We have now arrived at a point of very great importance in

---

[1] T. W. Manson, *Teaching*, pp. 281 f.

[2] References in H. B. Swete, *St Mark*, p. 186.

[3] So for example, in Britain, R. N. Flew, *Jesus and His Church*, [2]1943, p. 33: 'Platonic rather than Hebraic'; C. T. Cadoux, *Historic Mission of Jesus*, 1943, p. 117: 'Quite foreign to the Palestinian Jewish mind'; R. H. Fuller, *Mission and Achievement of Jesus*, 1954, p. 33; 'a wholly non-biblical, Platonic conception'. Similar judgments have been expressed in America by C. T. Craig, 'Realized Eschatology', *JBL* 56, 1937, p. 22; Floyd V. Filson, *JBR* 7, 1939, p. 62; Paul S. Minear, *JR* 24, 1944, p. 87.

[4] Davies, *Paul*, p. 315, referring primarily to I Enoch 71.15 and 39.4.

[5] *Paul and Rabbinic Judaism*, 1948, p. 320.

connection with the future element in the teaching of Jesus concerning the Kingdom of God. If it could be demonstrated that there was an element in Jewish apocalyptic which envisaged the final salvation state of men as being 'in heaven', i.e. in a transcendent realm beyond space and time, then this would open the way for an interpretation of the teaching of Jesus concerning the future like that of C. H. Dodd. If, however, this is not the case then Dodd's interpretation must be rejected, for there is no indication in the teaching of Jesus that a concept is being introduced which is new and radically different from that of his contemporaries concerning the Kingdom of God in its future aspect.

It is universally recognized that Jewish apocalyptic in general envisages the earth as the stage for the final act of the eschatological drama. To give a few examples:

And the earth shall rejoice,
and the righteous shall dwell upon it,
and the elect shall walk thereon.
                                    I Enoch 51.5.

. . . and the greatness of the kingdoms under the whole heaven shall be given to the people of the saints of the Most High.
                                                            Dan. 7.27.

And he shall purge Jerusalem, making it holy as of old so that nations shall come from the ends of the earth to see his glory.
                                                    Ps. Sol. 17.30 f.

The earth may be described as purged, transformed, renewed, even re-created, but it is nonetheless the earth, not a transcendent realm beyond it. In the classic passage in the Book of Revelation, itself characteristic in this regard of Jewish apocalyptic, we have the following description of the final state of things:

Then I saw a new heaven and a new earth, for the first heaven and the first earth had vanished and there was no longer any sea. I saw the holy city, new Jerusalem, coming down out of heaven from God, made ready for her husband. I heard a loud voice proclaiming from the throne: 'Now at last God has his dwelling among men! He will dwell among them and they shall be his people, and God himself shall be with them. He will wipe away every tear from their eyes; there shall be an end to death, and to mourning and crying and pain; for the old order has passed away!'
                                                    Rev. 21.1–4, NEB.

What the apocalyptist envisaged was a re-created universe in which
the barriers between heaven and earth were broken open and the
heavenly things descend to earth to play their part in the establishment of the final blessed state *on earth*. It has been argued, e.g., by
Charles, *Revelation ad loc.*, that the New Jerusalem referred to in
Rev. 21.1-4 is different from that described in Rev. 21.10-21. But
this is surely not necessary. The city described in the latter passage
is the city as it existed in heaven before it descended to earth, and
as it was descending to earth, in the final drama. In so far as an
apocalyptist could conceive of heaven he could conceive of it as a
realm in which were to be found the things that would come down
to earth with the breaking down of the barriers in the final acts of
the eschatological drama. That the Jews were thoroughly conversant
with such a conception can be seen from the readiness with which the
early Church accepted the idea of the ascension of Christ into heaven
until such time as he should return from there to earth.

New evidence for this understanding of heaven can now be found
in the Qumran texts. In 1QM (the War Scroll) 11.15-18 we read of
God manifesting himself as great and holy in the way in which he
fights 'from heaven' against his enemies. Further, in 1QM 12 we
read of the multitude of the Holy Ones, the armies of angels, who are
in heaven, and of the way in which these heavenly beings will
descend to earth to fight by the side of the Qumran community in the
holy war.[1] In this holy war all evil will be destroyed and the final
blessed state of the redeemed established *on earth*.

The fact that an apocalyptist could conceive of heaven as a realm
in which were to be found the beings and things that would come
down to earth at the End is the explanation for one of the passages
to which Davies calls attention: I Enoch 39.3-5:

> And in those days a whirlwind carried me off from the earth,
> And set me down at the end of the heavens
> And there I saw another vision, the dwelling places of the holy,
> And the resting places of the righteous.
> Here mine eyes saw their dwellings with his righteous angels,
> And their resting places with the holy.

Here we have the heavenly prototype of that which will be
established on earth when the End comes; there is no justification for
understanding these dwelling-places as existing permanently in a

---

[1] For the use of 'Kingdom of God' in this context see below, pp. 168 ff.

transcendent realm and for conceiving the righteous as being translated into this transcendent realm at death or at the End. Such a conception is foreign to the whole spirit of the Similitudes of Enoch (I Enoch 37–71) where again and again the earth is pictured as the place of final salvation (38.2; 45.5; 51.5), and the driving of sinners from the earth, *not* the taking of the righteous into heaven, is a necessary prerequisite of the establishment of the final blessed state (38.1; 45.6; 53.2; 69.27 f.).[1]

In calling attention to I Enoch 71.15,

And he said unto me:
He proclaims unto thee peace in the name of the world to come;
For from hence has proceeded peace since the creation of the world,
And so shall it be unto thee for ever and ever,

as evidence for the concept of a transcendent realm in Jewish apocalyptic, Davies is in very good company, for no less an authority than Paul Billerbeck has claimed that I Enoch 71, Slavonic Enoch (II Enoch) and Assumption of Moses together make up the evidence for the existence in Jewish apocalyptic of the idea 'that the consummation of salvation would take place not on earth but in heaven'.[2] But, in fact, this evidence cannot bear the weight here being put upon it.

I Enoch 71.15 says no more than that God has constantly intervened 'from heaven' on behalf of his people since the creation of the world; and v. 16,

And all shall walk in his ways since righteousness never forsaketh him;
With him shall be their dwelling places, and with him their heritage,
And they shall not be separated from him for ever and ever and ever,

is simply a prediction of the final blessed state of the righteous. The 'with him' in 16b does not necessarily involve the concept of being 'in heaven'; everywhere in apocalyptic we find the hope that the righteous will be with God for ever, but the place of this final union is the earth, and this is normally made clear by the texts themselves: I Enoch 45.6; 62.14; 105.1–2; Vita Adae et Evae 29.7, Test. Zebulun 9.8; Test. Dan 5.13; Test. Naphthali 8.3. In view of the unanimity of these texts in this regard we may surely interpret I Enoch 71.16b in

---

[1] Following N. Messel, *Die Einheitlichkeit der jüdischen Eschatologie*, 1915, pp. 79–84, although differing from him slightly in the interpretation given to I Enoch 39.3 ff.

[2] H. L. Strack and P. Billerbeck, *Kommentar zum Neuen Testament aus Talmud und Midrasch*, 4 vols., 1922–8 (= Billerbeck, *Kommentar*), here IV, p. 806.

this manner. In order to do otherwise we would have to have some specific reference to the righteous departing into heaven and this is not to be found here. Such a reference can be *read into* I Enoch 71 only by putting emphasis upon the fact that Enoch sees these things in heaven, but as we argued above in connection with I Enoch 39.3–5 he sees them there only as the heavenly prototype of that which will descend to earth at the End.

The crucial passage in the Assumption of Moses is chapter 10. In an earlier reference to this passage we argued that the reference here is to an intervention of God in history,[1] and it seems clear that the chapter offers us a series of three pictorial representations of this intervention and its consequences. In the first one (vv. 1–2) the Kingdom of God is manifested, Satan is defeated and Israel avenged of her enemies.[2] In the second (vv. 3–6) God arises from his throne and visits the earth with indignation and wrath on behalf of his sons, to the accompaniment of all kinds of astral and terrestrial phenomena. In the third (vv. 7–10) the Most High arises to punish the Gentiles and to make Israel happy; Israel is exalted to the stars and rejoices to see their enemies in Gehenna. Now the only way to read this as a reference to salvation in a transcendent realm is to take literally the reference to Israel's exaltation to the stars. In view of the frequency with which phrases like this are used as a simple metaphor for power and glory (Isa. 14.13; Obad. 4; Jer. 49.16, 51.53; Ps. Sol. 1.5; Luke 10.15) one wonders, with Messel,[3] why this reference should ever be read as anything other than the metaphor which it obviously is; certainly it provides no basis for positing a Palestinian Jewish belief in salvation in a transcendent, heavenly realm.

Slavonic Enoch (II Enoch) presents a different picture, but then this book is not evidence for the conceptions of Palestinian Judaism at the time of Christ; it should almost certainly be dated not earlier than the seventh century AD.[4]

It can be seen from this discussion that there is not to be found in Palestinian Judaism at the time of Christ any real evidence for a belief in a state of salvation to be experienced in a transcendent realm beyond time and space. Since there is no indication whatsoever in the

[1] See above, pp. 26 f.
[2] On this see further below, pp. 169 f.
[3] *Einheitlichkeit*, p. 73.
[4] For a review of the discussion leading to this conclusion see H. H. Rowley, *The Relevance of Apocalyptic*, ²1947, pp. 95 f. Rowley himself now no longer regards this book as part of Jewish apocalyptic, p. 8.

teaching of Jesus that he was introducing a new conception radically different from those of his contemporaries, this aspect of Dodd's 'realized eschatology' is to be rejected.

3. *The interpretation of the parables of the Kingdom*

The most important aspects of Dodd's work is undoubtedly his exegesis of the parables of the Kingdom; whatever may be the weaknesses of 'realized eschatology' at other points, here it has stood the test of subsequent discussion. Not only can there be no going back from Dodd's method of interpreting the parables in accordance with their *Sitz im Leben Jesu*, there can also be no denial of the fact that the parables do teach that the Kingdom of God is present in the ministry of Jesus. In this respect Dodd's work modified the Weiss-Schweitzer position once and for all, and subsequent attempts to maintain that the Kingdom was for Jesus a wholly future concept have largely been limited to the work of Bultmann, not in this respect now followed by the major members of his school,[1] and to the 'proleptic eschatologists' of whom the most important Anglo-American representative is probably R. H. Fuller.[2]

The parabolic teaching of Jesus has been subjected to further study since the publication of Dodd's *Parables of the Kingdom*, and in this field the definitive work is now that of Professor J. Jeremias of Göttingen. Beginning with a review of Dodd's book[3] he went on to his own work on the parables[4] in which he has shown that the parables do teach the Kingdom as present, in agreement with Dodd, and that there is also in them the Kingdom as future, in disagreement with Dodd. In the light of these findings he proposed the expression *sich realisierenden Eschatologie*[5] as a description of the emphasis of Jesus, an expression which Hooke aptly translates 'an eschatology that is in process of realization'.[6] Dodd has agreed in principle to this

---

[1] On Bultmann and the 'post-Bultmannians' see below, pp. 112–29.

[2] On Fuller's 'proleptic eschatology' see below, pp. 86 f.

[3] Jeremias, 'Eine neue Schau der Zukunftsaussagen Jesu', *Theologische Blätter* 20, 1941, pp. 216–22.

[4] Jeremias, *Die Gleichnisse Jesu*, [1]1947, [2]1947, [3]1954, [4]1956, [5]1960. Of these editions the second and the fourth were considerable revisions; the fifth edition has only bibliographical additions as compared with the fourth. The third German edition was translated into English by S. H. Hooke and published as *The Parables of Jesus*, 1954. We quote the English edition as *Parables* and the fourth German edition as *Gleichnisse*.

[5] *Gleichnisse*, p. 194, where he tells us that this term was suggested to him by Haenchen.

[6] *Parables*, p. 159.

modification,[1] which would seem to indicate that he himself would no longer maintain strictly the wholly present emphasis which we find in his earlier work, as indeed we have already noted in connection with his book *The Coming of Christ*.[2] Since the delineation of the element in the parabolic teaching of Jesus in which the Kingdom is present is and remains Dodd's most important contribution to the whole discussion, and since the establishment of this element as really to be found in the whole teaching of Jesus is essential to a true understanding of 'Kingdom of God' in that teaching, we propose here to summarize the evidence for it, with due acknowledgments to the work of Dodd and Jeremias[3] and with some additional emphases of our own.

SUMMARY OF EVIDENCE FOR THE KINGDOM AS PRESENT IN THE TEACHING OF JESUS

1. The presence of the Kingdom is a part of the message of the parables.

It is necessarily implied in the following parables:[4]

The Hid Treasure and the Costly Pearl (Matt. 13.44–46).[5]

The Tower-builder and the King Going to War (Luke 14.28–33).[6]

The Fig-tree (Mark 13.28 par.).[7]

The Lamp under the Bushel (Mark 4.21 par.).[8]

2. Jesus consistently speaks of himself and his work in eschatological imagery.

In the reply to the question about fasting (Mark 2.18–22 par.) the three pictures which Jesus uses of his work, Wedding Feast, New Patches and Old Garments, New Wine and Old Wineskins, all imply a claim that the Messianic times had begun in his work, and his disciples do not fast because the old order in which fasting had its part has passed away.[9]

---

[1] *The Interpretation of the Fourth Gospel*, 1953, p. 447 n. 1.

[2] See above, p. 67.

[3] W. G. Kümmel, *Promise*, pp. 105–40, has also presented a summary of this element in the teaching of Jesus.

[4] We quote only those parables which both C. H. Dodd and J. Jeremias interpret in this way.

[5] Dodd, *Parables*, pp. 112 f.; Jeremias, *Parables*, p. 140.

[6] Dodd, *Parables*, p. 114; Jeremias, *Parables*, p. 137.

[7] Dodd, *Parables*, p. 136; Jeremias, *Parables*, p. 96.

[8] Dodd, *Parables*, pp. 142 f.; Jeremias, *Parables*, p. 96 n. 34.

[9] Cf. Jeremias, *Jesus als Weltvollender*, 1930 (henceforth quoted as *Weltvollender*), pp. 21–31; art. *nymphios*, *TWNT* IV, pp. 1094 ff.; *Parables*, pp. 94 f.; Dodd, *Parables*, pp. 115–17.

Distinctively eschatological figures used by Jesus of himself and his work are:

The Shepherd (Matt. 9.36 par.; Matt. 10.6; 25.32; Mark 14.27 par.; Luke 15.3–7; 12.32).[1]

The Husbandman who sends out his servants to reap the harvest (Matt. 9.37 f.; Luke 10.1 f.).[2]

There are many others through which 'a thread of eschatological meaning runs'.[3]

3. Jesus applies to himself and to his ministry Old Testament prophecies traditionally referred to the joys of the Messianic age.

Luke 4.16–21 claims the fulfilment in the ministry of Jesus of Isa. 61.1 f.

Matt. 11.2–6 (cf. Luke 7.18–23) refers to the fulfilment in the work of Jesus of Isa. 35.5 f.; 61.1.[4]

This aspect of the evidence becomes particularly important when we compare it with what we find in Qumran. In Qumran prophecies of eschatological blessings are still referred to the future, e.g. 1QpHab 10.4–11.2, where, in commenting on Hab. 1.14, the knowledge of the glory of God is still a future expectation.

4. Jesus speaks of his ministry in terms which necessarily imply that with it the Messianic times have begun.

The Blessedness of the Disciples (Matt. 13.16 f. = Luke 10.23 f.) and the Greater than Solomon or Jonah (Matt. 12.41 f. = Luke 11.31 f.), both imply this.[5]

The gift of God's forgiveness was the supreme gift expected of the Messianic times. In Mark 2.5 par. this gift is available in the present.[6]

Together with the offer of God's (Messianic) forgiveness there is the whole emphasis upon the fact that salvation is sent to the poor and

---

[1] Cf. I Enoch 85–90; Ps. Sol. 17.40 f. Jeremias, art. *poimēn*, *TWNT* VI, pp. 484 ff.

[2] Dodd, *Parables*, p. 187; Jeremias, *Parables*, pp. 95 f.

[3] Jeremias, *Parables*, p. 97; cf. *Weltvollender*, pp. 33 f.

[4] Dodd, *Parables*, p. 47; Jeremias, *Parables*, p. 93.

[5] Dodd, *Parables*, pp. 46 f.

[6] Cf. J. Schniewind, *Das Neue Testament Deutsch* I, on Mark 2.12. Jeremias, *Parables*, pp. 98, 144. Evidence for the forgiveness of sins as an eschatological or Messianic hope in Judaism is to be found in *Pesiqta* 149a, where the tongue of the Messiah is forgiveness and pardon, and I Enoch 5.6:

> and there shall be forgiveness of sins,
> and every mercy and peace and forbearance;
> there shall be salvation unto them, a goodly light.

that Jesus has come as a saviour for sinners. How great a part this must have played in his ministry can be seen from the amount of offence which it caused, and the number of parables concerned to defend it.[1]

5. The Exorcisms of Jesus, and of his disciples, are a manifestation of the Kingdom of God in the present.

Matt. 12.28 = Luke 11.20 of the work of Jesus.[2]

Luke 10.18 of the work of his disciples.

With the defeat of Satan the eschatological time of salvation has begun, cf. the Binding of the Strong Man, Mark 3.27. Again, the Qumran texts help us to see how important this aspect of the evidence is. In Qumran the sect is very conscious of the fact that it suffers under the dominion of Belial, and longs for the day when that 'Kingdom' will be destroyed in God's eschatological visitation. Jesus is claiming that this visitation has begun in his own work, and in that of his disciples.

6. The Teaching of Jesus supersedes that of the Torah of Moses.

Jesus set his own concept of the will of God over against the Law as given through Moses, as e.g. in the dispute about divorce, Matt. 19.3–19 (cf. Mark 10.2–10). Similarly, he sets before his disciples the eschatological Torah, which is to supersede the Mosaic Torah as the revelation of the final and absolute will of God, Matt. 5.17 ff.[3] Again, the Qumran sect, on the authority of their founder, only obey the Mosaic Law the more earnestly, for them the eschatological Torah is an object of future expectation.

This last point concerning the eschatological Torah is one of very considerable importance and we must deal with it in some detail in order to justify the statements that we have made. The question is whether there was to be found in Judaism an expectation of a new Torah for the End-time, an eschatological Torah that would super-sede the Mosaic Torah. W. D. Davies has discussed the evidence in the Old Testament, in the apocalyptic and rabbinical literature, and in the Damascus Fragment,[4] and has come to the conclusion that the

---

[1] Among this number are some of the most important and distinctive of all the parables, e.g.: The Two Sons, the Two Debtors, the Wicked Husbandmen, the Prodigal Son, the Lost Sheep, the Lost Coin, the Labourers in the Vineyard, the Pharisee and the Publican. See Jeremias, *Parables*, pp. 99–120.

[2] Cf. Kümmel, *Promise*, pp. 105–9, 113 f.

[3] Jeremias, *Weltvollender*, pp. 61–69.

[4] In *Torah in the Messianic Age and/or the Age to Come* (Journal of Biblical Literature Monograph Series, Volume VII), 1952.

sources in general reveal 'the expectation that the Torah in its existing form would persist into the Messianic Age', but that at the same time 'there were elements inchoate in the Messianic hope of Judaism, which would make it possible for some to regard the Messianic Age as marked by a new Torah'.[1] The evidence for this latter 'cannot be regarded as very impressive', but it is none the less there and its comparative scarcity may be due to 'deliberate surgery' in the interests of an anti-Christian polemic. 'It is . . . the reaction against the New Law preached by early Christians which may have caused the comparative silence of the Rabbinic sources on the concept of a New Law.'[2]

With the publication of the Qumran texts the situation has changed, for here we find definite evidence for the expectation of a new, eschatological Torah. The relevant text is 1Q34 ii 2.5–8[3] which we may translate:

> In the time of thy good pleasure[4] thou wilt choose for thyself a people, for thou hast remembered thy covenant and thou wilt make them to be set apart unto thee as holy and distinct from all the peoples, and thou wilt renew thy covenant[5] unto them with a show of glory[6] and with words of thy holy spirit, with works of thy hand and a writing of thy right hand[7] to reveal to them the instructions of glory[8] and the heights of eternity . . . for them a faithful shepherd.[9]

Here we have a picture of things as they will be in the End-time. The faithful will be set apart and God will renew his covenant with them, and just as the provisions of the former covenant were given to the first Israel in the Torah, so the hand of God will write his laws

[1] P. 85.

[2] Pp. 86–90.

[3] Published *DJD* I, p. 154.

[4] *qṣ rṣwnk* obviously an expression denoting the End-time. *'t rṣwn* is found in the context of eschatological promise in the Old Testament, e.g. Isa. 49.8.

[5] *wṭhdš bryṭk*. The root *ḥdš* gives the adjective 'new'.

[6] Cf. Ex. 24.16–18; so Gaster, *The Scriptures of the Dead Sea Sect*, 1957, p. 298.

[7] An 'allusion au Decalogue', Milik, *DJD* I, p. 155.

[8] *yswry kbwdš* Milik, *DJD* I, p. 154, translates it 'les règles de gloire'. Cf. 1QS 3.1 which reads *yswry d'ʿt mšpty ṣdq*, 'instructions of knowledge of righteous judgments'. CD 7.5 reads *kl yswry bryṭ n'mnwṭ lhm* and Rabin (*The Zadokite Documents*, 1956, *ad loc.*) restores a further *bryṭ* and translates 'according to all instructions of the covenant, the covenant of God shall stand fast with them'. In this context *yswry* would appear to have a meaning similar to that of *yswdy*, Rabin refers from CD 7.5 to CD 10.6 *yswdy hbryṭ*, 'teachings of the covenant'.

[9] 'I.e., a new Moses. The lawgiver was known in late Judaism as "the faithful shepherd"; cp. Ex. 3.1.' So Gaster, *Scriptures*, p. 298. For 'the shepherd' as an eschatological figure see above, p. 75.

anew and the new Israel of the End-time will receive the Torah appropriate to that time.

A confirmation of the difference between the Torah appropriate to the present time and the Torah of the End-time is also to be seen in CD 12.23 and 14.19, where it is expressly stated that the laws in which the community is to walk are valid 'during the epoch of wickedness *until* there shall arise the Messiah of Aaron and Israel'. With the coming of the eschatological figure(s) the situation changes and the epoch of wickedness comes to an end. In 1QSa we have a picture of the Israel of the End-time[1] and here there is no reference to the 'era of wickedness' or to the 'domination of Belial'.[2] 'The provisions of the covenant'[3] are read to the community and 'the commandments of the Torah'[4] are the subject of discussion and decision; in the light of what we have seen above it is a fair assumption that these are references to the New Law appropriate to the new situation, although it must be admitted that 1QSa does not speak of *twrh ḥdšh*.

We would conclude from this discussion of the evidence in the Qumran texts that the expectation of a new, eschatological Torah was part of Jewish expectation at the time of Christ, and it is against the background of this expectation that we must set the ethical teaching of Jesus. In setting his own concept of the will of God over against the Mosaic Law, and in so carefully contrasting his teaching with that of the old Law,[5] he is claiming that his teaching is the New Law of Jewish expectation. In his work the End-time is beginning and in his teaching the Law appropriate to that time is being revealed.

Such then is the evidence for the Kingdom as present in the teaching of Jesus and, as we have already said, we believe that there is no going back from the recognition that this is an emphasis truly to be found in the teaching of Jesus concerning the Kingdom of God, and it is to the lasting credit of C. H. Dodd that he first called this emphasis decisively to the attention of modern New Testament scholarship.

---

[1] *'dt yšr'l b' ḥryt hymym*, 'the community of Israel at the end of the days'. 1QSa 1.1.
[2] Frank M. Cross, Jr., *Ancient Library of Qumran*, 1958 (= *Ancient Library*), p. 66.
[3] *ḥwqy hbryt* 1QSa 1.5.
[4] *mšptwt htwrh* 1QSa 1.11.
[5] See above, p. 76.

V

THE KINGDOM OF GOD AS BOTH PRESENT & FUTURE IN THE TEACHING OF JESUS

CADOUX, GUY, HUNTER, TAYLOR, FULLER

THE WORK OF C. H. DODD marked a new stage in the discussion of Kingdom of God in the teaching of Jesus; the discussion had moved from 'thoroughgoing eschatology' to 'realized eschatology', having left by the wayside 'the transformation of apocalyptic', 'the denial of apocalyptic' and the various other attempts to maintain the older views. Accepting Dodd's emphasis upon the Kingdom as present in the teaching of Jesus the discussion now turned upon the point as to whether or not this was the only emphasis in that teaching, and it gradually became established that it was not: the Kingdom of God is both present and future in the teaching of Jesus.

Since Dodd is a British scholar we are perhaps justified in restricting ourselves in the first instance to the British discussion of this point, and we shall concern ourselves first at this point with the following six works:

C. J. Cadoux, *The Historic Mission of Jesus*, 1943 (= *Mission*)
H. A. Guy, *The New Testament Doctrine of the Last Things*, 1948 (= *Doctrine*)
A. M. Hunter, *The Words and Works of Jesus*, 1950 (= *Words*)
Vincent Taylor, *The Gospel According to St Mark*, 1952 (= *St Mark*)
        The Life and Ministry of Jesus, 1954 (= *Life*)
R. H. Fuller, *The Mission and Achievement of Jesus* (= *Mission*)

Cadoux, Guy, Hunter and Taylor all follow C. H. Dodd in seeing the Kingdom of God as present in the ministry of Jesus.[1] Fuller sees

---

[1] Jesus is 'the person through whom the Kingdom became a reality among men' (Cadoux, *Mission*, p. 269). In some aspects of the teaching of Jesus 'the Kingdom is certainly thought of as a present reality' (Guy, *Doctrine*, p. 44). 'In some decisive

the matter differently; for him the Kingdom has not come in the ministry of Jesus, 'but it is near, so near that it is already operative in advance'.[1] But all five scholars are agreed that there are elements in the teaching of Jesus in which the Kingdom is certainly future. They point to Mark 1.15, which they interpret as having a future reference, and to Mark 9.1, which they insist cannot be interpreted in any other way than to a future coming of the Kingdom. They adduce the petition 'Thy Kingdom come' in the Lord's Prayer and the eschatological prospect at the Lord's Supper (Mark 14.25).[2] They argue that in the teaching of Jesus concerning 'entering' or 'receiving' the Kingdom of God in such sayings as Mark 9.47; 10.15 par.; 10.23–25 par.; Matt. 7.21; the reference is to the future.[3] They also see that a Kingdom in the future is implied in Jesus' expectation of a table-fellowship of the eschatological community with God (Matt. 8.11 par.; 22.1–10; Luke 14.15–24; 22.29 f.).[4]

In addition to the above both Guy and Fuller argue that the 'parables of growth' in Mark 4 imply that the 'climax' (Guy) or 'decisive event' (Fuller) lies in the future.[5] Fuller also finds a future reference in other parables and parabolic sayings of Jesus: the Fig-tree (Mark 13.28–29 par.), the Cloud and the South Wind (Luke 12.54–56, cf. Matt. 16.2 f.), Agree with Thine Adversary (Luke 12.58 f., cf. Matt. 5.25 f.), in all of which the decisive event is still in the future. The 'parables of decision' (the ten Virgins, Matt. 25.1–13, the Rich Fool, Luke 12.16–20, the Pearl and the Hidden

sense the Reign of God has come in the person and work of Jesus' (Hunter, *Works*, p. 74). 'He (Jesus) taught that the Kingdom was present in himself and his ministry' (Taylor, *Life*, p. 67).

[1] Fuller's position in this regard is part of his whole approach to the eschatology of Jesus and will be discussed later in this chapter. See below, pp. 86 f.

[2] Cadoux, *Mission*, pp. 198 f. Guy, *Doctrine*, pp. 48–50. Hunter, *Works*, p. 75. Taylor, *Life*, pp. 67 f. and *St Mark*, *passim*. Fuller, *Mission*, pp. 21–25, 27 f., 33.

[3] Guy, *Doctrine*, p. 49. Fuller, *Mission*, pp. 29–31. Taylor, *St Mark*, p. 423 (with reservations). This argument from these sayings goes back to H. Windisch, 'Die Sprüche vom Eingehen in das Reich Gottes', *ZNW* 27, 1928, pp. 163–92, who is followed by Jeremias, *Parables*, p. 100 n. 53.

[4] Guy, *Doctrine*, p. 50. Hunter, *Words*, p. 75. Taylor, *Life*, p. 68. Fuller, *Mission*, p. 33. The table-fellowship in this teaching is, of course, symbolic of the perfect personal relationship that will exist between God and that blessed eschatological community that will be for ever in his presence. On the necessity of our recognizing the nature of the symbolism of the teaching of Jesus in this context see Jeremias, *Weltvollender*, pp. 68 ff.

[5] Guy, *Doctrine*, p. 49. Fuller, *Mission*, pp. 44 f.

Treasure, Matt. 13.44–46) all call for decision in face of an impending but still future event. Also in the case of the Money in Trust (Matt. 25.14–30; Luke 19.12–27), the Marriage Feast (Matt. 22.2–14; Luke 14.16–24), and the Vineyard (Mark 12.1–9 par.) the decisive event lies neither in the present nor the past, but in the very near future.

The future reference is not certain in all of these cases; Professor Jeremias would, for example, refer the Fig-tree to the signs of the time of salvation in the ministry of Jesus, and the Pearl and the Hidden Treasure to the demand of Jesus for absolute self-sacrifice in response to the Good News in the present,[1] but there is sufficient evidence to make Fuller's point valid: the parables of Jesus do teach a future Kingdom of God and not only a Kingdom in the present.

JEREMIAS

The work of Professor Jeremias on the parables of Jesus, to which we referred in chapter IV above as being the definitive work on the parables since that of C. H. Dodd,[2] is also a major contribution to the discussion at this point, since it makes clear the fact that the message of the parables includes an emphasis upon the Kingdom both as present,[3] and also as future.[4] In the fourth German edition this has been made particularly clear; for the relationship of Jeremias's work to that of C. H. Dodd, and his emphasis upon the great crisis as present in the ministry of Jesus, could lead to the misunderstanding that he was not interpreting the teaching of Jesus as also looking forward to a crisis subsequent to his ministry, to the Kingdom as future.[5] So in the revised fourth edition there is now a new paragraph inserted into the discussion of the delay of the Parousia[6] in which Jeremias makes it quite clear that he believes that Jesus looked

[1] Jeremias, *Parables*, pp. 96, 140.

[2] See above, p. 73.

[3] *Parables*, pp. 93–99, 'Now is the Day of Salvation', and 99–120, 'God's Mercy for Sinners'. *Gleichnisse*, pp. 98–106, 107–27.

[4] *Parables*, pp. 89–92, 'The Great Assurance', and 120–6 'The Imminence of Catastrophe'. The illogical nature of the arrangement of these sections in *Parables* has been corrected in *Gleichnisse*, where the sections which in effect deal with the Kingdom as present (see previous note) are followed by those dealing in effect with the Kingdom as future, pp. 127–39, and 139–48.

[5] In fact, J. A. T. Robinson did so misunderstand Jeremias's interpretation of the so-called crisis-parables. See below, pp. 144 f.

[6] *Gleichnisse*, pp. 42 f. It would come after the end of the first paragraph on p. 41 of *Parables*.

forward to a crisis subsequent to his own ministry, and the sections
on the Message of the Parables have been revised and rearranged so
that the emphasis upon the Day of Salvation and God's mercy for
sinners as present is now followed by the emphasis upon the future
crisis.[1]

Jeremias's evidence for the future element in the eschatology of
Jesus is in two parts: (1) those parables which look forward to the
future for the fulfilment of that which has begun in the present, in
the light of which the present is a time of hope;[2] and (2) those which
look towards the future in expectation of an imminent catastrophe,
in the light of which the present becomes a time of crisis.[3] The first
of these parts is expanded in the fourth edition of the book and
includes both the four contrast parables (Mustard Seed, Leaven,
Sower and Patient Husbandman) which teach the unwavering
assurance that God's hour is approaching: 'Out of nothing, in spite
of apparent neglect, undeterred by failure, God is bringing in his
Kingdom',[4] and the parables of the Unjust Judge and the Friend at
Midnight,[5] which also reflect this unwavering assurance in regard
to the future, this time with the emphasis upon God's mercy towards
his own.[6] The second aspect of this future element is the imminence of
catastrophe, about which Jesus warns his contemporaries in the
parable of the Children in the Market-place (Matt. 11.16 f. par.,
Luke 7.31 f.), in the saying about the Signs of the Times (Luke
12.54–56) and similar sayings (Matt. 24.28; Matt. 6.22 f.; Luke
11.34–36), in the references to Sodom and Gomorrah (Luke 17.28 f.)
and the Flood (Matt. 24.37–39; Luke 17.26 f.), and in many other
parables and parabolic sayings.[7] In addition to these general warnings
we also find warnings directed to particular groups; to the enemies of
Jesus; to the leaders of the people and especially the scribes; to the
Sanhedrin and the Pharisees; to Jerusalem as representative of the
people; to the people of Israel as such; to the Messiah's generation,
and even to the Messianic community itself.[8]

[1] See p. 81 n. 4 above.
[2] *Gleichnisse*, pp. 127–39; cf. *Parables*, pp. 89–92.
[3] *Gleichnisse*, pp. 139–48; cf. *Parables*, pp. 120–6.
[4] *Parables*, p. 92; *Gleichnisse*, p. 133.
[5] Luke 18.2–8; 11.5–8; *Gleichnisse*, pp. 133–9. In the earlier edition these were
included under the parables designed to vindicate the Good News, *Parables*, 115–18.
[6] *Gleichnisse*, p. 139.
[7] *Gleichnisse*, pp. 139–44; *Parables*, pp. 120–4.
[8] *Gleichnisse*, pp. 144–8; *Parables*, pp. 124–6.

SUMMARY OF EVIDENCE FOR THE KINGDOM AS FUTURE IN THE TEACHING OF JESUS

There can be no doubt but that the parabolic teaching of Jesus does contain a major element that looks forward to a decisive eschatological event in the future, and we can add here other aspects of his teaching which carry the same message.

It is to be found in Jesus' expectation of a future state of things in which the present order of life would be reversed. This expectation we find in the Beatitudes (Luke 6.20–26; Matt. 5.3–12);[1] in Matt. 19.30 (the last shall be first and the first last); Matt. 10.26 par. (the hidden shall be revealed); Matt. 18.4 (the lowly shall be exalted, cf. Luke 14.11; Matt. 23.12; Luke 18.14).

It is implied in Jesus' expectation of a New Temple (Mark 14.58 par., 15.29 par.). The authenticity of this expectation is demonstrated by the use of it as an accusation at the trial of Jesus. The use of the symbol of the New Temple to describe the eschatological community in its perfect sacral relationship with God can now be illustrated from the Qumran texts where in 4Q Flor. 1.1–7 the blessed state of the community at 'the end of days' is envisaged in the imagery of a sanctuary.

It is to be seen behind the unfulfilled prediction of Matt. 10.23. That the whole passage in which this is to be found is not readily to be used to reconstruct the teaching of the historical Jesus we would agree, but such an unfulfilled prediction is not lightly to be brushed aside, whatever we may make of the passage as a whole.[2]

It is implied in the teaching of Jesus concerning future tribulation for the disciples, and the constant necessity of watchfulness in view of the suddenness of the end. That this is a major part of the teaching of Jesus as it was recorded in Q has been shown by T. W. Manson,[3] and it is especially to be found in Luke 12.35–46 par.; 12.49–53 par.; 13.22–30 par.; 17.22–30.

If we accept the position that the Kingdom is both present and future in the teaching of Jesus then we must immediately face the question:

---

[1] It has been pointed out by Frank M. Cross, Jr., *Ancient Library*, pp. 62, 67 n. 81, that the first and second Beatitudes (in the Lucan order) involve an eschatological interpretation of Psalm 37 in terms of the community that shall inherit the Kingdom of God and of the Messianic Banquet, an interpretation of this Psalm already to be found in Qumran, 4QpPs 37 1.8 f., and 2.10 f.

[2] On this point Schweitzer was surely right. See above, p. 32.

[3] *Sayings of Jesus*, 1949, pp. 114–48.

What is the relationship between these elements in the teaching concerning the Kingdom? Each of the scholars whose work we have reviewed in this chapter has attempted to answer this question.

RELATION BETWEEN PRESENT AND FUTURE EMPHASES IN THE TEACHING OF JESUS AS CONCEIVED IN BRITISH SCHOLARSHIP

C. J. Cadoux believes that Jesus concerned himself with the political condition of the Jews, that he worked for the coming of the Kingdom of God on earth through a re-awakened national sense of vocation in Israel. That which had begun in the ministry of Jesus would 'through the activity of Jesus himself, his disciples, and his re-awakened fellow-countrymen, extend throughout the earth, until the time was ripe for God to bring about the great climax. All thought of rebellion against Rome or of a war of vengeance to be waged on the Gentiles would vanish away. . . . The Son of Man, "the people of the saints of the Most High", would become the unofficial leaders and teachers of the race. In the shade of the great tree would the birds of heaven be glad to roost. God's will would be done at last by all mankind.'[1] All this is reminiscent of what we found earlier in the work of Bacon and others,[2] and as a picture of the expectation of the historical Jesus it is completely unacceptable. It attributes to him a *naïveté* about human nature that he certainly did not possess, and it offers us a travesty of his true attitude in that it puts all the emphasis upon man and what he may do and not upon God and what he is doing. The Kingdom of God in the teaching of Jesus is not something that God will 'bring about' on the basis of a world-wide movement for moral and spiritual renewal among men; it is the mighty power of God being revealed already in the ministry of Jesus, and shortly to be revealed completely in the final consummation of the Kingdom.

Both H. A. Guy and A. M. Hunter distinguish between different elements in the future expectation of the historical Jesus. Guy distinguishes between the expectation of the coming of the Kingdom and that of the coming of the Son of Man. 'The two themes should be treated separately.'[3] The Day of the Son of Man was expected shortly and the reference is to an act of divine judgment upon Jesus' contemporaries; this expectation was actually fulfilled in the

---

[1] C. J. Cadoux, *Mission*, p. 218.
[2] See above, pp. 51 f.
[3] Guy, *Doctrine*, p. 49.

destruction of Jerusalem. With regard to the present and future elements in the coming of the Kingdom, this tension is not to be resolved and indicates that it is possible that 'Jesus thought of the Kingdom as essentially timeless'.[1] A. M. Hunter distinguishes between the expectation revealed in Mark 9.1, which he refers to the Resurrection; that in the petition 'Thy Kingdom come' in the Lord's Prayer, which he refers to the Resurrection, Pentecost and the growth of the Christian Church; and that in Mark 14.25; Luke 22.16; 22.28 f.; and Matt. 8.11 par., which he refers to the transcendent order beyond time and space.[2]

These attempts to distinguish between various elements in the teaching of Jesus concerning the future fail to take into account the pictorial language of Jesus, and indeed of all Jewish apocalyptic. The future eschatological event could be spoken of as a 'coming of the Kingdom "in power"' (Mark 9.1), as the 'consummation of all things' (Mark 13.4), as the coming of the Son of Man (Mark 8.38; Matt. 10.23), or as the 'Day of the Son of Man' (Luke 17.24). Similarly the future eschatological state could be pictured as the complete reversal of the existing order of things (Luke 6.20–26; Matt. 5.3–12; etc.), in the imagery of table-fellowship between the eschatological community and God (Matt. 8.11 par., etc.), or in the imagery of a perfect sacral relationship between them (Mark 14.58 par.; 15.29). This use of different imagery in different sayings is an attempt to bring out various features in an event which by reason of its eschatological nature cannot be described in a factual manner; we are not justified in distinguishing between one picture and another as if they referred to different events. The different pictures refer to different aspects of the same thing, not to different things. That the coming of the Kingdom is synonymous with the coming of the Son of Man can be seen, for example, in the first occurrence of 'Son of Man' in an eschatological context, Dan. 7.13 f., 27, where the two are most definitely linked together. Thus we are not justified in distinguishing between various elements in the future expectation of Jesus and referring them to different events; nor may we seek to resolve the tension between the present and the future Kingdom in the teaching of Jesus by the introduction of such concepts as a 'timeless Kingdom' or a 'transcendent order beyond time and space'.

[1] Guy, *Doctrine*, pp. 75 f.
[2] A. M. Hunter, *Words*, pp. 75 f. For a discussion of somewhat similar views in the work of C. H. Dodd, see above, pp. 68 ff.

A 'timeless Kingdom' is as foreign to first-century Judaism as a 'transcendent order beyond time and space',[1] and if Jesus held such views he singularly failed to impress them upon his followers.

Vincent Taylor sees that Jesus 'thought that the Kingdom was present in himself and his ministry, but was also future in the sense that it was to be consummated by God'.[2] At the beginning of his work, during the Galilean ministry, the Kingdom is close at hand (Mark 1.15) and indeed present in Jesus' works (Luke 11.20). As the ministry develops the note of imminence in the future expectation becomes less marked. In Mark 9.1 the expectation is less immediate than at Mark 1.15, and in Mark 13.32 and Mark 14.25 is still less pronounced and everything is left to the good pleasure of the Father.[3] The difficulty with this view is the assumption that the sayings referred to have been preserved with sufficient accuracy for us to be able to detect such delicate nuances of meaning as the note of immediacy in them, and that the historical outline of the Gospel of Mark, and the placing of the sayings within that outline, is sufficiently accurate for us to be able to treat them as coming from definite points of time within the ministry, with a sequence and a time differential that can be known to us.[4] Mark 1.15 is, for example, a summary of what Jesus proclaimed; are we justified in assuming that such was his proclamation only at the beginning of his ministry? Again, Mark has introduced the saying in 9.1 at this point because he sees at least a partial fulfilment of it in the Transfiguration (9.2 8),[5] and 13.32 also owes its present position to the compiler of the Apocalyptic Discourse (13.1–37).[6] This being so, it is extremely difficult to see how they can be used as evidence for a progressive development in the expectation of Jesus. That the future Kingdom is to be viewed as the consummation of that which is manifested in the ministry of Jesus is obviously true, but beyond that Taylor's view must be regarded as being built on most insecure foundations.

FULLER: 'PROLEPTIC ESCHATOLOGY'

We noted at the beginning of this chapter that R. H. Fuller does not agree that the Kingdom of God is present in the ministry of Jesus, he argues that it may only be described as being so near that

[1] On the latter see above, pp. 68–73.
[2] Vincent Taylor, *Life*, p. 67.
[3] *Ibid.*, pp. 76 f.
[4] On the question of the historicity of the Marcan order, see below, p. 96.
[5] So Taylor himself, *St Mark*, p. 385.
[6] So, again, Taylor himself, *St Mark*, p. 522.

it is already operative in advance, so near that the signs of its coming are already apparent in the presence and activity of Jesus. Even Matt. 12.28 par. does not mean that the Kingdom is actually present. In this logion, as also in Luke 10.17 f., the exorcisms are only a vivid sign of the proximity of the Kingdom. 'The fact that the demons are yielding to his exorcisms is for Jesus so overwhelming proof, so vivid a sign, of the proximity of the Kingdom, that he speaks of it as though it had arrived already.'[1] Similarly, Matt. 11.12 shows that 'the Reign of God is already breaking in proleptically in the proclamation and signs of Jesus (that is the difference between the time of Jesus' ministry and the time of John the Baptist), but it would be to overstate the case to say that with Jesus the Kingdom of God had already come'.[2]

This seems to be going too far in a reaction against C. H. Dodd. The point at issue is whether in Matt. 12.28 and Luke 10.17 f. the exorcisms are a sign of the actual presence of the Kingdom or only of its imminence; has the Kingdom actually come or is it only 'casting its shadow before it'? The actual meaning of *ephthasen* in Matt. 12.28 is undoubtedly 'has come',[3] but Fuller attempts to surmount this difficulty by arguing that Jesus is using the 'familiar prophetic device' of speaking of the future as though it were already present.[4] Here one could reply that the exorcisms which occasioned the saying are not the product of a 'vivid prophetic imagination' but an indubitable fact in the present, and that this is a strong argument for taking the verb in its literal sense. But the decisive factor is to be found in the cumulative weight of the evidence in the teaching of Jesus for the fact that he saw the Kingdom as present in his ministry.[5] Matt. 12. 28 and Luke 10.17 f. do not stand alone; they are but a part of the whole evidence for this, and we would maintain that the weight of the whole evidence is such as to rule out Fuller's view of the Kingdom as only proleptically 'operative in advance' in the ministry of Jesus.

RELATION BETWEEN PRESENT AND FUTURE EMPHASES IN THE TEACHING OF JESUS AS CONCEIVED BY JEREMIAS, KÜMMEL AND CULLMANN

We noticed above that J. Jeremias has modified the work of C. H.

[1] Fuller, *Mission*, p. 26.
[2] *Ibid.*, p. 32.
[3] See the discussion above, pp. 64–66.
[4] Fuller, *Mission*, p. 26. He argues similarly in the case of Luke 10.18; the disciples' success 'is a sign of the approach of Satan's final overthrow ... which, with vivid prophetic imagination, he (Jesus) sees as an already accomplished fact' (p. 27).
[5] Summarized above, pp. 74–78.

Dodd on the parables in that he has argued for both a present and a future element in the parabolic teaching concerning the Kingdom.[1] In accordance with this he has suggested a modification of Dodd's terminology from 'realized eschatology' to 'eschatology that is in process of realization'.[2]

Jeremias's understanding of this is that the hour of fulfilment is here because the bringer of salvation is here; this is the basic message of the parables,[3] but it is not their whole message. Also in the parables is a teaching concerning a future in which that which has begun in the ministry of Jesus will reach its consummation. Jeremias here sees the teaching of the early Church as essentially true to that of Jesus: the present time of salvation would lead up to a time of catastrophe which would reach its climax in the eschatological triumph of God, the Parousia.[4]

This conception of the relationship between the present and future elements in the teaching of Jesus concerning the Kingdom as being that of the relationship between a present in which the long-promised eschatological salvation is known at a personal level in and through the ministry of Jesus and a future in which it will be manifested universally or cosmically through some climactic act of God, such as the early Church envisaged under the imagery of the Parousia, is a popular understanding of the relationship as modern scholars interpret it. W. G. Kümmel argues that Jesus sees the present as a time of eschatological fulfilment; understanding his present to be a particular period in God's salvation; seeing history as advancing swiftly towards the end, and the eschatological salvation is now fulfilling itself in his person; and all of this indicates the certainty of that moment in the future when what has begun in Jesus will be consummated in him. Present and future are related as present fulfilment carrying with it the certainty of future promise.[5]

Similarly, and following Kümmel, Cullmann sees the tension between present and future in the teaching of Jesus, and to explain it he uses a metaphor from warfare; a metaphor vivid to the generation that lived through the Second World War and knows the distinction between 'D-day' and 'VE day' or between 'VE day' and 'VJ day'.

---

[1] See above, pp. 73, 81f.
[2] In German the change is from *realisierter Eschatologie* to *sich realisierenden Eschatologie*. (Jeremias *Parables*, p. 159; *Gleichnisse*, p. 194.) See above, p. 73.
[3] The German word is *Grundton*, *Gleichnisse*, p. 194.
[4] Jeremias, *Gleichnisse*, pp. 42 f. See above, p. 81.
[5] Kümmel, *Promise*, pp. 141–55.

In the ministry of Jesus the decisive battle has been fought and won, Satan is fallen (Luke 10.18) and the power of the demons broken (Matt. 12.28), but the war none the less continues, and will continue, until the final 'Victory Day'.[1]

Finally, a modern Roman Catholic scholar, R. Schnackenburg, has argued that the presence of the Kingdom is, for Jesus, inextricably linked with his own person and work. God 'dynamically' works salvation in the present in Jesus although the consummation as judgment and (final) salvation remains in the future. We can best understand it either as a present time of Messianic fulfilment of the promise of salvation which is none the less not yet the consummation, or as the beginning of the eschatological salvation time which moves towards a new high point or climax.[2] Coming from a Roman Catholic scholar this is a most significant exegesis of the teaching of Jesus and a very welcome product of the renaissance of biblical studies in modern Roman Catholicism.

Such then is the present situation with regard to the understanding of the Kingdom as present and as future in the teaching of Jesus. However, there is one scholar who has consistently fought against the developing recognition of these two elements in the teaching of Jesus: Rudolf Bultmann. But Bultmann's position is complex and involves factors not yet taken into account in this review, and it seems best therefore to leave a consideration of his views, and those of his pupils until a later stage of this work.[3] For the sake of completeness in this chapter, however, we must say that some of the Bultmann *Schüler*, especially Fuchs, Robinson and Conzelmann, do see a tension between present and future in the teaching of Jesus but interpret it existentially.[4]

We turn then now to an important element in the discussion, an element closely related to the Kingdom as present and as future in the teaching, that of the Son of Man, and here we will begin with the most important English contribution to this aspect of the discussion, the work of T. W. Manson.

[1] Cullmann, *Christ and Time*, 1950, pp. 71 f., 83 f. This is an integral part of his interpretation of the eschatology of Jesus in terms of *Heilsgeschichte*, see below pp. 134 ff.

[2] R. Schnackenburg, *Gottesherrschaft und Reich*, 1959, pp. 77 ff., 87 f.

[3] See chapter VII below.

[4] See below, pp. 121 ff.

VI

T. W. MANSON AND VARIATIONS ON THE THEME 'SON OF MAN'

T. W. MANSON

IT IS OBVIOUS that an exegesis of the Kingdom of God in the teaching of Jesus is closely related to an understanding of Jesus' view of himself and his ministry, and this brings us inevitably to his teaching concerning the Son of Man. The English discussion of these sayings is not really important until we come to the work of T. W. Manson,[1] who sees the Kingdom as 'a present reality working towards a future consummation',[2] and offers a collective interpretation of the Son of Man sayings.

In order to appreciate fully Manson's interpretation of the Son of Man sayings we must begin with his understanding of Kingdom of God and note especially his emphasis upon the practice of the ministry of Jesus. 'The life and work of Jesus, his teaching, the mission of the disciples, the Cross and the Resurrection, are all of a piece. For Jesus the teaching is an essential part of his life-work; but it is not the whole. The whole is a manifestation of the Kingdom of God as a present reality. Origen was right when he called Jesus *autobasileia*—the Kingdom itself.'[3] Or, as he puts it elsewhere: 'The ministry with all its inevitable sacrifices *was* the true glory of the Messiah, the

---

[1] *The Teaching of Jesus*, [1]1931, [2]1935 (= *Teaching*); *The Sayings of Jesus*, 1949 (= *Sayings*), a reprint of his contribution to *The Mission and Message of Jesus* by H. D. Major, T. W. Manson, and C. E. Wright, 1937; 'The Son of Man in Daniel, Enoch and the Gospels', *BJRL* 32, 1949/50, pp. 171–93; 'The New Testament Basis of the Doctrine of the Church', *JEH* 1, 1950, pp. 1–11; *The Servant-Messiah*, 1952; 'Realized Eschatology and the Messianic Secret' in *Studies in the Gospels*. Essays in Memory of R. H. Lightfoot, ed. D. E. Nineham, 1955, pp. 209–22 (= *Lightfoot Festschrift*); 'The Life of Jesus: some tendencies in present-day Research' in *The Background of the New Testament and its Eschatology*, ed. by W. D. Davies and D. Daube, 1956, pp. 211–21 (= *Dodd Festschrift*).

[2] *Sayings*, p. 305.

[3] *Sayings*, p. 344.

authentic manifestation of the Kingdom of God in the world of men.'[1]

In what way was the Kingdom of God manifested in the ministry of Jesus? Manson examines all the sayings concerning the Kingdom of God in the Synoptic Gospels and comes to the conclusion that, in the earlier part of his ministry, Jesus spoke of the Kingdom as something that was coming (Mark 1.15, etc.), and, in the later part of his ministry, as something into which men enter (Mark 9.47, etc.).[2] He argues, further, that the proclamation of the coming of the Kingdom is made to the generality of the people, but the teaching with regard to the entering into the Kingdom is made only to the disciples.[3] The significance of the term 'Kingdom of God' is that it expresses a personal relationship between God as King and the individual as the subject of that Kingship. 'The claim on God's part to rule, and the acknowledgment on man's part of that claim, together constitute the actual Kingdom.'[4] During the early part of his ministry Jesus spoke of this Kingdom as still to come; during the later part he spoke of men entering it, which implies that it had now come. How are we to resolve this apparent antithesis? 'The most obvious solution of this problem is that Jesus held that the Kingdom had come in some real sense during his own ministry. . . . The most plausible conjecture will be one which equates the coming of the Kingdom with Peter's Confession. . . . Peter's Confession may fairly be regarded as just that acknowledgment that was needed to make the Kingdom *de jure* into the Kingdom *de facto*.'[5]

Manson supports this interpretation of the term 'Kingdom of God' by reference to the rabbinic literature where 'a similar notion' is to be found.[6]

[1] *JEH* 1, 1950, pp. 6 f.

[2] The major exception to this is the petition 'Thy Kingdom come' in the Lord's Prayer. But at the time he wrote *Teaching* Manson was inclined to argue that the inclusion of this petition at Luke 11.2 was the result of textual assimilation to the Matthaean version, and to doubt the authenticity of this particular petition in the Matthaean version (*Teaching*, pp. 128 f.). This is a bold and altogether improbable assumption and Manson did not repeat it in his later *Sayings*, pp. 169, 266.

[3] *Teaching*, p. 126. All through his work Manson emphasizes the difference between the teaching of Jesus addressed to the crowd and that directed to the disciples. He emphasizes, for example, the fact that the teaching on the Fatherhood of God is also confined to the disciples (*Teaching*, pp. 96, 101–15).

[4] *Teaching*, p. 131.

[5] *Teaching*, pp. 129–31.

[6] *Teaching*, pp. 120–32. He is here following Billerbeck, who searched the whole of the apocalyptic and rabbinical literature for references to the Kingdom of God and found:

The first manifestation of the Kingdom of God on earth is, then, to be seen in the obedience of Jesus and of his disciples to God as King, and this is the fulfilment of that Kingdom which is announced as imminent in Mark 1.15. 'Primarily the Kingdom of God is a personal relation between God as King and the individual as subject. Then it appears in the world as a society, something which might be called the people of God. This society consists of all those who are linked together by the fact of their common allegiance to one King.'[1] Here we are near to 'realized eschatology' and Professor Manson did once, in conversation with the present writer, refer to himself as 'a half-realized eschatologist'. But, unlike C. H. Dodd, Manson did not regard this coming of the Kingdom in the ministry of Jesus as the end of the matter. The Kingdom of God is a present reality in the ministry of Jesus, but it is 'a present reality in working towards a future consummation'.[2] This first manifestation of the Kingdom in the obedient community of Jesus and his disciples is 'an agent, an instrument in God's hands, a means towards a yet greater manifestation which still lies in the future'.[3]

Here we are at the heart of the matter, as far as Manson's interpretation is concerned; his emphasis is upon the community of Jesus and his disciples as the agent of God. It is at this point that he introduces his collective interpretation of Son of Man. He turns to

---

1. That the expression occurs only five times in the apocalyptic literature (reff. in *Kommentar* I, p. 179).

2. That in the prayers of the Synagogue the petition for God to establish his Kingship over Israel and in all the earth occupies a central place (reff., *Kommentar* I, p. 178).

3. That it occurs in three usages in the rabbinical literature.

    (a) It is used of the eternal sovereignty of God the creator over his creation, which sovereignty can be, and has been, both accepted and rejected by men (reff., *Kommentar* I, pp. 173 f.).

    (b) Developing out of this there arises the concept of accepting or rejecting the yoke of the Kingdom of God, i.e. accepting or rejecting the sovereignty of God as an individual and showing this in terms of service, chiefly in reciting the Shema (reff., *Kommentar* I, pp. 176–8).

    (c) Finally, there is the eschatological expectation of the day that will come when God will be universally acknowledged as King and his Kingdom therefore finally established in all its glory (reff., *Kommentar* I, pp. 179 f.).

Billerbeck writes in his introduction to the rabbinical citations: '*Die Gottesherrschaft realisiert sich eben überall da, wo sich ein Mensch bewussterweise dem Willen Gottes im Gehorsam unterstellt,*' and this is the point which Manson takes up and develops.

[1] *Teaching*, p. 134.
[2] *Sayings*, p. 305; see p. 90 n. 2.
[3] *Teaching*, p. 134.

the Old Testament and discusses the conception of the Remnant, showing that the Remnant becomes, in Isaiah, an eschatological idea, 'the nucleus of the future people of God'. He argues that in Deutero-Isaiah the conception of the Servant is a development of that of the Remnant: 'the Remnant was to be a *saved* few, the Servant of Jehovah is to be a *saving* few'. The Servant is a collective concept, a group, not an individual. So also the 'I' of the Psalms is to be interpreted collectively.[1] Finally 'Son of Man' as it occurs in Daniel and the Gospels is to be given the same collective interpretation. ' "Son of Man" in the Gospels is the final term in a series of conceptions, all of which are found in the Old Testament. These are: the Remnant (Isaiah), the Servant of Jehovah (II Isaiah), the "I" of the Psalms, and the Son of Man (Daniel). It has been argued above that it is the idea of the Remnant which is the essential feature about all of these, and it is now suggested that Son of Man in the Gospels is another embodiment of the Remnant idea . . . the Son of Man is . . . an ideal figure and stands for the manifestation of the Kingdom of God on earth in a people wholly devoted to their heavenly King.'[2]

This is Manson's collective interpretation of the Son of Man, and he discusses in detail the occurrences of the term in Daniel and in the teaching of Jesus in defence and explanation of this interpretation.[3]

The dedicated community, the Son of Man, is to be God's agent in bringing about the final consummation of that Kingdom which is first manifested in its obedience. The community is, in fact, Messianic; it is through the ministry of its obedience that the Kingdom is being manifested in the world of men, and this ministry, with all its sufferings, will, in the providence of God, lead to the final triumph.[4] But the disciples proved incapable of the obedience necessary to the fulfilment of the Son of Man ideal, and at Mark 14.62 'we have in fact reached the point at which the Son of Man becomes an individual person, not by a process of speculation, but by the logic of facts; not in apocalyptic theory but in life'.[5] But the obedience demanded of the Son of Man is still fulfilled, and Jesus looks towards the consummation in which this obedience will be vindicated. 'God will still have the last word, and he will vindicate the Son of Man.'[6] The key

[1] *Teaching*, pp. 176–83.
[2] *Teaching*, p. 227.
[3] *Teaching*, pp. 211–34; also *BJRL* 32, 1949/50, pp. 171–93.
[4] *JEH* 1, 1950, pp. 6 f.
[5] *Teaching*, p. 267.
[6] *Teaching*, p. 268.

to the whole is the obedience, individual and corporate, which manifests the Kingdom on earth and which will lead to the ultimate manifestation when God, in his own time, will vindicate that obedience. Jesus expected the ultimate vindication to take place at some time in the immediate future, and in this he was mistaken. But the essential eschatological note in his teaching remains true and must be maintained. 'If there is no final victory of good over evil, the Kingdom of God becomes an empty dream.'[1]

So for Manson the Kingdom .is both present and future: it is present as it is manifested through the obedience of the Son of Man and this obedience in turn is related to the future and ultimate manifestation. Before turning to the criticism of Manson's views there is one further aspect of his work that must be mentioned: the relationship which he envisages between eschatology and ethics in the teaching of Jesus. In this respect he takes a position similar to that of William Manson, and argues that the ethical teaching must be viewed in the context of the fact that the Kingdom was for Jesus, in one sense, a present fact.[2]

'The moral teaching of Jesus appears not as an independent ethic—either "interim" or any other sort—but as an integral part of his conception of the Kingdom of God. It is the way of the Kingdom . . . the way in which the subjects of the Heavenly King may show their loyalty to him through their obedience to his will.'[3] This is in line with the characteristic T. W. Manson emphasis upon the Kingdom as present in the new relationship which is established between God as King and man as subject, and he goes on to stress the fact that the ethical teaching of Jesus is an expression of the kind of moral conduct that should arise out of this new relationship. 'What Jesus offers in his ethical teaching is not a set of rules of conduct, but a number of illustrations of the way in which a transformed character will express itself in conduct.'[4] The similarity between the views of T. W. and William Manson is here obvious and the emphasis upon the fact that the ethical teaching of Jesus must be interpreted in the context of the Kingdom of God as present is surely valid. But T. W. Manson goes a step farther than his namesake in

---

[1] *Ibid.*, p. 284.

[2] *Teaching*, pp. 285–312: 'Religion and Morals'. Cf. also his essay 'Jesus, Paul, and the Law' in *Judaism and Christianity*, Vol. II, *Law and Religion*, ed. Rosenthal, London and New York, 1938, pp. 125–41.

[3] *Teaching*, p. 295.

[4] *Teaching*, p. 301.

that he argues that the ethical teaching of Jesus shares certain characteristics with the Torah of Moses. It is regarded as being of divine origin; it is given through one who regarded himself as being the agent of God's revelation of his will; and its application is primarily to the community to which it is addressed, the community of the Kingdom of God. 'The moral standard set up by Jesus is therefore to be conceived as given to the New Israel—the community of his followers—as the old Law was given to the Chosen People, to be the charter of their existence as a people of God.'[1]

Here we have a supremely important insight, the recognition of the fact that the ethical teaching of Jesus is not primarily directed to the general public but to the eschatological community of his disciples. It is not the case that the ethical teaching is independent of the eschatology, as the older liberalism had argued, nor is it the case that the ethical teaching is to be regarded as totally subordinate to the eschatology, as Schweitzer had argued; it is rather the case that the ethical teaching and the eschatology are inextricably woven together, for the ethical teaching is directed to the eschatological community and presupposes the situation in which that community finds itself, both in regard to God and the world.

CRITICISM OF MANSON'S INTERPRETATION OF 'KINGDOM OF GOD'

Criticism of Manson's work has been directed particularly at his collective interpretation of the Son of Man. Leaving that aside for the moment there are some other points in his work which call for further discussion, and the first of these is his interpretation of 'Kingdom of God' in the teaching of Jesus in terms of the use of this term in the rabbinical literature. We have already argued that this is an error and that the true background to the teaching of Jesus here is the apocalyptic rather than the rabbinical literature.[2] In the apocalyptic literature, in the Qumran texts and in the teaching of Jesus, the Kingdom of God is his kingly activity, and the coming of the Kingdom is, in fact, the decisive eschatological intervention of God in the affairs of men whereby he exercises his royal power on behalf of his subjects.[3] Manson's interpretation does not sufficiently take

[1] *Teaching*, p. 295.
[2] See above, pp. 24-27 in discussing the work of Dalman.
[3] See further below, pp. 160-178.

this into account. But he himself seems to have sensed this, for although the rabbinical understanding is in the forefront of his earlier work, *Teaching*, it recedes considerably into the background in *Sayings*, and is not found at all in *Servant-Messiah*, where he builds his presentation of the ministry of Jesus upon a foundation of the Messianic hope of apocalyptic, and speaks of the Kingdom as 'the actualization in history of God's power and wisdom'.[1] But in Manson's interpretation the early dependence upon the rabbinical usage does not lead to a modified Ritschlianism[2] and so the difference would be one of emphasis rather than substance: God acting as King in the ministry of Jesus and the believer responding to this in terms of obedience and service[3] rather than the manifestation of the Kingdom in the obedience of Jesus and his disciples.

More serious than this is Manson's dependence upon the historicity of the Marcan order. This he defended to the end, his last essay on Life of Christ research being concerned partly with its defence,[4] but in this he was fighting a losing battle. Mark is *kerygmatic* history rather than objective history,[5] the Marcan outline is the outline of the *kerygma*, and there is a steadily increasing recognition of the role of the early Church in the shaping and combining of the material in the Synoptic Gospels,[6] a tendency which is bound to be reinforced by the discovery of the Gospel of Thomas which presents us with synoptic material in different forms and different combinations from that of the Synoptic Gospels. Against all this Manson's argument, that he remembers the main course of the events of his own life in their proper order, and that the knowledge of the general outline of the ministry of Jesus would have been remembered because it was the property of a considerable number of people,[7] seems very weak.

[1] *Servant-Messiah*, p. 74.
[2] As it did in the case of Dalman, see above, p. 27.
[3] See, further, below, pp. 201-6.
[4] *Dodd Festschrift*, pp. 212 f.
[5] J. M. Robinson, *The Problem of History in Mark*, 1957 (= *Problem*), p. 15.
[6] Cf. J. M. Robinson's criticism of Manson, *A New Quest of the Historical Jesus*, 1959 (= *New Quest*), p. 38 n. 1.
[7] *Dodd Festschrift*, p. 213. C. H. Dodd has himself defended the Marcan order in an essay, 'The Framework of the Gospel Narrative', originally published in *ExpT* 43, 1932, pp. 396–400, and reprinted in a collection of his essays *New Testament Studies*, 1953. But D. E. Nineham has subjected Dodd's arguments to very searching criticism in the *Lightfoot Festschrift* (*Studies in the Gospels*, ed. Nineham, 1955), pp. 223–40. A more recent English writer, C. E. B. Cranfield, *The Gospel According to St Mark*, 1959, grants Nineham the best of the argument, but argues that Peter is likely to have remembered the general outline of the ministry (p. 18)

Manson's dependence upon the Marcan order leads him to put a lot of weight, as we have seen, upon the fact that the Kingdom 'came' at Caesarea Philippi with Peter's Confession. If the Marcan order is indefensible, then this distinction between before and after Caesarea Philippi must also be abandoned, as indeed it must also be abandoned on the grounds that it necessitates striking the petition 'Thy Kingdom Come' out of the Lord's Prayer.[1] The tension between present and future in the teaching of Jesus concerning the Kingdom is not resolved at Caesarea Philippi. Fortunately, again this does not make any vital difference to Manson's views; the essential point that the obedience-response of the believer to the kingly activity of God in the present is related to the ultimate manifestation of that activity is not itself dependent upon an acceptance of Manson's before and after Caesarea Philippi distinction.

CRITICISM OF MANSON'S INTERPRETATION OF 'SON OF MAN'

The collective interpretation of Son of Man which Manson proposed has been extensively criticized, especially by Erik Sjöberg, who maintained that the Son of Man in Jewish apocalyptic at the time of Christ is a pre-existent heavenly being and it must therefore be so interpreted in the Gospels.[2] The main evidence for this is the use of the term in the so-called 'Similitudes' of the Book of Enoch (I Enoch 37–71)[3] but there are a whole range of unsolved problems in connection with the Similitudes of Enoch and the use of Son of Man in them. In the first place there is the question of whether the references

---

and Mark is dependent upon his testimony. Dodd himself does not use this argument, and as Nineham says (*op. cit.*, p. 225) it would be interesting to know why not, but such a suggestion is wholly out of keeping with the modern understanding of the nature and history of the synoptic material, and of the theological motives at work in the *Aufbau* of the Marcan Gospel (see J. M. Robinson, *Problem*, and W. Marxsen, *Der Evangelist Markus*, 1959, *passim*). A further and still more devastating criticism of Dodd at this point is that by J. M. Robinson, *New Quest*, pp. 48–58.

[1] See p. 91 n.2 above.
[2] E. Sjöberg, *Der Menschensohn im aethiopischen Henochbuch*, 1946. Manson's lecture printed in *BJRL* 32, 1949–50, pp. 171–93, is largely directed against Sjöberg's arguments, to which Sjöberg replied in *Der verborgene Menschensohn in den Evangelien*, 1955, pp. 241 ff. See also S. Mowinckel, *He that Cometh* (English translation by G. W. Anderson of the Norwegian *Han som Kommer*, 1951), 1956, pp. 355 and 445–50.
[3] The expression also occurs in IV Ezra 13.3, 12, but it has been argued by Billerbeck that the usage here is different (*Kommentar* I, p. 958).

to Son of Man in these passages are to be interpreted as referring to a pre-existent heavenly being or whether they are to 'pre-mundane decisions in heaven which are destined to have their fulfilment on earth'.[1] This is the point at issue in the debate between Manson and Sjöberg and it is complicated by the additional question as to whether the Ethiopic version is a sufficiently accurate representation of the original text to allow for a decision on such a point. Then there is the problem of the date of the Similitudes of Enoch, which is obviously relevant to the question of their use as evidence for the circulation of the concepts contained in Judaism at the time of Christ. Here a new factor has recently been introduced into the discussion by the discovery of the Qumran texts. At Qumran the Enoch literature is represented fairly extensively, especially in the fragments from Cave 4, but as yet the Similitudes are conspicuous by their absence,[2] and it may be that the sect did not have this part of the Book of Enoch in their library. In the light of this the question of the date of the Similitudes has been re-discussed, but with no unity of conclusion. H. H. Rowley prefers a date in the second century BC,[3] O. Eissfeldt one in the first century BC,[4] and J. T. Milik one in the second century AD.[5] These variations of opinion among competent scholars are an indication of the complexity of the problems involved. Finally there is the problem of the literary structure of the Similitudes. In his review of Sjöberg's *Der Menschensohn im aethiopischen Henochbuch*[6] J. Jeremias called attention to this question, and to Sjöberg's failure to take it into account.

In English scholarship in the period under review there has been considerable reluctance to accept the derivation of Son of Man in the teaching of Jesus from the Book of Enoch. C. H. Dodd[7] points to the difficulty of determining that the similitudes of Enoch are pre-Christian in date, to the difficulty in determining the actual meaning and precise reference of the various Ethiopic expressions translated 'Son of Man', and to the fact that the Similitudes may represent an isolated and probably eccentric authority for the association of the title 'Son of Man' with an apocalyptic Messiah.

---

[1] Manson, *BJRL* 32, 1949–50, p. 182.
[2] Frank M. Cross, Jr., *Ancient Library*, p. 150 n. 7.
[3] *Jewish Apocalyptic and the Dead Sea Scrolls*, 1957, p. 9.
[4] *Einleitung in das Alte Testament*, ²1956, p. 766.
[5] *Ten Years of Discovery in the Wilderness of Judaea*, 1959 (ET by J. Strugnell of *Dix ans de Découvertes dans le Désert de Juda*, 1957), p. 33.
[6] In *TLZ* 1949, cols. 405 f.
[7] *According to the Scriptures*, 1952 (= *Scriptures*), pp. 116 f.

These difficulties in regard to the Similitudes of Enoch are sufficient to warrant caution about any claims that the concept of the Son of Man as a pre-existent heavenly being was at all a part of general apocalyptic thought at the time of Christ, and we may not therefore assume that the term, as it is used in the Gospels, must be interpreted in this way. On the other hand, evidence in support of Manson's communal interpretation is now coming to light in the Qumran texts, evidence to which Matthew Black has called attention.[1] He cites in particular 1QS 8.1 ff. where the sect or an inner *élite* of the sect, are 'to maintain faithfulness in the land with a steadfast purpose and a broken spirit; and they shall expiate iniquity by upholding the righteous cause and bearing the anguish of the refiner's furnace'.[2] There follows a description of the group in verse:

> As an eternal planting, an holy house for Israel,
> A conclave which is an holy of holies for Araon,
> Witnesses of truth concerning judgement,[3]
> And the chosen of grace to atone for the land,[4]
> And to render the wicked their desert,[5]
> This is the tried wall, the precious corner-stone,
> Whose foundations shall not be shaken,
> Nor be dislodged from their place.[6]

In this passage we have two things of real importance in support of Manson's interpretation of 'Son of Man'. The community has brought together aspects of the work of the Isaianic Servant[7] and of the Danielic Son of Man,[8] and it has applied them both to its own expected eschatological function *as a community*. So we have here:

[1] In 'Servant of the Lord and Son of Man', *SJT* 6, 1953–54, pp. 1–11.

[2] 1QS 8.3 f., Black's translation.

[3] Cf. Isa. 32.10, 12.

[4] The first part of this, 'chosen by divine grace', is strikingly reminiscent of what we read concerning the Servant in Isa. 42.1, 'my servant . . . my chosen', and the second part, 'to atone for the earth', parallels the thought of Isa. 53.

[5] This phrase, 'to render the wicked their desert' is a quotation from Ps. 94.2, which is also quoted in CD 7.9.

[6] 1QS 8.5–8. Black's translation.

[7] 'The chosen of grace to atone for the land.'

[8] 'To render the wicked their desert.' In Ps. 94.2, and at CD 7.9, this is used of God visiting the earth, but here the community is the means of this aspect of the eschatological visitation. In this concept of the eschatological visitation of the earth we are very near indeed to the thought of Dan. 7.14, where the Son of Man is given 'dominion, and glory and a kingdom, that all the peoples . . . should serve him', and to that of Dan. 7.26 f., where the dominion of the fourth beast is destroyed and the kingdom and the dominion passes to 'the people of the saints of the Most High'.

(1) evidence that the Suffering Servant and the Son of Man were linked in Judaism at the time of Christ; and (2) evidence that a collective interpretation of 'Son of Man' was to be found in Judaism at the time of Christ, something that Manson had had to argue was possible on the basis of the Old Testament and of the Hebrew concept of 'corporate personality'. Whether we are justified in speaking of an identification of the two figures will depend on how strictly we define the word 'identification'. Our evidence indicates that we can speak of them having predicates in common, that in the Similitudes of Enoch the language used of the Son of Man has links with the language used in Isaiah of the Servant, and that in Qumran eschatological functions proper to both are applied to the one group. This evidence shows that Manson's interpretation may not be described as 'strained',[1] nor may it be rejected on the grounds that the individual apocalyptic interpretation of the figure, as in Enoch, had become so influential as to rule out the possibility of a collective interpretation in the teaching of Jesus.[2] If the men of Qumran could think of themselves, as a community, exercising the eschatological function of the Son of Man, then certainly there is nothing strained or inherently improbable about a communal interpretation of the figure in the teaching of Jesus. Nor is it really relevant to argue, as does R. Newton Flew in rejecting Manson's interpretation, that 'to any student today the confusion caused by applying the title, now in the sense of a community, now in the sense of an individual, is evident', and it is therefore 'unlikely that Jesus . . . would clothe his thought in such an ambiguity'.[3] Modern conceptions of the sharp distinction between the individual and the community are simply irrelevant in first-century Judaism. It is more to the point to recognize, with Vincent Taylor, that 'community' and 'personal' are not mutually exclusive categories and that it is therefore possible that 'by the Son of Man Jesus sometimes meant himself, but sometimes the community of which he is the head'.[4]

---

[1] As it is by T. F. Glasson, who rejects Manson's view, *The Second Advent*, 1945, p. 54.

[2] So, in effect, John Knox, *The Death of Christ*, 1958, p. 61.

[3] R. Newton Flew, *Jesus and His Church*, ²1943, p. 54.

[4] Vincent Taylor, *The Names of Jesus*, 1953, p. 32. A particularly good example of the former, i.e. a reference to Jesus himself, is Mark 2.10. Here T. W. Manson originally favoured the meaning 'man' in a general sense (*Teaching*, p. 214), but later changed his view and saw the reference as being to the community (*BJRL* 32, 1949–50, p. 191).

THE DERIVATION OF 'SON OF MAN' IN THE TEACHING OF JESUS

With regard to the whole discussion of Son of Man in the teaching of Jesus since T. W. Manson's work we may say that the most of it has revolved around the questions of the *derivation* of the term in the teaching of Jesus and of the *authenticity* of the various sayings. Three derivations have been proposed—from Ezekiel, from Daniel and from the Similitudes of Enoch—and the sayings have been divided into groups and the question of their authenticity argued on source-critical grounds. The majority of scholars have agreed that Jesus did use the term as a title.[1] A derivation from Ezekiel leads to an emphasis upon the term as expressing a prophetic consciousness; a derivation from Enoch leads to an emphasis upon the apocalyptic nature of the figure, and to a tendency to doubt the authenticity of the usage in any other context than an apocalyptic one; a derivation from Daniel leaves room for either a corporate or an individual interpretation and also for the possibility of a fusion of the Son of Man with the Suffering Servant of Isaiah.

Two scholars who have maintained the derivation from Ezekiel are George S. Duncan[2] and J. Y. Campbell.[3] Duncan thinks that the expression represents 'man as he ought to be in accordance with the purpose of God, and as he may be when he becomes filled with the divine Spirit'.[4] We must not look for conscious reference to Daniel or Enoch, because the term as Jesus used it is not apocalyptic although

---

[1] An exception is Pierson Parker, 'The Meaning of Son of Man', *JBL* 60, 1941, pp. 151–7, who argues that Son of Man as used by Jesus and his predecessors carried no Messianic implication at all. In Dan. 7.13 it is a description, not a title; it indicates that the figure looked like a man, and has no other meaning. Its use in Enoch 'is without technical significance, and is in no wise a messianic title' (p. 154). In the Gospels the only places where 'it is given a messianic turn' are Mark 13.26; 14.62 and Matt. 24.30. All of these are 'unauthentic'; the first is in the Little Apocalypse, the second is in a story for which the disciples had no eye-witness testimony, and the third is in Matthew's special material which is generally untrustworthy (p. 156). In all other instances the reference is such that there is 'little eschatology, and no apocalyptic in the context', usually 'the context is a parable or the emphasis is ethical' (p. 155). When Jesus uses the term of himself it indicates simply prophetic leadership and not Messiahship. This contribution deserves preservation as a curiosity of modern New Testmanent studies, but so extreme a position, and such arguments, could not be expected to influence very greatly the subsequent discussion.

[2] George S. Duncan, *Jesus, Son of Man*, 1947 (= *Jesus*).

[3] J. Y. Campbell, 'Son of Man' in *A Theological Word Book of the Bible*, edited by A. Richardson, 1950, pp. 230–2.

[4] Duncan, *Jesus*, p. 147.

it is eschatological, by which Duncan means that it is used in the context of the fulfilment of God's purposes for mankind. 'God's final purpose may be described as the establishment of his Kingdom. His more immediate purpose is the creation, or the evolution, or (as Christian theology prefers to call it) the redemption of a new order of mankind; and this requires that there should be raised up a perfect man.'[1] In his use of Son of Man of himself 'Jesus had in mind that in and through a new type of man God's purposes for mankind are to be fulfilled'.[2] This is an attempt to put the clock back to the time before the coming of Schweitzer's theory, and to interpret the eschatology of Jesus in terms of an evolutionary Christian humanism; in 1947 it could only be described as an anachronism.

Campbell argues that Jesus used Son of Man of himself and that in so doing he indicated at once his prophetic consciousness and his consciousness of his solidarity with his fellow men; '. . . it was a fitting self-designation for him who was made in all points like his brethren, the sons of man, that he might make them sons of God.'[3]

There are two objections to this derivation of Son of Man in the teaching of Jesus from Ezekiel. In the first place, there is no indication in the recorded teaching of Jesus of any dependence upon Ezekiel, but there are two specific quotations from Dan. 7.13,[4] which indicates a dependence upon Daniel rather than Ezekiel. In the second place, the usage of Son of Man by Jesus is such as to indicate something more than that the Son of Man is called to the service of God as the prophet Ezekiel was called. There is nothing in the Ezekiel usage of the term to prepare us for the Son of Man who 'must' suffer (Mark 8.31 etc.), or for the Son of Man who comes in apocalyptic glory (Mark 8.38 etc.).[5]

THE AUTHENTICITY OF VARIOUS GROUPS OF 'SON OF MAN' SAYINGS

The view that Son of Man in the teaching of Jesus is derived from the Book of Enoch had been put forward in America as early as 1920 by F. J. Foakes Jackson and K. Lake.[6] They distinguished between three

[1] *Jesus*, p. 267.
[2] *Jesus*, p. 148.
[3] Campbell, *op. cit.*, p. 232.
[4] Mark 13.26 par.; 14.62 par. Cf. C. H. Dodd, *Scriptures*, p. 117, and R. H. Fuller, *Mission*, p. 101.
[5] Cf. R. H. Fuller, *Mission*, pp. 131 f.
[6] In *Beginnings of Christianity*, Part 1: *The Acts of the Apostles*, Vol. 1, 1920, pp. 368–84.

usages of the term in the teaching of Jesus: (1) a 'present' usage, e.g.
Mark 2.10; 2.28; (2) a 'Parousia' usage, e.g. Mark 8.38; 9.9; 13.26,
etc.; (3) a 'suffering' usage, e.g. Mark 8.31, 9.12, etc. According to
this view the 'present' usage represents a misunderstanding of the
original Aramaic which, on the lips of Jesus, meant 'man' (e.g. Mark
2.10, 28). The 'Parousia' usage goes back to Jesus himself, who used
the term of a coming eschatological figure similar to that referred to
in the Book of Enoch, but who did not identify himself with that
figure. The 'suffering' usage is due to the disciples who developed
what were originally quite general predictions of suffering in
accordance with the *ex post facto* knowledge of the Passion. In the
course of the development of the tradition 'Son of Man' was added
where Jesus had originally used the first person singular. Jesus had
not thought of the sufferings as those of the Servant in Isaiah 53.

This view is supported by the following arguments. (*a*) The
'Parousia' usage is found in both of the earliest sources, Mark and Q,
and is immediately explicable by reference to contemporary Judaism.
(*b*) In such key-sayings as Mark 14.62; 13.26; 8.38 Jesus did not
identify himself with the Son of Man. (*c*) The tendency to introduce
'Son of Man' into sayings in the course of the tradition can be clearly
seen in Matt. 12.31 f., cf. Mark 3.28. (*d*) The Passion sayings, by
their very precision, are clearly *vaticinia ex eventu*, and the reference
to the disciples not understanding at the time (Mark 9.10 and 9.32)
is evidence that the sayings have been interpreted in the light of
subsequent events.[1]

A similar view was put forward again by John Knox in America
in 1958.[2] He prints the sayings in three groups: A. Apocalyptic,

---

[1] The position of Foakes Jackson and Lake is similar to that represented in
Germany by R. Bultmann, *Theologie des Neuen Testaments*, 3rd ed., 1958, pp. 27–33
(cf. ET of 1st ed. by Kendrick Grobel, *Theology of the New Testament*, Vol. I, 1952, pp.
26–32), and *Geschichte der synoptischen Tradition*, 3rd ed., 1957 (ET by John Marsh,
History of the Synoptic Tradition, 1963), *passim*. In comparison with Jackson and Lake,
Bultmann does not concern himself with the possibility that the 'suffering' usage
goes back to Jesus in any form, but roundly declares that all such sayings are
vaticinia ex eventu, creations of the Hellenistic Church (*Theologie*, pp. 31 f.; ET, pp.
30 f.). He also stresses more than do Foakes Jackson and Lake that the 'Parousia'
and 'suffering' sayings form two separate groups, never being found together, and
that the former is found in every stratum of the tradition and the latter only in
Mark.

[2] John Knox, *The Death of Christ*, 1958 (= *Death*). We shall discuss this book
further, together with two other books from the same scholar, in chapter IX,
pp. 152-5, below.

B. Suffering, C. Remaining (= Foakes Jackson and Lake's 'present' usage), and restates the positions and arguments that we find earlier in the works of Foakes Jackson and Lake, and Bultmann. The first group is authentic, but in the original form of these sayings the apocalyptic Son of Man is not identified with Jesus himself; the second group represents a 'Marcan contribution to the tradition' and is noticeably absent from Q; in the third group 'Son of Man' has been editorially substituted for an original 'I' or 'man'.[1]

A most important question raised by this aspect of the discussion is that of the authenticity of the 'suffering' Son of Man sayings, questioned by Foakes Jackson and Lake, by Bultmann, and by Knox. The main arguments against their authenticity are, as we have seen, that they are necessarily *vaticinia ex eventu*, and that they are not found in Q. In the English discussion R. H. Fuller has investigated these sayings and shown that when every specific reference to an event of the Passion has been removed from them there still remains a hard core of prediction which seems to reflect the Hebrew text of Isaiah 53.[2] They seem to reflect two stages of composition: (*a*) a first stage in which they are prediction of suffering couched in general terms and showing reflection on the Hebrew text of Isaiah 53; (*b*) a second stage in which these predictions are made more pointed in view of the events of the Passion.[3] That both stages have occurred in the development of the tradition in the later community is, of course, possible, but in view of the evidence brought forward by J. Jeremias[4] for the fact that Jesus did think of his own mission and death in terms of the Suffering Servant, this is a viewpoint that it is becoming increasingly difficult to defend.[5] That the sayings could have developed in

---

[1] *Death*, pp. 89–102.

[2] Fuller, *Mission*, pp. 55–58. He also points out that the prophecy of the 'killing' of the Son of Man has been retained without making any mention of 'crucifixion'. This last point is one of some importance and an indication that we must not be too ready to speak of these sayings as *vaticinia ex eventu*. For sayings composed after the event they are curiously indefinite in their reference to the form of Jesus' fate.

[3] Fuller, *Mission*, pp. 58 f.

[4] In *TWNT*, V, pp. 709–13 (ET, W. Zimmerli and J. Jeremias, *The Servant of God* [= *Servant*] 1957, pp. 98–104).

[5] Further support for the argument that Jesus did predict his sufferings and death in general terms can be found in the fact that, as J. Jeremias points out in *Servant*, pp. 98 ff., there is evidence in the New Testament that some of the expectations of Jesus concerning his fate were not in fact fulfilled. He was not stoned as a false prophet (Luke 13.34, cf. Matt. 23.37 par.); he was not buried as a law-breaker (Mark 14.8 par.); and the disciples were not called upon to share his fate (Mark 10.32–40 par.). This last point is important when we consider the objection

the Hellenistic Church is quite impossible, since they reflect the
Hebrew and not the LXX text of Isaiah 53, and one of them, Mark
9.31, has an Aramaic play on words.[1]

The fact that these sayings are not to be found in Q is not so
remarkable if we take into account that Q was not a Gospel but a
collection of the general teaching of Jesus, having no Passion narrative. Now the Passion sayings are obviously out of place in a
collection which, no doubt deliberately, excluded the Passion, and it
can occasion no surprise therefore that they are not to be found in Q.
No one maintains that Q was the whole authority for the teaching of
Jesus among any group of Christians. It was simply part of that
authority, a part which did not include either the Passion narrative
or the Passion sayings. Again, the Passion predictions belong to the
esoteric teaching of Jesus to his disciples, not to his general teaching
to the people,[2] another reason for their not being included in a quite
general collection of his teaching. It would seem, therefore, that their
absence from Q is no sufficient ground for rejecting the authenticity
of the 'suffering' Son of Man sayings.

The majority of British scholars have favoured the third suggestion,
that the term in the teaching of Jesus is derived from Daniel, and
especially from Dan. 7.13.[3]

William Manson has presented succinctly what is probably the
most popular view among British scholars, and he defends it against
the scepticism of Form-criticism. 'Son of Man' is taken from Daniel,
but not Enoch, and it was used by Jesus as his favourite self-
designation. It was a designation which could absorb all other aspects
of the Messianic idea and is used by Jesus in three main ways: (i) as a

---

that Jesus could not have prophesied his sufferings, otherwise the disciples would
not have been so shocked and confused by what happened. It has been suggested
by T. W. Manson (*JEH* I, 1950, p. 6, followed by Jeremias, *Servant*, p. 101 n. 472)
that the disciples expected a corporate suffering that would be a mere preliminary
to, and would be followed quickly by, a corporate triumph. What they were not
prepared for was the Cross for Jesus alone, accepted by him as an essential part of
the ministry and glory of the Son of Man, and without any immediate evidence
that the triumph was at hand.

[1] Jeremias, *Servant*, p. 102.
[2] Jeremias, *Servant*, p. 104.
[3] So, for example, C. H. Dodd, *Scriptures*, p. 117; Vincent Taylor, *Jesus and His
Sacrifice*, 1937, p. 26; R. Newton Flew, *Jesus and His Church*, 1938, [2]1943, pp. 54 f.
(with reservations); C. J. Cadoux, *The Historic Mission of Jesus*, 1941, p. 90; Wm.
Manson, *Jesus the Messiah*, 1943, p. 120; T. Francis Glasson, *The Second Advent*,
1945, [2]1947, pp. 61 f.; R. H. Fuller, *Mission*, p. 102.

simple self-designation (e.g. Matt. 8.20 par.; 11.19 par.; 12.32 par.); (ii) to express his final assurance of his Messiahship and of his ultimate vindication by God (e.g. Mark 14.62); (iii) infused with ideas taken from the fifty-third chapter of Isaiah to express his approach to his own death (Mark 8.31, etc.).[1]

'SON OF MAN' AND 'SUFFERING SERVANT'

In connection with this view that Jesus reinterpreted the Son of Man in terms of the Suffering Servant of Isaiah, an important question is whether the concepts of the Davidic Messiah, the Servant of the Lord, and the Son of Man were brought together in pre-Christian Judaism. William Manson discussed the question in an Appendix to his book, *Jesus the Messiah*,[2] in which he showed that the three figures have many traits in common. They are each, 'endowed with righteousness', 'chosen and exalted by God', 'to be worshipped by kings', 'to be the light of the Gentiles', 'the hope of the troubled', 'anointed of the Lord', and 'endowed with wisdom'.[3]

H. H. Rowley published a characteristically thorough discussion of the question in 'The Suffering Servant and the Davidic Messiah'.[4] He pointed out that although the Targum on Isaiah 53 equates the Servant with the Messiah it does not present a suffering Messiah, and he insists that neither here nor in the Book of Enoch is there evidence for the identification of the Son of Man with the Suffering Servant. 'The fact that something is predicated of the one figure which is predicated of the other does not involve the conclusion that the two are to be identified.'[5] The evidence in the New Testament itself

---

[1] Wm. Manson, *Jesus the Messiah*, pp. 101–3, 113–19. An example of a similar view from America is John W. Bowman, *The Intention of Jesus*, 1945, who argues along lines similar to those of Wm. Manson. He lays great stress on Jesus' activity being in the tradition of the Hebrew prophets. Since Jesus' thinking was prophetic, and the Son of Man concept was apocalyptic it was natural that he should have transformed the Son of Man concept as he used it (*op. cit.*, p. 132). Note the characteristically American stress on Jesus as a prophet.

[2] Wm. Manson, *Jesus the Messiah*, Appendix C II, pp. 173 f.

[3] For the actual references to the Old Testament and the Book of Enoch see Wm. Manson, *loc. cit.*

[4] One of a number of essays by H. H. Rowley collected together and published in a volume *The Servant of the Lord and Other Essays in the Old Testament*, 1952 (= *Servant*).

[5] Rowley, *Servant*, p. 78, referring especially to the evidence for a connection between the Suffering Servant and the Son of Man in the Similitudes of Enoch adduced by J. Jeremias, *Deutsche Theologie* 2, 1959, pp. 109 ff. Jeremias has since restated the evidence in *Servant*, pp. 58 ff.

indicates that the disciples were always confused and bewildered when Jesus spoke of his mission in terms of suffering, and also that Jesus used the title Son of Man of himself, but deliberately avoided that of Messiah. This would indicate that 'Son of Man' was not equated with 'Messiah' in contemporary expectation, nor was it linked with the concept of the Suffering Servant.[1] The Messianic use of 'Son of Man' and the association with it of the concept of the Suffering Servant are the work of Jesus himself. But both the concept of the Davidic Messiah and that of the Servant of the Lord may well have their roots in the royal cultic rites of ancient Israel, from whence they developed along separate lines until they were reintegrated in the thought of our Lord.[2]

CULLMANN: *Christology of the New Testament*

All of this discussion has revolved around the questions of derivation and authenticity and this phase of the discussion may perhaps be said to have reached its climax in O. Cullman's *Christology of the New Testament*,[3] where a modified form of the interpretation most popular in Anglo-American scholarship has been presented in a definitive manner. Combining a derivation from Daniel and Enoch, Cullmann argues that Son of Man was an eschatological title in apocalyptic Judaism, designating a heavenly being now hidden who would appear at the end of time and identified with the first man at the beginning of time. Accepting all three usages in the teaching of Jesus as authentic Cullmann further argues that Jesus identified himself with this figure and reshaped the concept involved in terms of that of the Servant of the Lord. Thus Jesus used the title to express his consciousness of having to fulfil the vocation of the Heavenly Man both in glory at the end of time and also in the humiliation of the

---

[1] An indication of the complexity of the problems involved in this discussion is the fact that both of the factors in the New Testament to which attention is here being drawn are themselves the subject of debate. The problems connected with the gospel evidence for Jesus' reticence in using the term 'Messiah' were raised by W. Wrede in *Das Messiasgeheimnis in den Evangelien*, 1901, and are still being discussed. (For two recent English discussions see Vincent Taylor in *ExpT* 65, 1953–54, pp. 246–50, and T. W. Manson's contribution to the Lightfoot *Festschrift*.) A different explanation for the bewilderment of the disciples at Jesus' teaching concerning his sufferings has been given by T. W. Manson, *JEH* 1, 1950, pp. 6 f.

[2] Rowley, *Servant*, p. 87.

[3] ET, 1959, by Guthrie and Hall of the German *Die Christologie des Neuen Testaments*, 1957; see pp. 137–92.

incarnation among sinful men. Cullmann also combines elements
from the collective interpretation of T. W. Manson with the representative interpretation of the liberals, suggesting that in the light of
the collective use of the title in Dan. 7.13 the idea of the Son of Man
as representing the remnant of Israel and through it all mankind is
not completely foreign to Jesus.

THE NEED FOR A NEW METHODOLOGY: JAMES M. ROBINSON

A review of the discussion from the work of T. W. Manson to that of
Cullmann shows that various positions can be taken up, attacked,
defended and modified without any one view prevailing over the
others. Any given student may prefer to follow T. W. Manson,
Bultmann or Cullmann, but no one can claim that the arguments
in favour of the positions of any of these scholars are such as to render
the others untenable. The research into the Son of Man question has
not revealed decisive evidence or arguments as has, for example, the
research into the question of the apocalyptic or non-apocalyptic
nature of the Kingdom of God. The one thing that the discussion of
the last quarter of a century has revealed is that in this field we badly
need a new methodology. This has been pointed out by J. M.
Robinson in an article 'The Historical Jesus and the Church's
Kerygma'[1] where he notes the 'scholarly impasse' that has arisen in
connection with 'Son of Man' in the teaching of Jesus, suggests that
it is due to 'limitations imposed by scholarly methodology',[2] and
urges a new approach to the problem. The present methodology is
to be supplemented by a consideration of the relationship between
the teaching of Jesus and the Church's kerygma. This may be
especially fruitful at the level of meaning, for when we carry out such
an investigation we find that the Messianic and divine titles attributed
to Jesus in the kerygma 'are a development inaugurated within the
humble self-consciousness of Jesus'.[3] In his later book *A New Quest of
the Historical Jesus*, 1959, Robinson takes a step farther along this new
path and argues that the relationship between Jesus' understanding
of himself and the later kerygmatic understanding of him is such that
we may say that Jesus himself 'assumes the eschatological selfhood

[1] *Religion in Life* 26, 1957, pp. 40–49.
[2] *Ibid.*, pp. 42 f.
[3] *Ibid.*, p. 46.

which ultimately found expression in the title "Son of Man" '.[1] This development is wholly in keeping with that going on within the 'Bultmann school', of which it may indeed be said to be a part. H. Conzelmann has argued for an 'indirect christology' in Jesus' own understanding of the relationship between his ministry and the manifestation of the Kingdom of God.[2] E. Fuchs has stressed the fact that the parables reveal an attitude of Jesus in which he acts as if he stood in the place of God himself, and that the hidden element in the parables of the Kingdom is Jesus himself, who in attitude and deed is the secret and yet present content of the message of the Kingdom of God.[3] This development is part of the post-Bultmannian movement and will be discussed in some detail in our next chapter.

H. E. TÖDT: *Der Menschensohn in der synoptischen Überlieferung*

Another new beginning on the Son of Man problem in the teaching of Jesus has been made by H. E. Tödt, whose book *Der Menschensohn in der synoptischen Überlieferung*, 1959, is much the most important work on the subject in recent times and is likely to remain so until Professor Jeremias completes his proposed work on *huios anthrōpou* for Kittel's *Theologisches Wörterbuch*. Tödt is a second-generation member of Bultmann's school in that he is a student of Günther Bornkamm in Heidelberg, and the importance of his work is that he makes a significant 'break-through' in the study of the individual sayings. He studies them from the point of view of '*Redaktionstheologie*', i.e. he examines and classifies them in accordance with their theological emphasis and setting, and in this way he reaches new criteria for authenticity. The authentic sayings of Jesus are: Matt. 24.27 par.; Matt. 24.37, 39 par.; Luke 17.30, the comparison-sayings (*Vergleiche*); Luke 11.30, the menace-saying (*Drohwort*); Matt. 24.44 par., the warning-saying (*Mahnung*); Luke 12.8 f. par.; (Mark 8.38 par.), the promises (*Verheissungen*).[4]

These sayings are authentic for the following reasons: (1) they lack any reference to scripture for authentication and therefore represent

---

[1] See Robinson, *New Quest*, p. 108.

[2] *RGG*, 3rd. ed., II, 1958, 667 f., and III, 1959, 631. Cf. Robinson, *New Quest*, p. 111 n. 3.

[3] E. Fuchs, 'Die Frage nach dem historischen Jesus', *ZTK* 53, 1956, pp. 210–29, especially 218–21; 'Bemerkungen zur Gleichnisauslegung', *TLZ* 79, 1956, pp. 345–68, especially 348. Cf. Jeremias, *Gleichnisse*, p. 194 n. 1, and Robinson, *New Quest*, pp. 14–16.

[4] Tödt, *Menschensohn*, p. 206.

the sovereign authority and certainty of Jesus' teaching concerning the Kingdom and concerning the Son of Man; (2) they show no apocalyptic colouring (*Ausmalung*), being concerned solely with the significance of the coming of the Son of Man for men, in this respect being like the challenge: Repent for the Kingdom of Heaven is at hand; (3) they reflect the combination of warning and promise that is characteristic of the whole teaching of Jesus.

Two further points about these sayings are important: (4) they reflect the demand of Jesus for allegiance to himself, not to the Son of Man, on the basis of which men may be divided into two groups: those who confess their allegiance to Jesus and for whom the eschatological future holds promise; and those who do not, for whom it holds catastrophe. (5) They have no *christological* content; Jesus does not directly claim to be Messiah (Son of Man/Son of God). Their content is *soteriological;* like the remainder of the teaching of Jesus they promise an inheritance in the Kingdom of Heaven to those who respond in the right manner to the challenge of the present.[1]

So for Tödt there is in the Son of Man teaching of Jesus an essential relationship between the present and the future: 'the future of the Son of Man is already anchored in the present';[2] the coming of the Son of Man is the eschatological cosmic consummation of that which begins in the ministry of Jesus, and the relationship to Jesus in the present determines one's fate at that consummation. Similarly in the Kingdom of God teaching: the Kingdom of God is known in the present in fellowship with Jesus, for the Kingdom has come for those who in their relationship with Jesus are freed from the demons (Luke 11.20), for those tax gatherers and sinners who find fellowship with him (Matt. 11.19 par.), and for those who come to know the healing power of God through him (Matt. 11.5 par.). This fellowship with Jesus in which the Kingdom is known will not pass away with this generation, but will be confirmed by the Son of Man and will be authenticated in the presence of God at the consummation.[3]

Here we have an exciting characteristic of the newer research: radical scepticism with regard to the authenticity of given sayings and yet conclusions wholly in accordance with the deepest insights of Christian faith; insights the surer for having been so radically tested. Whether Jesus taught that he himself was Son of Man is compara-

---

[1] *Menschensohn*, pp. 206 f.
[2] *Ibid.*, p. 239.
[3] *Ibid.*, pp. 239 f.

tively unimportant: that the kingly activity of God was manifest in him to those who responded to the challenge of his ministry, and that in fellowship with him the believer looks towards the final consummation with confidence and hope; this is a note upon which we may gladly take leave for the moment of the continuing discussion of 'Son of Man' in the teaching of Jesus.

VII

BULTMANN AND THE 'BULTMANN SCHOOL' ON KINGDOM OF GOD AND SON OF MAN

BULTMANN

AS WE NOTED at the end of chapter V, there has been one notable exception to the developing tendency among scholars to recognize the Kingdom as both present and future in the teaching of Jesus: Rudolf Bultmann.[1]

[1] Bultmann has been such a prolific writer that it is virtually impossible to list here his contributions to the discussion. A bibliography of his writings to August 1, 1954, is to be found in *Theologische Rundschau* 22, 1954, pp. 3–20. A bibliography from that date to 1960 is given in *Existence and Faith* (Shorter Writings of Rudolf Bultmann selected, translated and introduced by Schubert M. Ogden), Living Age Books 25, Meridian Books, New York, 1960, pp. 317 ff. In this chapter reference will be made especially to:

'Die bedeutung der Eschatologie für die Religion des Neuen Testaments', *ZTK* 27, 1917, pp. 76–87.

Die Geschichte der synoptischen Tradition (= *Tradition*), [1]1921, [2]1931, [3]1957; ET, *History of the Synoptic Tradition*, 1963.

Jesus, [1]1926, [2]1951; ET, *Jesus and the Word*, 1934, 1958.

Glauben und Verstehen, (Collected Essays) I, 1953, [3]1958, II 1952, III 1960; ET of Vol. II, *Essays*, 1955.

'Zur eschatologischen Verkündigung Jesu' (review of Kümmel, *Verheissung und Erfüllung*, [1]1945), *TLZ* 72, 1947, 271–4.

'Heilsgeschichte und Geschichte' (review of Cullmann, *Christus und die Zeit*, [1]1946) *TLZ* 73, 1948, 659–66; ET in *Existence and Faith*, pp. 226–40.

Theologie des Neuen Testaments, [1]1948–[2]53, [3]1958. ET, *Theology of the New Testament*, 2 vols. I 1952, II 1955.

'Weissagung und Erfüllung', *ZTK* 47, 1950, pp. 360–83.

Das Urchristentum im Rahmen der Antiken Religionen, [1]1949, [2]1954; ET, *Primitive Christianity in its Contemporary Setting*, 1956.

'History and Eschatology', *NTS* 1, 1954–5, pp. 5–16 (originally written in English).

The Presence of Eternity: History and Eschatology, 1957 (the Gifford Lectures 1955, and originally written in English; published in Britain as *History and Eschatology*).

Jesus Christ and Mythology, 1958 (originally written in English).

Das Verhältnis der urchristlichen Christusbotschaft zum historischen Jesus,·[2]1961.

In considering Bultmann and his school careful attention must always be given to the language they are using. For this reason all references in this chapter are to the German edition of the works concerned, except in the case of work originally

Bultmann traces the conception 'Kingdom of God' through the Old Testament, seeing in it a basic belief in the Kingship (*Königtum*) of Jehovah over his people in the world whereby he orders their lives and protects and helps them. In the course of time this conception becomes eschatological, and the hope is for a future in which God will manifest himself as King over his people and bring them salvation (*Heil*). So Deutero-Isaiah looks to a future redemption of Israel from their captivity which will be the beginning (*Anbruch*) of the salvation-time. By the time of Christ this eschatological expectation had developed into two forms: the nationalistic expectation which was eschatological in the sense that it looked forward to a final stage in history, and the apocalyptic expectation which was eschatological in the stricter sense that it looked forward to an event whereby history would be brought to an end and something begun which would be essentially trans-historical. In the nationalistic expectation God would become King through the coming of a Messianic King, the Son of David, who would destroy all the enemies, establish the world rule of Israel, gather the twelve tribes into a transformed Holy Land where they would know eternal joy, great riches and everlasting peace. However much this hope might be coloured by supernatural elements it was essentially an historical hope; it was the hope of a new epoch in history, albeit the final epoch; it was the hope of a continuation of earthly life and being, albeit in a transformed state. In the apocalyptic expectation, on the other hand, God becomes King through a series of wholly supernatural events: the coming of a pre-existent Son of Man, a general resurrection, a final Judgment, the breaking-down of the barriers between earth and heaven. In this expectation God does not transform the world and usher in the final epoch of history. He suddenly puts an end to the world and to history. He does not transform earthly life and being, but makes an end of it. The apocalyptic eschatological hope is concerned with the 'wholly other' (R. Otto), with the absolute antithesis of any 'Here and Now', with something supernatural and superhistorical.[1]

It is this apocalyptic hope that is the true background to the

---

written in English, and translations offered in the text are by the present writer. References to the English editions are added for convenience only.

[1] *Jesus*, pp. 33–36 (*Jesus and the Word*, pp. 35–38); *ZTK* 47, 1950, pp. 373–7; *Jesus Christ and Mythology*, p. 12; *Presence of Eternity: History and Eschatology*, pp. 29–33.

proclamation of Jesus concerning the Kingdom of God. Consciously
following Johannes Weiss Bultmann argues that the hope of Jesus is
the hope of apocalyptic Judaism with its coming of the Son of Man
(Mark 8.38), its resurrection and non-worldly trans-historical life
(Mark 12.18–27) and its final judgment (Luke 11.31 f.).[1] Jesus
rejected the nationalistic type of expectation[2] and although he
accepted the apocalyptic hope he also modifies it by rejecting all
apocalyptic speculation concerning the coming of the End (Luke
17.20 f.; 17.23 f.), by claiming that he in his own person was the sign
of the End and by proclaiming that the Kingdom was imminent.[3]

The new note in the proclamation of Jesus is, above all, that of the
imminence of the Kingdom. What the apocalyptists expected of the
future Jesus proclaimed as at the very door, as even now breaking in
(Luke 10.23 f. par.; Luke 6.20 f.; Luke 10.18; Luke 17.21), and as
breaking in in his person, in his deeds, in his message (Matt. 11.5
par.; Luke 11.30; Mark 3.27).[4] But this does not mean that it is
already present; it is already dawning, but not yet present; it is like a
train coming into a station, but not yet having arrived at the plat-
form.[5] Bultmann thus sets his face firmly against all who would see an
element in the teaching of Jesus in which the Kingdom is present;
on this point the arguments and evidence adduced by Dodd,
Jeremias, Kümmel *et al.* leave him quite cold.

At this point, however, we must be careful not to misunderstand
Bultmann's position. Although he does reject the evidence adduced
by Dodd, Jeremias and Kümmel,[6] one gets the impression when

---

[1] *Jesus*, pp. 37–42 (*Jesus and the Word*, pp. 38–45); *Urchristentum*, p. 94 (*Primitive
Christianity*, p. 87); *Jesus Christ and Mythology*, pp. 12 f.
[2] At this point Bultmann contrasts the Eighteen Benedictions with the Lord's
Prayer. *Jesus*, p. 39 (*Jesus and the Word*, p. 39 f.).
[3] *Theologie des NT*, pp. 3–8 (*Theology of the NT* I, pp. 6–10); *Urchristentum*,
pp. 94–96 (*Primitive Christianity*, pp. 87–90).
[4] *Theologie des NT*, pp. 5–7 (*Theology of the NT* I, pp. 6 f.).
[5] *TLZ* 72, 1947, cols. 272 f., in discussion of the *ephthasen* in Matt. 12.28.
[6] For example in *Tradition*, [3]1958, *Ergänzungsheft*, p. 19 (ET, Appendix to p. 123),
the interpretation of Mark 13.28 f. by Dodd and Jeremias as originally referring
to the presence of the salvation time in the ministry of Jesus is 'doubtful'. Matt.
25.1–13 and Mark 12.1–9, both of which Dodd interpreted of the Kingdom as
present (*Parables*, pp. 172, 124) and Jeremias of the Kingdom as future (*Parables*,
pp. 132, 124), are, for Bultmann products of the early community. The former is
designed to meet the situation created by the delay of the Parousia and the latter
is an allegorical presentation of the *Heilsgeschichte. Ibid.*, pp. 27, 28. In *TLZ* 72,
1947, cols. 272 f., he discusses Kümmel's interpretation of Matt. 12.28, but rejects
it in favour of an interpretation of the *ephthasen* here in terms of the *ēggiken* in
Mark 1.15.

reading him that this is not in itself the important thing so far as he is concerned. What is important is to reject anything that would bring back the older ideas of the Kingdom as something that grows or develops.[1] The crucial thing is to maintain the fact of crisis produced by his proclamation and his ministry; whether this be the crisis of an imminent Kingdom or of a Kingdom in some sense present is unimportant compared with the fact that it is a crisis and so demands a decision of those who come to face it.[2]

The crucial thing for Bultmann is that the proclamation of the Kingdom by Jesus, and the signs of the Kingdom in his person and ministry, demand a decision of Jesus' hearers. Questions as to whether Jesus thought of the Kingdom as imminent or present, or as to his view of his own person, are not so important as the recognition that the Kingdom is eschatologically conceived and that Jesus understood his time as the time of decision and that he thought that men's attitude to himself and to his message was decisive for them.[3] The future element in the proclamation is not so much temporal as existential; it is future in the sense that it is coming towards men and demanding a decision of them.[4]

It is here that we have the much-discussed use by Bultmann of the categories of Heideggerian existentialism. What is happening is that he is accepting the *konsequente Eschatologie* of Weiss and Schweitzer and interpreting it in terms of the *Daseinsanalyse* of Martin Heidegger's *Sein und Zeit*, 1927. He does this quite consciously,[5] and especially in his understanding of 'future'. For Bultmann, following Heidegger, the future (*Zukunft*) is that which is coming upon man

---

[1] To give one example of this: In *Tradition*, [2]1931, pp. 216 f. (ET, p. 200), he discusses the parables of the Sower, Mustard Seed and Leaven and is not able to determine their original meaning. In the *Ergänzungsheft* to the third edition, 1958, p. 30, he quotes as 'doubtful' the interpretation of them by Dodd and Jeremias as parables of crisis or contrast. But this is almost in passing; his main interest is to reject a recent attempt by Dahl to interpret the Sower as a parable of organic growth and in this way to argue for the presence of the Kingdom. He reacts much more strongly against this than he does against the work of Dodd and Jeremias.

[2] So, for example, in *Tradition*, [2]1931, p. 103 (ET, p. 98), he discusses Mark 3.27 and says that the saying may well originally have meant that 'Jesus' victory over the demons proves that God has already overthrown the devil's rule'. Now Dodd, Jeremias and Kümmel have argued that this indicates the presence of the Kingdom in the ministry of Jesus and in the *Ergänzungsheft* to the third edition of 1958 Bultmann quotes this opinion, but without comment; he does not argue against it.

[3] *Presence of Eternity: History and Eschatology*, pp. 31 f.

[4] *Jesus*, p. 46 (*Jesus and the Word*, p. 51).

[5] 'Theology as a science can make fruitful use of the philosophical *Daseinsanalyse*' (*ZTK* 11, 1930, p. 343).

(*Zukommendes*), and this future determines the present, or may even be said to be a mode of the present, for in the light of that which is coming upon him a man makes the existential decision which determines the difference between potential existence (*Sein-Können*) and real existence (*Dasein*) for that man.[1] This is the background to Bultmann's definitive statement of the significance of the future Kingdom in the proclamation of Jesus:

> The Reign of God[2] is a power which wholly determines the present although in itself it is entirely future. It determines the present in that it forces man to decision: he becomes one thing or the other, chosen or rejected, his entire present existence wholly determined by it. . . . The coming of the Kingdom of God is not therefore actually an event in the course of time, which will come within time and to which a man will be able to take up a position, or even hold himself neutral. Rather, before he takes up a position he is already revealed for what he is, and he must therefore realize that the necessity for decision is the essential quality of his being. Because Jesus so sees man as standing in this crisis of decision before the activity of God, it is understandable that in him the Jewish expectation becomes the absolute certainty that now the hour of the breaking-in of the Reign of God has come. If man stands in the crisis of decision, and if this is the essential characteristic of his being as a man, then indeed every hour is the last hour, and it is understandable that for Jesus the whole contemporary mythology should be pressed into the service of this conception of human existence and that in the light of this he should understand and proclaim his hour as the last hour.[3]

It is difficult to determine how far Bultmann regards Jesus as the author of this existentialist understanding of eschatology. From the passage just quoted one would get the impression that Jesus himself thought in terms of a twentieth-century philosophy and used first-century categories only as a means to serve this understanding. But in other places Bultmann speaks of Jesus as really expecting the end of all history in the imminent future, and as mistaken in this expectation,[4] or of this understanding as an *interpretation* of Jesus' mythological eschatology, as an arrival—by the process of de-mythologizing—at its 'deeper meaning'.[5] In any case it is Bultmann's understanding

---

[1] For an extended discussion of this see Körner, *Eschatologie und Geschichte. Eine Untersuchung des Eschatologischen in der Theologie Rudolf Bultmanns*, 1957, pp. 69–87.

[2] Bultmann consistently uses *Gottesherrschaft* rather than *Gottesreich*.

[3] *Jesus*, pp. 46 f. (*Jesus and the Word*, pp. 51 f.).

[4] *Urchristentum*, pp. 99 f. (*Primitive Christianity*, p. 12).

[5] *Jesus Christ and Mythology*, p. 31.

of the proclamation of Jesus, and in the light of it all else in his interpretation of Jesus and his ministry falls into place. In demanding this decision of men Jesus is conscious that he is, in his own person, the 'sign of the time', that his cry is God's last word before the end.[1] But this does not mean that Jesus was conscious of being the Messiah, indeed his whole ministry is notably non-Messianic in character. Jesus appears as a prophet, in his proclamation of the imminence of the Kingdom, as a rabbi, in his radicalization of the demands of God, and as an exorcist; but not as the traditional Messianic king. Nor did Jesus regard himself as Son of Man, for he did not appear as judge of the world and supernatural bringer of salvation and he did not identify himself with the Son of Man whose coming he foretold.[2]

With regard to the relationship between eschatology and ethics in the teaching of Jesus, the centrality of the demand for decision, and the existential nature of that decision, is the key to understanding this relationship. Jesus did not teach an 'interim ethic', rather his proclamation of the Kingdom faces man with that crisis of decision which in itself is the means of salvation, and only he who can accept the radical demands of Jesus' ethical teaching can also accept the challenge of the crisis of decision. So the two things—ethical demand and demand for decision—both bring man into the presence of God, both direct him into his now as the hour of decision. This is not 'interim ethic' because 'interim ethic' means fulfilling an irksome requirement, for example the command to love, while directing one's attention to something different, the coming of the Kingdom, whereas in truth the radical ethical demand and the proclaimed coming of the Kingdom come together in the crisis of decision.[3]

BULTMANN'S VIEWS SUMMARIZED

Having reviewed Bultmann's contribution to the discussion of 'Kingdom of God' in the teaching of Jesus we may perhaps summarize it as follows:

1. He accepts the contention of *konsequente Eschatologie* that 'Kingdom of God' is an apocalyptic conception and argues that it is eschatological in the sense that it brings history to an end; it is essentially a supernatural and superhistorical expectation.

---

[1] *Theologie des NT*, p. 8 (*Theology of the NT* I, p. 9).
[2] *Ibid.*, pp. 27–34 (ET, I, pp. 26–32).
[3] *Ibid.*, pp. 19 f. (ET, I, pp. 20 f.).

2. The Kingdom is proclaimed by Jesus as imminent in the future, as indeed already dawning but not yet actually present. This imminent future is, however, not to be understood as temporal but as existential; the Kingdom cannot by its very nature come in the course of time, its imminence confronts man with the crisis of decision.

3. Jesus is conscious of his mission as the bearer of the last word of God before the End, and of his own person and work as the 'sign of the time', but his ministry is not Messianic and he neither claims Messiahship nor does he identify himself with the coming Son of Man.

4. The relationship between eschatology and ethics in the teaching of Jesus is such that both the proclamation of the Kingdom and the radical ethical demands find their unity in the crisis of decision before God.

The very least that can be said about this contribution to the discussion is that it is immensely important and tremendously stimulating. Its importance is that it defines the issues that must now be faced, as in all of Bultmann's contributions to New Testament studies; its stimulation is that it raises questions in the mind of the reader at every possible level, as again is always the case in Bultmann's work.

In the case of the first point there can be no doubt but that 'Kingdom of God' is an apocalyptic conception in the teaching of Jesus; our review of the discussion has shown the gradual but complete victory of this contention put forward by Johannes Weiss in 1892, Albert Schweitzer in 1907 and Bultmann himself in 1926. But if this be accepted the question that must then be faced is the one which Bultmann raises: What is the essential nature of this apocalyptic expectation? He claims that it is essentially a super-natural and superhistorical expectation, concerned with something which by its very nature cannot come in the course of time. Is he justified in this? To answer this question we must turn again to the vexed question of the content of the Kingdom concept in the teaching of Jesus, this time with the issue sharply defined for us by Bultmann.

With regard to the second point Bultmann again defines the issue for us. We have seen that to see the Kingdom both as present and as future in the teaching of Jesus is, on the basis of the evidence we have, much the most reasonable view, and Bultmann's rejection of this is not really the point at issue, as indeed he himself seems to feel. The point at issue is the significance of the Kingdom, present or future or both, for the men to whom the message concerning it is addressed. It is to this point that Bultmann's understanding of the Kingdom as future, and of the existential significance of this future Kingdom, is addressed, and it is this point that must be faced by any interpreter of the message of Jesus concerning the Kingdom of God.

The question of Jesus' consciousness of his mission is raised by Bultmann in a most challenging and fruitful manner, for he turns the discussion away from the older and by this time somewhat excessively well-worn paths to a newer and potentially more promising approach. His own conclusions proved too negative to stand the brunt of further discussion, but the decisive advance has been made along the lines laid down by him of considering the significance of Jesus' eschatological message for his, and our, understanding of his person and his mission rather than, for example, by putting all the weight upon the question of the derivation of Son of Man and the authenticity of the various groups of Son of Man sayings.

Finally, the relationship between eschatology and ethics remains for further discussion. Bultmann's understanding of this relationship may not finally be acceptable, but any other that is proposed to take its place must do at least equal justice to the dynamic unity between ethical demand and eschatological proclamation in the teaching of Jesus.

We do not propose at this point to take up a discussion of these questions, rather that will come at the end of our work;[1] at this point we must concern ourselves with the modifications of Bultmann's position that have taken place within the 'Bultmann school'.

THE 'BULTMANN SCHOOL'

Not the least of Bultmann's contributions to New Testament scholarship has been the fact that he attracted to himself a group of students who themselves in turn became significant New Testament scholars, and that he so trained them that they have shown a very considerable degree of independence from their teacher whilst maintaining his basic insights and emphases.[2] Four of these Bultmann *Schüler* are particularly important to our discussion: Ernst Käsemann of Tübingen, Günther Bornkamm of Heidelberg, Ernst Fuchs of

---

[1] See chapter X below.
[2] Cf. Ernst Käsemann's tribute to Bultmann in *ZTK* 54, 1957, p. 101.

Marburg, and Hans Conzelmann of Göttingen. In addition we must consider the work of an American New Testament theologian who shares the insights of the group, and who has made significant contributions both to their discussion and to the understanding of it in the world of Anglo-American theological scholarship: James M. Robinson of Claremont, California.

The main point at which these scholars have moved away from their master has been on the 'question of the historical Jesus'. Here they are engaged upon what J. M. Robinson has aptly called 'a new quest of the historical Jesus' in which they are departing from Bultmann's position as to our knowledge of the historical Jesus, although remaining true to his basic insights as to the nature of this knowledge and the nature of the kerygma and Gospel materials from which we derive it. This movement, now called 'post-Bultmannian', has been carefully described and brilliantly interpreted for English readers by J. M. Robinson, *A New Quest of the Historical Jesus*, 1959, who has himself made a significant contribution to it, especially in the German edition of this book, *Kerygma und historischer Jesus*, 1960, pp. 135–82, where he considerably expands and develops what is to be found in pp. 111–25 of the English edition.

We may not concern ourselves here with this discussion as such, although it may well turn out to be the most important development in New Testament theology in the mid-twentieth century, but only with those aspects of it which bear upon the subjects of 'Kingdom of God' and 'Son of Man'.[1]

This we can best do by considering the work of the 'school' at each of the four points which constituted our summary of Bultmann's contribution to the discussion.

1. *The Nature of the Kingdom*

All the *Schüler* agree with the master that 'Kingdom of God' is an apocalyptic concept in the teaching of Jesus, and that the expectation

---

[1] Works to be considered are: E. Käsemann, *Exegetische Versuche und Besinnungen* I, 1960 (includes his famous essay 'Das Problem des historischen Jesu' originally printed *ZTK* 51, 1954, pp. 125–53); 'Neutestamentliche Fragen von Heute', *ZTK* 54, 1957, pp. 1–21; E. Fuchs, *Zur Frage nach dem historischen Jesu*, 1960 (a collection of all his essays on the subject; ET in preparation); G. Bornkamm, *Jesus von Nazareth*, [1]1956, [2]1957 (ET directed by James M. Robinson, *Jesus of Nazareth*, 1960); H. Conzelmann, 'Gegenwart und Zukunft in der synoptischen Tradition', *ZTK* 54, 1957, pp. 277–96; 'Eschatologie: IV Im Urchristentum', *RGG*[3] II, 1958, cols. 665–72; 'Jesus Christus', *ibid.*, Vol. III, 1959, cols. 619–653; 'Reich Gottes', *ibid.*, Vol. V, cols. 912–18.

involved is a supernatural one, an expectation of something coming into history from outside.[1] However, they do not stress as much as does Bultmann the essentially superhistorical nature of this expectation. Bornkamm in particular is prepared to see the Kingdom as at any rate in part to be fulfilled in history,[2] and Fuchs remarks on this 'correction' of Bultmann's position, suggesting that Bultmann may have been '*zu dialektisch*' in his presentation of the proclamation of Jesus.[3] The change here does not come about because of a new study of the Kingdom concept itself, but rather because of a lessening of the emphasis upon a wholly future Kingdom in the teaching of Jesus. There is a new preparedness to see God as already beginning his reign in the ministry of Jesus and the Kingdom therefore as already being experienced in history, which carries with it the necessary correlate of a lessening emphasis upon the transhistorical nature of the Kingdom.

2. The Coming of the Kingdom

The change that has taken place here can be seen from the fact, often noticed,[4] that whereas Bultmann sees Jesus as looking forward to the decisive event in the future and Paul as looking back upon it in the immediate past,[5] Bornkamm sees the decisive event taking place in the ministry of Jesus, interpreting Matt. 11.12 to mean that John is the one who 'stands guard at the frontier between the aeons' and yet is overshadowed by Jesus 'in whose word and works the Kingdom, hidden, is breaking in'.[6] This is the difference we pointed out under (1) above, and it is a change in emphasis in which one of the major grounds for criticism of Bultmann has been removed. Bultmann's view has been criticized as not doing justice to the New Testament evidence for the fact that there is a tension between an aspect of the salvation activity of God already being fulfilled in the ministry of Jesus and the still future aspect of the Kingdom.[7] The Bultmann *Schüler* in their change of emphasis now do more justice to this aspect

---

[1] A contrary opinion on this point would be hard to find in Germany (see above, p. 57) and quite impossible within the Bultmann school!

[2] *Jesus von Nazareth*, chapter IV, and pp. 93 f. (*Jesus of Nazareth*, p. 102).

[3] *Zur Frage nach dem historischen Jesu*, p. 184 n. 34.

[4] E.g. by J. M. Robinson, *New Quest*, p. 17.

[5] *Glauben und Verstehen* I, pp. 200 f., 316.

[6] *Jesus von Nazareth*, p. 40 (*Jesus of Nazareth*, p. 51). Käsemann interprets the saying in a similar manner, *Exegetische Versuche*, p. 210. Robinson, *New Quest*, pp. 116–19, gives an extensive discussion of this aspect of the interpretation of Matt. 11.12.

[7] E.g. O. Cullmann, *TLZ* 83, 1958, col. 10 and W. G. Kümmel, *Coniectanea Neotestamentica XI* (Festschrift A. Fridrichsen), 1947, pp. 118 f.

of the evidence. Käsemann claims that Jesus meant, by the saying Matt. 11.12, that in his words the Kingdom came to his hearers.[1] Bornkamm speaks of the conflict and victory that is already present in Jesus by means of which the present contains the decisions of the ultimate future; the Kingdom is present in this sense in the ministry of Jesus, hidden but beginning. The future of God is salvation to those who recognize the presence of God in Jesus, whose present is the hour of salvation.[2] Conzelmann discusses the various attempts to synthesize the elements of present and future in Jesus' teaching and argues that any such attempt which continues to stress the time element must be unsatisfactory. Jesus, in fact, superseded the time element; he did not sharpen the degree of imminence in the Kingdom expectation, but proclaimed it as bound up with his own person. The message of Jesus was therefore not only a call for decision but also a proclamation of salvation.[3]

This change of emphasis is most radical in the work of Ernst Fuchs, which in itself is a very interesting fact, since in Germany he is generally regarded as being the Bultmann *Schüler* who is most truly developing the insights of his teacher.[4] Fuchs contrasts Jesus with the Qumran sect as one who not only challenged men to repentance in face of the future but gathered those who responded, not into a monastery to await the future but into a group who celebrated with him the presence of the Kingdom. They are not the last who shall know the Kingdom, but they are the first.[5] In 1960 Fuchs further announced that he could no longer rest content with Bultmann's understanding of the eschatological teaching of Jesus. There is, he says, an essential difference between a present leading towards a future, or determined by a future coming towards it, and a present which is determined and stamped by that future, in some sense already 'fulfilled'. Parables such as the Hid Treasure and the Pearl of Great Price go beyond teaching the necessity to sacrifice in a crisis of decision; they point to something found in the present, to a gift which is the activity of God now being experienced by men.[6] The preaching

---

[1] *Exegetische Versuche*, p. 211.

[2] *Jesus von Nazareth*, chapter IV, *passim*.

[3] *ZTK* 54, 1957, pp. 286 ff.

[4] The present writer had the privilege of spending a year at the *Kirchliche Hochschule* in Berlin while Fuchs was teaching there.

[5] *Zur Frage nach dem historischen Jesus*, pp. 253 f. (from an essay 'Jesus und der Glaube' originally published in 1958).

[6] *Zur Frage nach dem historischen Jesus*, pp. 326–35. Fuchs's indebtedness to Jeremias is here obvious and acknowledged by him (p. 334).

of Jesus creates a new existential relationship for men with the Kingdom as God acts for them in the present. The future element is not to be overlooked or explained away, but the miracle of the call in the present is intimately related to the equal miracle of the coming of God in the future. The whole is involved in the beginning, and the beginning is in the ministry of Jesus and in the fellowship of the called with him.[1]

Now at this point it must be made clear that although this new emphasis in the work of the post-Bultmannians is a modification of Bultmann's original position, it is not an acceptance of the position of scholars such as Jeremias or Kümmel. The post-Bultmannians can speak of present and future elements in the teaching of Jesus, but for them the reference is not temporal but existential. This can perhaps be seen most clearly in Fuchs's review of Kümmel's *Verheissung und Erfüllung*.[2] He points out that Kümmel speaks of the future element in the teaching of Jesus as the consummation of history, and that through the coming of Jesus as judge of the world. But Jesus himself, Fuchs argues, is not concerned with chronological history or world history but with man himself as the essential content *(Inbegriff)* of history. This can be seen in sayings such as Matt. 16.25 and the Beatitudes, and in the stylistic construction of the sayings of Jesus with their parallelism of present/future, finding/losing, which later was quite properly understood in terms of the paradox Gospel and Law, or Death and Life: Jesus was not concerned with the 'consummation' of world history but with the twofold 'end' of history for the person in either death or life.

This same point has been made in more detailed form by James M. Robinson in the German edition of his work on *The New Quest of the Historical Jesus*. He has a section on 'The Existential Interpretation of Eschatology by the Historical Jesus'[3] in which he examines the formal structure of the sayings of Jesus showing that a characteristic form is one in which the personal subject of the sentence is directly related to the predicate, the Kingdom (e.g. Matt. 21.31b; Mark 10.23; Mark 10.25; Luke 9.62; Matt. 18.3.). In these sayings we can see the 'eschatological polarity' of the message of Jesus whereby the present is explicitly brought under the aspect of the Eschaton and 'the entry into the Kingdom of God becomes a turning-point in

[1] *Ibid.*, pp. 346–59.
[2] In *Zur Frage nach dem historischen Jesus*, pp. 66–78.
[3] Robinson, *Kerygma und historischer Jesus*, pp. 161–6.

the destiny of the individual'.[1] The dialectic in the message of Jesus—present/future, find/lose, hunger/be filled, be humbled/exalted, last/first—is an existential dialectic.[2]

3. *The mission consciousness* (Sendungsbewusstsein) *of Jesus*

The three points about Bultmann's position here that have been taken up by his *Schüler* are: the contention that Jesus did not himself claim to be the Messiah, the scepticism with regard to the Son of Man sayings, and the implication of Jesus' consciousness of his mission as the bearer of the last word of God before the End.

In regard to the first of these points all the *Schüler* are unanimous in maintaining this scepticism with regard to Jesus' *specific* claims concerning his own person and work:[3] that they are also unanimous in regard to the significance of *implied* claims will become evident as we proceed.

The scepticism concerning the Son of Man sayings is one point upon which the *Schüler* are not unanimous. Conzelmann, following Vielhauer,[4] has argued that none of the Son of Man sayings are authentic, largely on the grounds that Jesus' understanding of the Kingdom was such that it cannot be reconciled with the apocalyptic concept of a climactic coming of the Son of Man.[5] This radicalization of Bultmann's own scepticism was hinted at by Käsemann,[6] but is not accepted by Fuchs and Bornkamm. Fuchs is not convinced that the early Church was the first to speak of the coming Son of Man[7] and Bornkamm accepts as authentic some of the apocalyptic Son of Man sayings and lays great stress upon those which relate the judgment of the coming one so very closely with Jesus' own person (e.g. Luke 12.8).[8]

It can be seen that the discussion of the actual Son of Man sayings within the 'school' is not taking us very much farther forward; here the important work has been done in the second generation by the

---

[1] *Ibid.*, p. 161.

[2] *Ibid.*, p. 166. Conzelmann makes exactly the same point in *RGG* V, col. 915.

[3] Käsemann, *Exegetische Versuche*, p. 206, 210 f.; Bornkamm, *Jesus von Nazareth*, p. 156 (*Jesus of Nazareth*, p. 170); Fuchs, *Zur Frage nach dem historischen Jesus*, *passim*; Conzelmann, *RGG* III, cols. 629 ff.

[4] P. Vielhauer, 'Gottesreich and Menschensohn in der Verkündigung Jesu', *Festschrift für Gunther Dehn* (ed. Schneemelcher), 1957, pp. 51–79.

[5] Conzelmann, *RGG* III, cols. 630–2.

[6] *Exegetische Versuche*, p. 211.

[7] *Zur Frage nach dem historischen Jesu*, p. 343 n. 69.

[8] *Jesus von Nazareth*, pp. 161–3, 206–8 (*Jesus of Nazareth*, pp. 175–7, 228–31).

Bornkamm *Schüler*, H. E. Tödt, as we pointed out in chapter VI above.[1] But in connection with the third point, the implications of Jesus' consciousness of his mission, there has been a most important development. Beginning from a statement in Bultmann's *Theologie des Neuen Testaments*, 'Jesus' call to decision implies a Christology',[2] the 'school' has gone on to develop these implications very considerably indeed, and to develop them in regard to Jesus' understanding of the significance of his mission.

Käsemann began the process of change by arguing for the authenticity of the first, second and fourth antitheses of the Sermon on the Mount, for the authenticity of the fact that Jesus claimed freedom in regard to the Sabbath commandments and the purification laws, and for the historicity of the fact that Jesus cast out demons and claimed to do so by means of the Spirit of God with which he was filled. He also pointed to the directness and authority with which Jesus proclaimed his knowledge of the will of God, and especially to his remarkable use of 'Amen' in introducing his own sayings. All of this, together with the fact that Jesus claimed that in his Gospel he was bringing the Kingdom to his hearers, indicates that Jesus viewed himself as more than a rabbi, wisdom teacher or prophet. The only category that can be valid in response to claims such as these is that of Messiah; irrespective of whether or not Jesus explicitly claimed Messiahship, his words and work imply such a claim.[3] Following upon Käsemann, Bornkamm accepts the points that he had made and goes on to add some others, especially stressing that in offering the forgiveness of sins, in proclaiming salvation to the people, and in celebrating table-fellowship with tax-collectors and sinners in the name of God and in close connection with the proclamation of Kingdom of God Jesus was usurping the prerogatives of God. In Jesus and his ministry the dawn of the Kingdom of God becomes a reality; he awakened Messianic hopes and expectations of salvation, he taught that decisions made in regard to his person and message would be confirmed at the Last Judgment, and although he did not claim Messiahship the essentially Messianic character of his being is contained in his words and deeds and in the unmediated character

---

[1] See above, pp. 109 ff.

[2] 3rd Edition, p. 46 (*Theology of the NT* I, p. 43). Here the reference occurs in a discussion of the understanding of the early Church, but in *Glauben und Verstehen* I, p. 216, it occurs in a discussion of the historical Jesus.

[3] Käsemann, *Exegetische Versuche*, pp. 206–12.

of his historic appearance.[1] Conzelmann speaks of the 'indirect' Christology to be found in Jesus' linking of the salvation hope with his own person, in the way in which he sees the Kingdom at work in his own deeds and in the way in which he understands his message as the last word of God before the End.[2]

Again at this point it is Fuchs who goes farthest along this new road of 'post-Bultmannianism'. Twice he quotes Bultmann's 'Jesus' call to decision implies a Christology', but each time he corrects it to 'Jesus' *conduct (Verhalten)* implies a Christology'.[3] He stresses the fact that Jesus' conduct is the actual context of his teaching, that, for example, the parable of the Prodigal Son is set in the context of Jesus' (eschatological) table-fellowship with sinners, and defends this conduct by referring to it as a direct exhibition of the will of God. 'Jesus dares to assert the will of God, as if he himself stood in the place of God!'[4] Jesus' conduct in regard to sinners actually implies more than would have been involved in an explicit claim to be Son of God or Son of Man.[5] The post-Resurrection proclamation of the Gospel of Christ by the early Church is in continuity rather than discontinuity with the conduct of the historical Jesus. The apocalyptic promises which were ascribed to Jesus by the early Church are false in the sense that Jesus did not actually say these things, but they are true in the sense that they represent what is implicit in Jesus' conduct and in his absolute certainty concerning the will of God.[6]

In one sense the work of Fuchs completes a circle: Bultmann began by rejecting all that the Gospels record of Jesus except his demand for a decision in the light of the coming Kingdom of God, and Fuchs has restored it all as authentic—the salvation which Jesus brought, the claims that he made, even the apocalyptic promises for the future that he uttered. But he has restored it in a manner that is entirely his own, and to which no report can pretend to do justice. It would be unfair to say that he is starting from radical presuppositions and reaching conservative conclusions, for this would imply a distinction between the presuppositions and the conclusions, an implication which Fuchs would strenuously, and rightly, deny. He is not bringing

---

[1] Bornkamm, *Jesus von Nazareth*, pp. 73 f., 155–63 (*Jesus of Nazareth*, pp. 80 f., 109–78).
[2] Conzelmann, *RGG* II, cols. 667–8; IV, cols. 629–33.
[3] Fuchs, *Zur Frage nach dem historischen Jesus*, pp. 185 n. 36, 403 n. 9.
[4] *Ibid.*, p. 154, cf. J. M. Robinson, *New Quest*, pp. 14 f.
[5] Fuchs, *op. cit.*, p. 156.
[6] *Ibid.*, p. 395.

comfort to conservatives, but challenging them to see the existential significance of the New Testament narratives, when these narratives are approached critically and in the spirit of demythologizing. It is far too soon to be able to judge the long-term significance of the approach of which he is the leading representative, but one tribute must be paid to it: it offers a most challenging presentation of Jesus.

4. *Eschatology and Ethics*

Bultmann's emphasis upon the unity of the eschatological proclamation and the radical ethical demand being found in the crisis of decision before God has been maintained by his *Schüler*, although they have introduced modifications at this point in accordance with their readiness to see the present of Jesus' ministry as the time of salvation. As we pointed out under (2) above, they see a dialectic tension between present and future in the message of Jesus, a tension which they interpret existentially, and it is in this context that the relationship between eschatology and ethics becomes clear for them. They point out that the Weiss-Schweitzer *Interimsethik* breaks down when applied to the teaching of Jesus because the ethical demands of Jesus are not, in fact, derived from the proclamation of the nearness of the Kingdom, but from the unmediated will of God. Although the general challenge to repent is set in the context of the imminence of the Kingdom (Mark 1.15), all of the specific ethical demands for love, purity, faithfulness, truth are rooted in the direct will of God.[1] The challenge of the eschatology and the challenge of the ethics are analogous confrontations with the unmediated will of God.[2]

Thus far the *Schüler* are following the teacher, but now comes the difference made by the fact that they are prepared to see the present of Jesus' ministry as a time not only of decision but also of salvation. Let us begin at this point with Bornkamm, who has discussed this in some detail. He contrasts Jesus' call for repentance with that of John the Baptist; repentance no longer means simply to prepare for a future act of God, it means to lay hold of the present salvation offered by God. Jesus' call to repentance is a demand for decision and action by man, but it is set in the context of a prior decision and action by God in manifesting the Kingdom as salvation in Jesus. Repentance

---

[1] Bornkamm, *Jesus von Nazareth*, p. 202 (*Jesus of Nazareth*, p. 223); Conzelmann, *RGG* III, col. 637.
[2] Conzelmann, *ibid.*

and salvation have now changed places; as compared with John the
Baptist, the call to repentance has become the call to salvation: the
call to recognize the grace of God, to accept it joyfully and to live in
this joy.[1] The burden of the message of Jesus is that the future is God's
future, and the future of God is salvation to the man who recognizes
the present as God's present and responds to it as the hour of
salvation. Similarly the future of God is judgment to the man who
does not recognize the present as the Now of God but clings to his
own present.[2] Those who lay hold of the present as the Now of God
are also called upon to fulfil the will of God with all their might,
because to respond to the will of God in the Now of Salvation must
mean also to respond to that same will in the commandments, since
Jesus reveals the same unmediated will of God in the present call to
salvation and in his interpretation of the commandments. So the
doing of the commandment will of God with all our might becomes
the means whereby we truly respond to the salvation will of God.
We must bring to our knowledge of the salvation love of God the
preparedness to love our neighbour, as we must come to the altar of
God with a preparedness to be reconciled with our brother, and as we
must accept God's forgiveness with a preparedness to forgive.[3]

Fuchs has criticized this presentation of the relationship between
eschatology and ethics, and especially the reference to fulfilling the
will of God with all one's might, on the ground that it does not do
justice to the eschatological dialectic between present and future in
the message of Jesus.[4] He himself prefers to express the matter in a
much more existentialistic manner and does so in an important
essay 'Das Zeitverständnis Jesu'.[5] Here he argues from the parables of
the Hid Treasure and Pearl that the challenge of Jesus is not a call
to preparedness to sacrifice (*contra* Bultmann) but a challenge to
accept what God has done for man in order to draw him to his side.
Jesus' proclamation creates a new existential relationship with the
Kingdom for the man who responds to the call, giving him a new
status and demanding of him a new obedience. The salvation which
this man knows in the present requires from him even the love of
enemies. Through the call in his present he comes to know the will

---

[1] Bornkamm, *Jesus von Nazareth*, pp. 74–79 (*Jesus of Nazareth* pp. 82–86).
[2] *Ibid.*, p. 82–87 (ET, 90–95).
[3] *Ibid.*, pp. 87–105 (ET, pp. 95–115).
[4] Fuchs, *Zur Frage nach dem historischen Jesus*, pp. 168–218 (an *Auseinandersetzung*
with Bornkamm's book), especially pp. 198–203.
[5] Printed in his book, pp. 304–76.

of God as love, he experiences this love as it determines his present situation; he comes to know what this love requires of him and to find in the existential situation created for him by it the freedom to respond to it. For those whose hearts are filled by this love there is obviously no divorce, no hate.[1]

One who stands outside this 'school' may perhaps be forgiven for feeling that there is here a difference in emphasis between Bornkamm and Fuchs that is comparatively unimportant in view of what they have in common. Their recognition of the essential relationship between eschatology and ethics in the teaching of Jesus as deriving directly from the unmediated will of God revealed in both, and their careful attempt to do justice both to the dialectic between present and future and to that between gift and demand, represent a very real contribution to what is probably the most difficult, and certainly not the least important, aspect of this whole discussion.

This review of the work of Bultmann and his *Schüler* has brought us down to the present day, but before we can turn to a final discussion of the teaching of Jesus concerning the Kingdom of God there are two further aspects of the discussion which call for notice: work done in recent time on 'Jesus and the Parousia', and the work of a group of American scholars who share a common emphasis upon 'Jesus as a prophet'.

[1] *Ibid.*, pp. 327, 336, 346, 350 ff.

VIII

JESUS AND THE PAROUSIA

BEASLEY-MURRAY

A PARTICULAR POINT in connection with the eschatology of
Jesus that has been the subject of recent discussion is that of
the Parousia. Did Jesus expect and teach a future consummation in the form of a Parousia, a Second Coming or Second
Advent? This question has been answered in the affirmative by
G. R. Beasley-Murray[1] and O. Cullmann,[2] and in the negative by
T. Francis Glasson,[3] J. A. T. Robinson,[4] and Erich Grässer.[5] Each of
these scholars has introduced different emphases in his answer to the
question, with the result that the issues involved have been more
clearly defined.

Beasley-Murray is concerned to establish Mark 13 as authentically
a part of the teaching of Jesus and with it the Parousia as taught in
that chapter. He reviews the whole discussion of the chapter in
modern New Testament scholarship, beginning with D. F. Strauss's
Life of Jesus, 1835, seeking to expose as invalid the various theories
that have been suggested to account for the existence of it on grounds
other than that it goes back to the authentic teaching of Jesus. Then
he attempts to demonstrate the authenticity of the chapter by
showing that its teaching 'approximates so closely to the otherwise
attested teaching of our Lord as to preclude the necessity for postulat-
ing an extraneous origin for it'.[6]

It must be said at once that the portrayal of the discussion is very

---

[1] G. R. Beasley-Murray, *Jesus and the Future*, 1954 (= *Future*); *A Commentary on
Mark Thirteen*, 1957.

[2] O. Cullmann, 'The Return of Christ' in *The Early Church*, a collection of his
essays edited by A. J. B. Higgins, 1956, pp. 141–62.

[3] T. F. Glasson, *The Second Advent*, [1]1945, [2]1947 (= *Advent*).

[4] J. A. T. Robinson, *Jesus and His Coming*, 1957 (= *Coming*).

[5] E. Grässer, *Das Problem der Parusieverzögerung in den synoptischen Evangelien und
in der Apostelgeschichte*, 1957 (= *Problem*).

[6] *Future*, p. 172.

well done. It seems to encompass every possible contribution, and what might well have been a chaos of differing opinions is firmly reduced to clarity and order. It is also quite brilliantly written; there are many examples of a liveliness of style unusual in English theological writing.[1] For all the author's industry and brilliance, however, the authenticity of Mark 13 is very far from being re-established. There are two main arguments against it, or, more accurately, against the apocalyptic discourse which it contains:[2] the language, and especially the vocabulary, of this passage; and the use of the LXX within it. The present writer investigated the former point and found that of the 165 words in the Nestle text of Mark 13.5–27, 35 (= 21.2 per cent) do not occur elsewhere in the Gospel, and of these 35 words 15 are to be found in the Book of Revelation.[3] A similar investigation of the vocabulary of Mark 13.28–37 reveals a total vocabulary of 79 words, of which 13 (= 16.4 per cent) do not occur elsewhere in the Gospel. Of these 13 words only 2 are to be found again in Revelation. The significance of these percentages can be seen when they are compared with R. Morgenthaler's[4] similar investigations of Mark 16.9–20 and John 7.53–8.11, both of which are generally recognized as not originally belonging to the Gospels in which they are found. Mark 16.9–20 has a vocabulary of 92 words of which 16 (= 17.2 per cent) do not occur elsewhere in Mark; John 7.53–8.11 has a vocabulary of 82 words of which 14 (= 17.2 per cent) do not occur elsewhere in John. It can be seen at once that Mark 13.5–27 has a much higher percentage of words not found elsewhere in the Gospel (21.2 per cent) and Mark 13.28–37 a somewhat lower percentage (16.4 per cent). It might be argued that Mark

[1] One example from the many possible: 'Acknowledging the interest and value of this treatment, we must yet confess that the net result is to dismember the original Little Apocalypse and put its head and legs together, minus its torso; how well it walks, we are not sure.' *Future*, pp. 107 f., of Vincent Taylor's treatment of the chapter in his *St Mark*, 1952.

[2] I.e. Mark 13.5–27. The parable of the Fig-tree, vv. 28 f., the disclaiming of knowledge of the time of the End, vv. 30–32, and the injunctions to watchfulness, vv. 33–37, are not part of the discourse proper, and they may well have a basis in the authentic teaching of Jesus.

[3] The 35 words are as follows (the numbers in brackets indicate the number of occurrences to be found in the Book of Revelation): *akron, apoplanan, astēr* (14), *bdelygma* (3), *gastēr, goneis, dōma, eklegesthai, eklektos* (1), *epanistasthai, erēmōseōs, hēgemōn, thēlazein, thlipsis* (5), *throeisthai, koloboun, ktizein* (2), *limos, misein* (3), *planan (seducere)* (6), *polemos* (9), *prolegein, promerimnan, saleuein, seismos* (7), *selēnē* (4), *skotizesthai* (4), *telos* (as term. techn. of apoc.) (3), *teras, hypomenein, pheggos, cheimōn, pseudoprophētēs* (3), *pseudochristos, ōdin*.

[4] R. Morgenthaler, *Statistik des Neutestamentlichen Wortschatzes* 1958.

13.5–27 deals with a subject not found elsewhere in the Gospel, and this could account for the different vocabulary. But Morgenthaler has also investigated Luke 2.1–20 which equally deals with a subject not found elsewhere in the Gospel. Here the total vocabulary is 156 words, of which 22 (= 14.1 per cent) are not found elsewhere in the Gospel.

It would seem therefore, that the vocabulary of Mark 13.5–37 does bear out the general assumption that this apocalyptic discourse is secondary material; secondary, that is, as compared to the rest of Mark's Gospel, and secondary therefore to the authentic teaching of Jesus recorded in Mark.

Beasley-Murray does not investigate the vocabulary of Mark 13; with regard to the language he contents himself with pointing to the Semitisms in the Greek, while admitting that no great weight can be put on them.[1]

The second point is the use of the LXX; in order to be able to see this in perspective we must first see what is the use of the LXX in the teaching of Jesus as it is recorded in Mark before we come to chapter 13. It is usually the case that specific quotations from the Old Testament are given in the LXX version (e.g. 12.10, 11; 12.26; 12.36), but it is only to be expected that the early Church, which used the LXX, should accommodate the language of specific quotations to this version. So there is no difficulty here; nor is there any difficulty in the many instances of reminiscence of the Old Testament where the language is from the LXX but the Hebrew gives the same meaning (e.g. 2.26; 4.29; 4.32; 6.34; 9.12; 10.4, 7, 8; 12.1; 12.19; 12.31). Other instances are more worthy of note. In 4.12 we have a dependence upon the Aramaic Targum, rather than upon either the Hebrew or the LXX.[2] In 8.18 the reference is similar to that in 4.12. The reference in 7.6 is certainly dependent upon the LXX of Isa. 29.13, but the Hebrew text yields the same point.[3] Again in 7.10 we have quotations from the LXX of Ex. 20.12 and 21.16, but the point of the argument demands the Hebrew verb of the latter (*m⁽qalēl*) which can be rendered 'he that curseth' rather than the LXX (*kakologōn*) which means 'he that speaks evil of'. In Mark 12.29 f. the reference to Deut. 6.4 f. agrees neither with the Hebrew nor with the LXX; it adds *ischuos* to the three nouns of the LXX

---

[1] *Future*, pp. 246–50.
[2] So T. W. Manson, *Teaching*, pp. 75–80.
[3] See V. Taylor, *St Mark*, *ad loc*.

(*kardias psychēs dynameōs*) and to the three of the Hebrew (*lēbāb nephesh m^e'ōd*).

It can be seen, therefore, that until we come to chapter 13 we have no case of dependence upon the LXX in the recorded teaching of Jesus where that version differs from the Hebrew or does not yield the same point. In Mark 13 all this changes.[1] 13.7 quotes the LXX of Dan. 2.28, where the LXX and Theodotion read *dei genesthai*:[2] the Aramaic has the simple future. 13.13 'the end' corresponds to the climax of the time of tribulation in Dan. 12.12, 13; Theod. has *ho hypomenōn* (Mark *ho hypomeinas*), the Hebrew has 'he that waiteth'. 13.14 *to bdelygma tēs erēmōseōs* is from Dan. 12.11 LXX and Theod.; the Hebrew is 'the abomination that maketh desolate'. 13.19 reflects Dan. 12.1 (Theod. rather than LXX); here the Marcan *thlipsis hoia ou gegonen* is *verbatim* from Theod., the Hebrew could be otherwise rendered and indeed LXX has *hoia ouk egenēthē*. 13.25 reflects the LXX of Isa. 34.4 and agrees with the LXX against the Hebrew on three separate counts: it has (1) 'the powers of the heavens' (Hebrew 'the host'): (2) 'the stars' (Hebrew 'their host'): (3) 'shall be falling' (Hebrew 'shall fall away'). 13.27 is from the LXX of Zech. 2.6; the Hebrew is different (v. 10): 'I have spread you abroad as the four winds of heaven.'

In Mark 13, therefore, we do not have a series of quotations which could have been accommodated to the text of the LXX in the course of transmission, nor do we have a series of quotations or allusions which could equally well have been made originally from the Hebrew; we have a series of quotations and allusions woven into the text of the chapter and taken *verbatim* from the LXX or Theod., which is often quite different from the Hebrew (or Aramaic). We have no single instance of necessary dependence upon any text other than the Greek. All this is absolutely different from the usage elsewhere in the recorded teaching of Jesus in Mark.

Beasley-Murray's attempts to deal with these facts are as ingenious as they are unconvincing.[3] In v. 14, for example, he argues for an original Marcan reading (without a shred of textual evidence) *to sēmeion tou bdelygmatos* which he thinks referred to the standards of the Roman Army, and which would not be a quotation. In v. 19 he

---

[1] We are now following Glasson, 'Mark 13 and the Greek Old Testament', *Exp T* 69, 1957–58, pp. 213–15.
[2] This phrase is also to be found in Rev. 1.1; 4.1; 22.6.
[3] *Future*, pp. 246–50, 255–8.

suggests that the nearness to the Theod. rather than the LXX text could quite well be due to an independent use of the Hebrew text, since the Theod. text is of the second century AD.[1] In v. 27 he notes that Kittel recommends modifications of the Hebrew text in accordance with the Greek version and so he suggests that here the reference is to a pre-Massoretic Hebrew text of Zech. 2.6. One suspects that if such arguments had been used in support of the Little Apocalypse theory, Beasley-Murray would have found some biting phrase with which to dismiss them!

The two points that we have discussed are not the only arguments that can be brought against the authenticity of Mark 13, but they are certainly sufficient to show that the apocalyptic discourse in Mark 13.5–27 may only be used with the very greatest caution as a source for the eschatological teaching of Jesus. As it stands it reflects a vocabulary and a dependence upon the Greek Old Testament markedly at variance with the recorded teaching of Jesus in the remainder of the Gospel.

Beasley-Murray's work therefore does not take us very much farther forward in the discussion of Jesus and the Parousia, except in so far as his failure to demonstrate the authenticity of the Marcan apocalypse confirms the almost universal tendency of modern New Testament scholarship not to rely upon it in any attempted reconstruction of the teaching of Jesus. The work of Cullmann[2] is much more important, for here we have what is probably the most significant modern attempt to preserve and interpret the Parousia element in the teaching of Jesus.

CULLMANN: *Heilsgeschichte*

Cullmann's aim is confessedly to interpret the teaching of Jesus in

---

[1] The fact that the Greek Old Testament version used in Mark 13 often seems to be Theod. rather than LXX is indeed worthy of note, but it cannot be assumed that the text of Theod., especially in the Book of Daniel, did not exist before the second century AD. C. H. Dodd points out that all through the New Testament the Greek version of Daniel known and used seems to be that of Theodotion rather than the Septuagint (*According to the Scriptures*, p. 69 n.). Two leading editors of the Greek Old Testament, A. Rahlfs in Germany and H. B. Swete in England, have agreed that Theodotion did not provide an entirely new translation but rather a correction of an existing text (A. Rahlfs, 'Geschichte des Septuaginta-Textes' in his *Septuaginta*, Editio Quinta, 1952, I, p. x; H. B. Swete, *Introduction to the Old Testament in Greek*, 1900, p. 47).

[2] For an earlier mention of Cullmann's work see above, pp. 88 f.

terms of the *Heilsgeschichte*.[1] He argues that eschatology is 'an absolutely chronological concept'[2] and that the eschatological teaching of Jesus must therefore be understood to have a chronological frame of reference.[3]

The Jewish expectation is characterized by Cullmann as concerned with linear time, but with linear time which could be regarded in two ways. Looking at it in one way we have a line divided into three parts by two decisive events: Creation and the Parousia (coming of the Messiah). We have therefore three periods: time before the Creation, time between Creation and the Parousia, and time after the Parousia. Looking at it in another way we have a line divided into two by the decisive redemptive activity of God, a line of what might be called 'redemptive time' to be divided into two: the time before the decisive redemptive activity of God and the time after it. The Jews expected that the Parousia would be the decisive redemptive act of God and so for them the two lines coincide: the time between Creation and the Parousia was also the time before the decisive act of redemption, and the time after the Parousia would be the time of redemption.[4]

Jesus' understanding was different from this in that he regarded the decisive redemptive activity of God as already taking place in his own ministry; for him this did not coincide with the Parousia. The teaching concerning the Kingdom as present determines the present as the time of redemption, as his teaching concerning the Kingdom as future looks to the Parousia as the beginning of the third and final period of linear time. So Jesus still expected the Parousia, and sayings such as Mark 10.23; 13.30; 9.1; 14.62 contemplate a period of time elapsing between his ministry and the Parousia. The prophecies of the Passion, which Cullmann accepts as authentic,[5] indicate that Jesus regarded his Cross and Resurrection as constituting the decisive stage in the coming of the Kingdom, so the decisive mid-point in redemptive time is, for Jesus and the early Church, the ministry which culminates in the Easter events.[6] This ushers in the

---

[1] There seems to be no unanimity with regard to an adequate English translation of this most expressive German word. Cullmann himself seems to prefer 'redemptive history' (*Early Church*, p. xii).

[2] *Early Church*, p. 144, *contra* Bultmann.

[3] *Christ and Time*, pp. 41, 43, 71 f.

[4] *Christ and Time*, pp. 81–83.

[5] For Cullmann on the Son of Man sayings see above, pp. 107 f.

[6] *Early Church*, pp. 150 ff.

final period of redemptive time, but does not invalidate the Parousia hope; the war must continue until the end, although the decisive battle has already been fought and won.[1]

There can be no doubt but that Cullmann has presented vividly a view of 'redemptive history' that is characteristic of some New Testament writers, if not all,[2] but the question arises as to whether such a view is to be found in the teaching of Jesus. In this connection two particular factors have to be weighed: does the teaching of Jesus presuppose an eschatological continuation of linear time; and did Jesus foresee a period of time elapsing between his ministry, and especially his death, and the Parousia? Bultmann would answer both of these questions in the negative[3] and Cullmann in the affirmative. They are important questions and we shall take them up in our final discussion.[4]

GLASSON

T. Francis Glasson has argued that Jesus did not expect a Parousia; he expected a new state of things after his death, an expectation which was, in fact, fulfilled by Pentecost and the coming into being of the Church. The doctrine of the Parousia was read back into the tradition by the early Church, where it was derived from the Day of the Lord passages in the Old Testament, Jesus being identified with the Lord. 'Jesus comes not because he is Christ, but because he is Lord.'[5]

In arguing for this interpretation of the teaching of Jesus Glasson discusses three things that are important to our discussion: the Parousia sayings themselves; Mark 14.62; and the 'parables of crisis'. His arguments about Mark 14.62 and the crisis parables are taken up and developed by J. A. T. Robinson and we will discuss them therefore in the context of his work;[6] at this point we concern ourselves with Glasson on the Parousia sayings.

[1] *Christ and Time*, p. 84.
[2] R. Bultmann, 'Heilsgeschichte und Geschichte' (a review of Cullmann's, *Christus und die Zeit*), *TLZ* 73, 1948, col. 663, argues that it may be true that such a conception is to be found in Paul, Hebrews, Matthew, Luke, Acts, but certainly not in John.
[3] As he does in his review of Cullmann's work quoted in the previous note.
[4] See below, pp. 160 ff.
[5] Glasson, *Advent*, p. 171. On this view, very popular among British writers, that the actual course of events—Resurrection, Pentecost, the history of the Church—corresponds to the expectation of Jesus concerning the future, see above, p. 67, where Glasson is one of the writers mentioned in n. 6.
[6] See below, pp. 140–45.

He argues that references to the Parousia have been introduced into the Gospel tradition in the course of its transmission,[1] and that the references in the synoptic apocalypses cannot be accepted, since it is widely held that these passages are secondary. Luke 17.22–37 originally referred to the destruction of Jerusalem and was Jesus' warning to his followers not to be involved in the city's fate. The Parousia references in the parables are either later additions, e.g. Luke 18.7 f., or they are cases of original references to the crisis in the ministry of Jesus being applied to the Parousia, e.g. the Ten Virgins (Matt. 25.1–13). Mark 13.32 appears to apply to the Parousia, but we have no means of knowing what the original reference was; 'the words are apparently a reply to a question and we have no means of finding out what the question was'. In Matt. 23.37–39 'Jesus was simply referring in the course of one visit to Jerusalem to his absence until the feast of the Passover'. Matt. 10.23, crucial to Schweitzer's theory, reflects the harassment of the early Christians under persecution. Matt. 25.31, and indeed the whole passage, vv. 31–46, 'owes a good deal to the Evangelist'.[2]

Glasson also argues that Jesus' teaching concerning the Kingdom of God does not require a Parousia; Mark 9.1 is to be seen as a reference to Pentecost and the subsequent history of the Christian Church.[3] A final indication of the fact that Jesus did not look towards a Second Advent is provided by the fact that there are three elements in his teaching which are incompatible with the assumption that he expected a speedy end of the world. These are (a) his ethical teaching;[4] (b) the New Israel;[5] and (c) the fact that his purpose embraced the Gentiles. Actually, far from proving that the teaching of Jesus is incompatible with the assumption that he expected a speedy end of the world, these three aspects of his teaching tend to prove the exact opposite! They do, in fact, show us how thoroughly eschatological his teaching was. The New Law is the eschatological Torah, which replaces the old Torah because the End-time has come; the New Israel is the eschatological community,

---

[1] E.g. at Matt. 16.28, cf. Mark 9.1; Matt. 24.42, cf. Mark 13.43; Mark 8.38 par., cf. Matt. 10.32 = Luke 12.8 f. (Q).

[2] *Advent, pp.* 103–5.

[3] As we noted above, p. 67.

[4] 'Why should Jesus take the trouble and risk of revising a legal code, which had existed for centuries, if he expected the end of the world in a short time?' (p. 137).

[5] 'The Church spoke of itself as the New Israel, e.g. Gal. 6.16, and it seems certain that this thought goes back to Jesus himself' (p. 139).

the Israel of the End-time; and although the purpose of Jesus embraced the Gentiles, he expected that they would be brought into the Kingdom by an eschatological act of God.[1]

There can be no doubt but that Glasson is right in one respect: Parousia references *have* been introduced into the Gospel tradition in the course of its transmission. But this does not necessarily mean that all references to a future consummation can be so readily explained away or referred to the post-Easter course of events. The great argument against seeing them as a reference to the post-Easter events is the fact that the early Church did not so see them,[2] and Glasson's ingenuity in explaining away those that cannot be so referred is commendable as ingenuity but suspicious as argument. It is essential to Glasson's position that he should accept Dodd's 'realized eschatology', as he does,[3] but once this exclusive emphasis upon the Kingdom as present in the teaching is abandoned, as it must be in light of the discussion and arguments reviewed in chapter V above, then what remains of Glasson's position is scarcely defensible. That the Matthaean reinterpretation of this in terms of this Parousia is secondary would be generally admitted,[4] but this does not alter the fact that Mark 9.1 itself looks towards a future consummation of that which had begun in the ministry of Jesus. Dodd's earlier position with regard to this saying has been rejected, and abandoned by him,[5] and his later reference of it to Pentecost and the era of the Church, which Glasson follows, is also to be rejected.[6] There is also the possibility that we should reject the Marcan saying altogether as *Gemeindebildung*, as do Bultmann and his school in arguing that the saying has been produced by the early Church as a word of encouragement in the situation created by the delay of the Parousia.[7] This is indeed possible, but it seems extremely unlikely that a saying created by the early Church to meet a given need should have been so formulated as to create the difficulties found in it by Matthew and

---

[1] Jeremias, *Jesu Verheissung für die Völker*, 1956, pp. 47–62 (ET by S. H. Hooke, *Jesus' Promise to the Nations* (= *Promise*), 1958, pp. 55–73).

[2] See above pp. 67 f.

[3] *Advent*, p. 94 n. 1.

[4] This does not mean that Matthew was necessarily wrong in this interpretation of Mark. See C. K. Barrett, *The Holy Spirit and the Gospel Tradition*, 1947, p. 73.

[5] See above, pp. 67 f.

[6] See above, p. 68.

[7] Bultmann, *Tradition*³, p. 128 (ET, p. 121), and *Ergänzungsheft*, p. 18; G. Bornkamm, *In Memoriam Ernst Lohmeyer*, 1951, pp. 116–19; E. Fuchs, *Zur Frage nach dem historischen Jesus*, p. 67; For Grässer on this see below, pp. 145 ff.

Luke and leading them to reinterpret it.[1] We will discuss it in more detail when we consider the work of E. Grässer. If we, however, follow Kümmel in accepting the authenticity of this saying in its Marcan form[2] then we must recognize that what we have here is an emphasis upon the future aspect of the Kingdom as manifest to all in contrast with the present aspect about which there can be argument.[3] Jesus might proclaim the forgiveness of sins, but it could be argued that he was blaspheming (Mark 2.1–12); he could interpret his exorcisms in terms of the coming of the Kingdom (Matt. 12.28 par.), but his opponents could argue that the power was of Beelzebub, not of God (Mark 3.22). Out of this situation Jesus looks to a future consummation of that which has begun in his own ministry about which there can be no further argument, only the acceptance of judgment based upon the attitude one has taken to the present manifestation (Luke 12.8 f. par.).

That there is in the teaching of Jesus a characteristic contrast between a hidden (perhaps better 'debatable') present and a manifest future has been argued by C. K. Barrett,[4] and this is certainly the message of the 'contrast-parables'.[5] Now if this be accepted as the proper interpretation of Mark 9.1, then we have in the teaching of Jesus the prediction of a future consummation of that which had begun in his own ministry, a prediction that has been further defined by Matthew in terms of the Parousia. Similar is the case of Mark 8.38, where we find an expression of Jesus' expectation of the eschatological judgment of the Son of Man. Matthew (16.27) has again sharpened the reference in accordance with his expectation of the Parousia of the Son of Man, but to acknowledge this does not alter the fact that Jesus did expect a future eschatological event in which the Son of Man would exercise his function as Judge. This expectation is far too widespread in the tradition for it to be dismissed as no part of the expectation of the historical Jesus. It is one of the themes of the

---

[1] Kümmel, *Promise*, p. 27.

[2] Kümmel rightly rejects a suggestion that the 'in power' is an addition by the evangelist, *Promise*, p. 26.

[3] This is surely the significance of the similar 'in power' in Rom. 1.4. There the Resurrection does not make Jesus Son of God in a way that he was not before, such a suggestion would be foreign to the theology of the kerygma and of Paul; it designates him Son of God manifestly to all who accept the fact of his Resurrection. From this point there can be argument about the Resurrection but not, if the Resurrection be accepted, about Jesus being Son of God.

[4] *The Holy Spirit and the Gospel Tradition*, pp. 73 f.

[5] Jeremias, *Parables*, pp. 89–92.

parables (Matt. 25.31–46), it is the theme of the one group of Son of Man sayings accepted as authentic by so sceptical a scholar as Bultmann,[1] and a part in it is promised to the disciples (Matt. 19.28).[2]

We can see therefore that although there is a tendency in the tradition to insert Parousia references there is none the less firm evidence for the fact that Jesus expected in the future an event which would mark the end of the existing order of things and bring to consummation that which had begun in his own ministry. This evidence is not only to be found in the Parousia sayings themselves but in all those aspects of the teaching of Jesus in which the Kingdom is future.[3] This future event could be referred to in several ways; it could be pictured in imagery like that of the New Temple, or of the eschatological table-fellowship with God, or of the complete reversal of the existing order of things. It could be referred to as 'the consummation of all things', the coming of the Kingdom 'in power', or the 'coming' or the 'day' of the Son of Man; or the term 'Kingdom of God' could be used in contexts in which it is necessarily a future hope. The important thing is that all of these are different ways of expressing the same conviction, that what had begun in his ministry would necessarily issue in a final and perfect consummation; the Kingdom of God was both a present reality and a future hope.

It is this teaching concerning a future eschatological event that gave rise to the developed Parousia expectation of the early Church. That Jesus taught a Second Advent doctrine in this form seems to be doubtful; in so far as he denies this Glasson has right on his side; but what seems to be beyond doubt is that one of the ways in which Jesus phrased his future expectation is as the coming of the Son of Man.

J. A. T. ROBINSON

We turn now to J. A. T. Robinson who, like Glasson, is concerned to show that the Parousia doctrine of the early Church does not correspond to the expectation of the historical Jesus. Unlike Glasson, he is prepared to admit that the historical Jesus did expect a future 'consummation of all things in the final vindication of God and his

---

[1] See chapter VII above for the not altogether successful attempt by Vielhauer to radicalize the scepticism of the Bultmann school in this regard.

[2] On this saying see T. W. Manson, *Teaching*, pp. 268 ff., *Sayings*, pp. 216 f.

[3] See above, pp. 80–84.

saints', that he used of this future consummation the traditional imagery of the heavenly banquet, that he thought in terms of a distinction between 'this age' and 'the age to come', and that he visualized history as bounded by the final judgment, which would be marked by a general resurrection and a final separation of the saved and the lost.[1]

In the expectation of Jesus two elements are distinguished, both of them part of the traditional Parousia expectation. These are, on the one hand, the element of *vindication*—of victory out of defeat—and, on the other hand, the element of *visitation*—of a coming among men in power and judgment. Robinson's argument is that although both of these elements are to be found in the expectation of Jesus, neither of them necessitates a future 'coming'. Jesus expected an *immediate* vindication out of his sufferings, not a future event, a 'coming', in which he would be vindicated; and the visitation of which he spoke was the visitation which took place in his own ministry. 'There is in his teaching no "coming of the Son of Man"', which does *not* refer to this ministry, its climax and its consequences. The visitation of which he spoke would merely be *set in motion* by his rejection. Its outworking, like his own vindication, would take place "from now on".'[2]

It is extremely difficult to see how Robinson reconciles this view of the expectation of Jesus with the admission that Jesus expected a final consummation. Having once admitted that Jesus expected a final consummation he never again mentions it, and he says nothing whatever about the relationship between what is 'set in motion' by Jesus' rejection and the final consummation. Presumably the inevitable process continues until God winds up all things in the final consummation. But what is the role of Jesus, or the Son of Man, in this final consummation?

This is the basic weakness of Robinson's approach to the expectation of the historical Jesus, as distinct from his approach to the question as to whether Jesus expected a Second Advent. He makes a sharp distinction between the expectation of Jesus concerning a final consummation and his expectation concerning vindication and visitation. But this distinction is a false one; because the expectation of Jesus concerning his vindication is part of his whole expectation concerning the final consummation, and the visitation that took place

[1] Robinson, *Coming*, pp. 36 f.
[2] *Coming*, p. 81 (Robinson's italics).

in his ministry does not exclude the expectation of a future visitation.

With regard to the element of vindication, the most important saying is the solemn adjuration at the trial of Jesus, Mark 14.62 par. After a detailed discussion of this saying Robinson concludes that the reference is not to a vindication in the sense of a future coming from God, but vindication in the sense of an immediate going to God. The saying indicates that Jesus expected 'the immediate vindication of his person and cause . . . what is most important is what I believe is most certain: that we have here a saying not of visitation from God but of vindication to God'.[1] Jesus' expectation of vindication through and out of his sufferings is also to be seen in the sayings at Mark 8.31; 9.31; 10.33 f., and parallels; also at Luke 12.50; 13.34. Jesus expected 'that there would indeed be a Parousia, in the sense of a coming to appear before the presence of God, and that it would be inaugurated "henceforth" (Matt. 26.64; Luke 22.69) through his own redemptive death'.[2]

This argument concerning Jesus' expectation of a vindication through and out of his sufferings that would follow as a climax to the sufferings, and that would involve an appearing before the presence of God rather than a coming to the world in triumph, is not new in British New Testament scholarship. Robinson can, and does, claim the support of C. H. Dodd, T. W. Manson, Vincent Taylor, T. F. Glasson, and G. S. Duncan at various points.[3] The crux of the matter is undoubtedly the saying at Mark 14.62; whatever interpretation we give to the 'coming of the Son of Man' here can also be given to all the other sayings with a similar reference. Here Robinson, T. W. Manson,[4] Vincent Taylor,[5] T. F. Glasson,[6] and C. H. Dodd[7] are at one in seeing the reference to Psalm 110.1 and to Dan. 7.13 as parallel expression referring to a vindication that would follow the sufferings of Jesus, and not implying a Parousia.

---

[1] *Coming*, p. 50.
[2] *Ibid.*, p. 58.
[3] *Ibid.*, pp. 43, 45, 49, etc.
[4] *BJRL* 32, 1950, p. 174. 'It cannot be too strongly emphasized that what Daniel portrays is not a divine, semi-divine, or angelic figure coming down from heaven, to bring deliverance, but a human figure going up to heaven to receive it.'
[5] *St Mark*, p. 569: '. . . . the conjunction of Ps. 110.1 and Dan. 7.13 shows that a spectacular descent is not contemplated. . . . The emphasis lies on enthronement, and on enthronement as the symbol of triumph.'
[6] See above, p. 136.
[7] Robinson claims that C. H. Dodd now accepts a view similar to his own, *Coming*, p. 43.

But although this is a widely held opinion in British New Testament scholarship there is a strong argument against it: the fact that in the Jewish interpretation of Dan. 7.13, as soon as the text was interpreted Messianically it was interpreted in terms of a *coming* on the clouds of heaven.[1] The importance of the Jewish interpretation here is that in Mark 14.62 the saying is addressed to a Jew[2] and it is therefore a strong presumption that it is intended to mean what it would have meant to the person to whom it was addressed. In view of the unanimity of the Jewish interpretation there can be no doubt but that the High Priest would have understood it as referring to a vindication at a future 'coming' of the Son of Man. Another indication that the reference here is to Dan. 7.13 as it was interpreted in the Jewish tradition rather than as it could be interpreted on the basis of the MT of Daniel is the fact that the text of Dan. 7.13 presupposed by Mark 14.62, and all other references to it in the New Testament, is a text in which the adverbial phrase 'with (or 'in') the clouds' has been moved from its original place in the sentence and brought into close conjunction with the verb 'coming'. This is the word order presupposed by the Jewish interpretation of Dan. 7.13, but not the word order of the MT of that verse, nor of the Greek versions.[3]

[1] So, e.g., II (4) Ezra 13.1 ff., and the rabbinical references given in Billerbeck, *Kommentar* I, pp. 956 f.

[2] Neither Robinson, nor the other scholars quoted above, doubt the authenticity of the narrative at this point.

[3] R. B. Y. Scott, ' "Behold, he cometh with clouds",' *NTS* 5, 1958–59, pp. 126 ff. Cf. also H. K. McArthur, 'Mark XIV. 62', *NTS* 4, 1957–58, pp. 156–58, who offers three considerations in support of the parousia exegesis of Mark 14.62: (i) When the New Testament quotes an Old Testament passage it is precarious to determine the New Testament meaning by the Old Testament context; and the fact that Dan. 7.13 is interpreted of the Messiah in Mark 14.62 indicates that 'Mark 14.62 does not repeat the original meaning of Daniel'. (ii) the Jewish interpretation: 'when Dan. 7.13 was applied to the Messiah in the literature of the period it referred to a Parousia rather than an enthronement in heaven.' (iii) 'The enthronement interpretation of Mark 14.62 is converted by the order of the phrases quoted from Psalm 110.1 and Dan. 7.13 respectively. If Glasson's view were correct, the verse should have read, "I am; and you will see the Son of Man coming with the clouds of heaven and sitting at the right hand of power." ' To this Glasson replied, *NTS* 7, 1960–61, pp. 88–93. He argues (i) that the literal Parousia interpretation of Mark 14.62 is difficult because of the 'from now on' and because of the co-ordinate participles 'sitting' and 'coming'; (ii) that the difficulty seen by McArthur in the order of phrases is not a fatal difficulty (but he does not deal with Scott's point and even quotes the Danielic passage in the NT order!): (iii) that the Jewish interpretation of Dan. 7.13 is symbolic rather than literal; he gives modern and medieval Jewish authority for this. These do not seem to be strong arguments: (ii) would be stronger if he could deal with Scott's point, and (iii) if he were not relying on late Jewish authorities.

We would argue, therefore, that Mark 14.62 does have reference to the vindication of the Son of Man at a future 'coming', and that this is one of the ways in which Jesus spoke of the future consummation which he expected. The Parousia interpretation of this saying is to be held, not only because it best fits this saying, but also because the saying is but one of many in which a Parousia reference is to be found.

The second element in the Parousia expectation is that of visitation, and here Robinson argues that Jesus saw his own ministry as God's visitation of the Jewish people. He finds confirmation of this in Jesus' act of prophetic symbolism at the Triumphal Entry and the Cleansing of the Temple, in the parable of the Husbandmen (Mark 12.1–12 par.), and in the following sayings: Matt. 23.34–38 (= Luke 11.49–51 and 13.34–35a), where 'this generation' is the one of which the blood of the prophets will be required, and Jesus' ministry is the climax of all that has gone before; Luke 19.41–44; Luke 12.49; Matt. 10.34 par.; Matt. 10.35 cf. Luke 12.52 f.; Matt. 5.17; Mark 2.17 par.; Matt. 11.19 par.; Mark 10.45 par.; Luke 19.10. These sayings, which are widespread and well attested throughout the Gospel tradition, occurring in all four sources, indicate that Jesus comprehended his own work as the 'coming' of the Son of Man to 'this generation', 'the generation upon which the long-awaited blessing and judgment of God at last has fallen'.[1]

Having found that the parable of the Husbandmen refers to the visitation in the ministry of Jesus, Robinson finds a similar reference in the 'crisis parables',[2] following C. H. Dodd and arguing that the early Church is responsible for the change in emphasis that now relates these parables to the Parousia. He refers to the work of both C. H. Dodd and J. Jeremias in this connection,[3] but as we pointed out earlier[4] he misunderstands Jeremias here in so far as he argues from Jeremias's conclusions in support of a view that there was no further visitation to be expected beyond that of the ministry of Jesus. What Robinson is in effect doing at this point is to point to

---

[1] Robinson, *Coming*, p. 64.

[2] The Nocturnal Burglar, Matt. 24.43 f.; Luke 12.39 f.; the Ten Virgins, Matt. 25.1–13; the Door-keeper, Mark 13.33–37; Luke 12.35–38, cf. Matt. 24.42; the Servant entrusted with Supervision, Matt. 24.45–51; Luke 12.41–46; the Talents, Matt. 25.14–30; Luke 19.12–27.

[3] Robinson, *Coming*, p. 67, quoting Dodd, *Parables*, pp. 146–53 and Jeremias, *Parables*, pp. 47–51.

[4] See above, p. 81 n. 5.

those elements in the teaching of Jesus from which it may properly be argued that Jesus regarded the Kingdom as present in his ministry and then to go on from there to argue that there is in the teaching of Jesus no reference to a crisis, or to a visitation, or to a coming of the Son of Man, which is not a reference to 'those climactic events in which he himself stood'.[1] Now if this is meant to deny the fact Jesus taught a Parousia in the sense of a future consummation of that which has begun in his own ministry, as it seems to be, then it is going too far. The crisis parables, upon which both Glasson and Robinson build at this point, should not be interpreted to exclude a future consummation, and the whole future element in the teaching of Jesus is far too strong to be discounted as Glasson and Robinson discount it.

GRÄSSER: *Parusieverzögerung*

Finally in this chapter we turn to the work of Erich Grässer which is important as the one full-scale work to come from Germany on a theme about which one hears a good deal in these days, especially among the Bultmann *Schüler*: the delay of the Parousia. Setting his face against all the work of Dodd, Jeremias and Kümmel, Grässer holds fast to the position that Jesus taught only a futuristic eschatology: the Kingdom is at hand, is already breaking in, but has not yet come.[2] There is no tension between present and future in the teaching of Jesus, but only the imminent future dominating all else as it dominates the ethical teaching.[3] Such was the eschatological teaching of Jesus, but then the early Church was faced with the problem that the end did not come and sought to come to terms with it. This was done in a variety of ways, a study of which shows the development of the early Church's understanding of the Parousia. First, sayings were produced and put into the mouth of Jesus which showed uncertainty about the time of the coming of the Kingdom, e.g. Mark 13.32 par. This uncertainty with regard to the time of the coming of the Kingdom led to an emphasis upon watchfulness which in turn produced the sayings demanding watchfulness (Mark 13.33-37; Luke 12.35) and the parables having the same emphasis (Doorkeeper, Mark 13.34-36; Waiting Servants, Luke 12.36-38, etc.). The

---

[1] Robinson, *Coming*, p. 82.
[2] Grässer, *Problem*, pp. 3-8.
[3] *Problem*, p. 76: 'The Kingdom is the event in the future (eschatology) which reveals its claim in the present (ethic).'

next stage is to be found in the Lord's Prayer, where the early Church prays for the coming of the Kingdom, something that would have been quite unnecessary for Jesus. Finally the Church comes to the idea that the Lord is delaying the promise, and in this spirit produces the parables of the Faithful and Wise Servant (Matt. 24.45–51 par.), the Talents (Matt. 25.14–30 par.) and the Ten Virgins (Matt. 25.1–13).[1] Having reached the stage of believing that the Lord was delaying his promise the Church was faced with the problem of convincing her members that the promise was none the less to be believed. This situation produced the *Trostwort*, a saying put on the lips of Jesus which promised that although the End was delayed it would none the less come, and that in this present generation. So we are to understand Mark 13.30 par.; Mark 9.1 par.; Matt. 10.23 and Luke 18.7, 8a. Similarly, and to meet the same need, the Church produced the contrast parables.[2] But finally even this did not serve, for the End was ever more delayed, and so the Church turned to Jewish apocalyptic and produced the synoptic apocalypses to show all that must happen before the End could come.[3]

If we are to follow Grässer, then we may not accept the idea that Jesus taught a Parousia that would bring to fulfilment that which had begun in his own ministry, for nothing began in his ministry; there is in his teaching no tension between present and future, all is future. But Grässer's work can scarcely be said to be convincing; indeed, Cullmann has subjected it to a searching criticism which exposes its weaknesses.[4] Grässer sets up the hypothesis that there is no tension between present and future in the teaching of Jesus, but to do this he has again and again to ascribe to the early Church sayings which he himself admits *could* have come from Jesus,[5] and he makes no attempt to deal explicitly with the arguments of Dodd, Jeremias, and Kümmel at this point. It really is too late in the day to claim that there is nothing in the teaching of Jesus to indicate that the present of his ministry is different from, for example, that of John the Baptist,[6] and Grässer's attempt to do this must be rejected, not only in view of the arguments of Dodd, Jeremias, Kümmel and

---

[1] *Problem*, pp. 77–127.

[2] *Ibid.*, pp. 128–49.

[3] *Ibid.*, pp. 151–78.

[4] O. Cullmann, 'Parusieverzögerung und Urchristentum', *TLZ* 83, 1958, cols. 1–12.

[5] Grässer, *Problem*, pp. 57, 81 f., 91 f., 94, 112, 130; Cullmann, *op. cit.*, col. 7.

[6] Cullmann, *op. cit.*, cols. 10 f.

Cullmann, but also in view of the more recent developments among the Bultmann *Schüler*. We may no longer deny the tension between present and future in the teaching of Jesus; our problem is to understand it. As for Grässer's hypothetical reconstruction of the various stages in the Church's attempts to deal with the situation created by the delay of the Parousia, and the corresponding stages of activity in creating sayings, parables and discourses, a bare statement of his theory is sufficient to ensure its general rejection. Not only does he have to ascribe to the early Church sayings which he himself admits could have come from the historical Jesus, as Cullmann points out, but he also has to ascribe to the early Church such varied material as Mark 9.1, the Lord's Prayer, the synoptic apocalypses and the contrast parables. With regard to the synoptic apocalypses his point is well taken, but by no means new;[1] with regard to Mark 9.1 he has the Bultmann school on his side, but does not meet the point of the difficulty of this saying;[2] with regard to the Lord's Prayer he is likely to find little support, especially in view of Jeremias's work on it;[3] and with regard to the contrast parables he is a voice crying in the wilderness and likely to remain so.

RESULT OF THIS DISCUSSION

The result of this discussion of Jesus and the Parousia has been, we believe, to establish the fact that Jesus did look forward to a consummation in the future of that which had begun in his own ministry, a consummation that is variously described in his teaching. The discussion must now turn to the interpretation of this teaching; attempts on the one hand to insist that it is to be interpreted strictly in terms of the Second Coming, and on the other hand to deny that it exists at all, have proven equally unsuccessful.

[1] See above, pp. 130–34, for Beasley-Murray's unsuccessful attempt to rehabilitate Mark 13 as authentic.

[2] See above, pp. 68 ff.

[3] Jeremias, 'The Lord's Prayer in Modern Research', *ExpT* 71, 1959–60, pp. 141–6.

IX

THE AMERICAN VIEW OF JESUS
AS A PROPHET

WE HAVE ALREADY NOTED at several points in our work that a constant tendency in the American discussion has been to see Jesus as a prophet, to emphasize that in his work he was concerned with a redemption that would show itself in this world, and to interpret his eschatology in terms of a continuing world order. We now turn to a discussion of this approach to the teaching of Jesus as it is to be found in the following works:

C. C. McCown,   *The Genesis of the Social Gospel*, 1928.
                'The Eschatology of Jesus Reconsidered', *JR* 16, 1936, pp. 30–45.
                The Search for the Real Jesus, 1940.
                'Jesus, Son of Man. A Survey of recent discussion', *JR* 28, 1948, pp. 1–12.
F. C. Grant,   *The Gospel of the Kingdom*, 1940 (= *Gospel*).
John Knox,   *The Man Christ Jesus*, 1941 (= *Jesus*).
                Christ the Lord, 1945 (= *Lord*).
                The Death of Christ, 1958 (= *Death*).
Amos N. Wilder, *Eschatology and Ethics in the Teaching of Jesus*, [1]1939, [2]1950 (= *Eschatology*).

MCCOWN

McCown paid tribute to Schweitzer as the one who made the eschatology of Jesus a subject of general discussion;[1] but in his own approach to the eschatology of Jesus, argues McCown, Schweitzer was 'wrong on two counts. . . . Both his logic and his history were consistently and thoroughly mistaken.'[2] His logic was wrong because

[1] *JR* 16, 1936, p. 30.
[2] *Ibid.*, p. 31.

his argument takes the form of a series of disjunctive syllogisms. His major premise is that Jesus was either eschatological or non-eschatological. The Gospels show that he was not non-eschatological. 'Therefore Jesus was a thorough-going eschatologist—note the illogical addition to the conclusion.'[1] His history was wrong in that he understood Jewish eschatology as being thoroughly transcendental at the time of Christ. In fact, there were many at the time of Christ, including Rabbi Akiba, who were political messianists, that is, they expected God to interfere in the affairs of this world. Jesus also expected 'some kind of divine intervention in the affairs of the world in a short time'.[2] He expected the reign of God, but this does not mean that he expected that God would reign only in an other-worldly, transcendental realm. 'Jesus expected the divine power to work on earth.'[3] We cannot know exactly what the eschatology of Jesus was, because the views of his followers have unconsciously modified their reports of his sayings. But in the last resort this does not matter, because it is not the programme of Jesus that is available and important to men, but his religious dynamic. Not being bound by any programme of Jesus we are free to interpret this eschatological dynamic in terms of cultural evolution in a continuing world.

McCown's basic assumption is that the eschatology of Jesus is such that he conceives of the power of God working within the context of a continuing world-order. This was also the view, according to McCown, of Rabbi Akiba and the political messianists. But the point about all messianic pretenders was that they believed that God would intervene in the affairs of the world on their behalf in order to establish the perfect Kingdom of God. After this intervention things would be radically different from what they had been before. The expectation, as we can see from the Assumption of Moses, II (4) Ezra, the Apocalypse of Baruch, and the other apocalyptic literature, is full of things like the appearance of supernatural beings, the total destruction of the Gentiles except for the few who will be spared to act as servants of Israel, a general resurrection, an everlasting Kingdom of perfect bliss with a supernatural abundance of every good thing, and so on. That there is a great deal in this expectation that is purely symbolic is certainly true, but it is not symbolic of political and cultural changes; it is symbolic of a new and perfect

[1] *Ibid.*, p. 32.
[2] *Ibid.*, p. 39.
[3] *Ibid.*, p. 46.

state of things radically different from anything that ever was, or from anything that ever could be; a new and perfect state of things that could only come into being through the supernatural activity of God. Similarly with the expectation of the historical Jesus. We gathered together above[1] the evidence concerning his expectation for the future. Here again we have symbolism: the coming of the Kingdom 'in power', the 'Day of the Son of Man' and his judgment, the eschatological table-fellowship with God, the New Temple, the End that could come like a thief in the night, and so on. But can this symbolism be reduced to terms of political development or cultural evolution, however much these may be inspired by the spirit of Christ? Can it be reduced to terms of the mission and life of the Church? The symbolism seems to imply something more than, and something different from, anything possible in a world of space and time. Not that the symbolism is to be referred to an eternal order beyond space and time, as it is by C. H. Dodd and other British scholars;[2] it is rather that Jesus expected God to intervene in the affairs of the world to establish something new and something radically different, something that could only be expressed in pictures. To this point we shall return in our last chapter.

F. C. GRANT

Frederick C. Grant is a most uncompromising opponent of the eschatological approach to the ministry of Jesus. He thinks that recent New Testament studies have been 'milling around in a cul-de-sac', having been led into it by 'the fundamental insincerity of "thorough-going eschatology" '.[3] For Grant the 'Gospel of the Kingdom . . . was originally a this-worldly expectation . . . it was not other-worldly, nor was it apocalyptic. The Gospel was a message of social redemption from the start . . . closer to normal or normative Judaism—even in criticizing it—than to the wild, feverish, bizarre dreams of deluded fanatics.' Grant comes back to this point again and again; apocalypticism was a deluded fanaticism, so Jesus, himself supremely sane, could not have been in any sense an apocalyptist.[4]

That Grant is here making a modern value-judgment the basis for

---

[1] See above, pp. 83 f.
[2] See above, pp. 61, 67, 85.
[3] *Gospel*, p. viii.
[4] *Gospel*, pp. 63, 67 f., 153, 156.

an historical judgment is obvious, and he moves with a similar readiness from a modern, liberal-Christian approach to world problems to the message of Jesus. 'What is really needed in our distracted world is a complete submission of human motives to the will of God, a complete and radical renovation of human society, refashioning it upon the principle of faith in the righteousness of God and a determination to live in accordance with his revealed purposes. That was Jesus' program. . . .'[1] The only question here is: Was this Jesus' programme according to the New Testament texts, or was it Jesus' programme according to a modern view of what that programme ought to have been?

The Gospel narratives as a whole do not support this view of the intention of Jesus; this Grant freely admits, and to get over the difficulty he suggests that there were two centres in which the Gospel tradition took form. One was in Jerusalem, and the other in Galilee. In Jerusalem there was a great interest in Jewish Messianic ideas, and in Galilee a similar interest in apocalypticism. So in Jerusalem the original tradition of a prophetic social reformer was transformed in terms of 'Messiah' and 'Son of God', and in Galilee it was transformed in terms of the apocalyptic 'Son of Man'. The idea that the earliest Gospel tradition took form in two separate centres, Galilee and Jerusalem, originates with Lohmeyer,[2] but it has not found general acceptance,[3] and Grant's version of it is too obviously concerned to maintain an original picture of Jesus as a prophetic social reformer to be acceptable.

---

[1] *Gospel*, p. 134.

[2] Lohmeyer, *Galiläa und Jerusalem*, 1936. He begins from the fact that the New Testament reports resurrection appearances of Jesus from both Galilee and Jerusalem; Luke appears to know only of appearances in Jerusalem (Acts 1.4) while Matthew reports an appearance in Galilee (Matt. 28.16–20) and Mark presupposes such an appearance (Mark 16.7; cf. 14.28). Lohmeyer found that these differences in the place of the appearances are accompanied by theological differences in the narratives (p. 23) and from this he argued for two different centres in the earliest Christianity; one in Galilee with a particular emphasis upon eschatology and upon Jesus as Son of Man and Lord, and one in Jerusalem where the emphasis was upon the Cross and upon Jesus as Messiah (p. 100).

[3] A recent discussion of it is that by H. Grass, *Ostergeschehen und Osterberichte*, 1956, pp. 123 ff. He shows that there is not sufficient support for it in our sources, and that Lohmeyer must read more into the New Testament evidence than the texts themselves justify. To take one example from his discussion, Lohmeyer argued from Acts 1.8 ('You shall be my witnesses both in Jerusalem, and in all Judaea and Samaria, and unto the uttermost part of the earth') that Galilee was not an area of missionary work during the period of the Acts of the Apostles, because it was already *terra christiana* (*op. cit.*, pp. 51 f.). Grass retorted, surely rightly, that the

The inherent weakness of all views of the Kingdom of God in the teaching of Jesus which see it as a theocratic, reformed social order is that they cannot be supported by a detailed exegesis of the New Testament texts. An exegesis of the parables of the Kingdom, or of the eucharistic words, or of such a logion as Matt. 11.12 par, or a consideration of Jesus' actual expression of his expectation of the future, simply rules out views such as Grant here presents.

KNOX

John Knox reviewed Grant's book and expressed himself in general agreement with the belief that 'Jesus stands much nearer to the prophets than to the apocalyptists and that for him the Kingdom was a this-worldly order', but he added: 'It seems to me, however, that apocalypticism had a larger influence upon Jesus' thinking than Dr Grant appears to allow. Elements of both propheticism and apocalypticism—perhaps quite incompatible elements—were almost certainly present. We must avoid the error of attributing absolute consistency to Jesus, whether in his acceptance of apocalypticism or in his independence or repudiation of it.'[1]

In his own books Knox expands these themes. He writes: 'There is every reason to believe that Jesus looked forward to a time when, as a result of a new and mighty creative act of God within history, God's purpose for mankind should be fulfilled; when all men should know him, and his law should be written in their hearts.'[2] This is, in fact, significantly different from Grant's position; a 'mighty creative act of God within history' can be defended as a modern statement of the apocalyptic hope of the coming of the Kingdom of God, and, where Grant poured scorn upon the idea that Jesus could have had anything to do with the deluded fanaticism of apocalyptic, Knox quietly writes: 'That Jesus was influenced by such ideas is not to be denied; but that they do not represent his most

---

listing of places in Acts 1.8 is intended to exhibit the spread of Christianity from the Jewish centre through the *Halbheiden* Samaria to the *Vollheiden* wider world, and that this is the plan followed by the story of Acts as a whole. We may not therefore draw from this text conclusions about the relative dates of the founding of Christianity in Judaea and Galilee respectively.

[1] *JBL* 60, 1941, pp. 74 f.
[2] *Jesus*, p. 38.

characteristic way of thinking about the Kingdom is, I believe, almost equally certain.'[1]

In *Christ the Lord*, Knox presents his views of Jesus' most characteristic way of thinking about the Kingdom. He suggests that the Aramaic phrase rendered in Greek by *basileia tou theou* has a full or varied significance which in English has to be rendered by three separate expressions; (i) the eternal, ultimate sovereignty of God; (ii) the rule of God in and among men in so far as God's sovereignty is acknowledged and his will is done; (iii) the complete and perfect establishment of God's will in the 'age to come'. There is no reason to choose among these views, no reason to assume that Jesus' use of the term was either simple or consistent. 'He doubtless employed the phrase in all three of the senses we have been discussing.'[2] This is, of course, nonsense. Jesus' use of the phrase is consistent, and wholly in accord with its use in apocalyptic, as we hope to show in our next chapter.

A major problem for those who would think of the work of Jesus in terms of a prophetic activity aimed at the reformation of a continuing world-order is the problem of the death of Jesus. If the sacrificial interpretation of the Cross goes back to Jesus himself, if he saw the climax of his work in terms of the Suffering Servant of Isaiah 53, then obviously there is much more to his work, as he saw it, than the 'Jesus as a Prophet' school would generally allow. John Knox addresses himself to this problem in his recent book, *The Death of Christ*. Here he devotes a whole chapter to arguing the *possibility* that the sacrificial interpretation of Jesus' death arose in the Christian community in the decade or so between the death of Christ and the establishment of the Eucharist in the Church.[3] He then devotes a further chapter[4] to the psychological implausibility of the conception of Servant-Messiah as a mode of Jesus' own self-consciousness. His point is: 'Such an understanding of his destiny is compatible with the theology—and the psychology—of the Church. But is it compatible with the mental health of the man Jesus?'[5] One feels that both of these chapters are totally irrelevant except in so far as they serve to establish a prejudice in advance of the discussion of the New Testament evidence. The question is not, 'Could these ideas have arisen

---

[1] *Jesus*, p. 39.
[2] *Lord*, p. 27.
[3] *Death*, pp. 35–51.
[4] *Death*, pp. 52–76.
[5] *Death*, p. 76.

in the early community?'; but, 'Did they?' It is not a question of whether Jesus should have thought of himself as Servant Messiah according to a modern view of what makes for a healthy psychological attitude; but, Did he?

After forty pages of preliminary discussion, Knox finally comes to a discussion of the evidence in the Gospels.[1] He argues that Jesus did not think of himself as 'Messiah'. At Caesarea Philippi, according to the Marcan account, he rejects the term and the view of his mission that it would imply; Mark 14.62 is a lone example of acceptance of the title and therefore outweighed by the ambiguity of his reply at every other place where the Messiahship is an issue. In the accounts of the Triumphal Entry and the Cleansing of the Temple one can see an increasing emphasis on Jesus' Messiahship in the later accounts, and one is therefore bound to recognize the probability that even the earliest form of the story is not free from the same effects.[2]

The weakness of this argument is that far too little of the New Testament evidence is discussed. If we are to make any decision about the claims that Jesus was making concerning his person then we have to consider what is implicit in all of the things that he said of his mission and its significance. The total evidence for the fact that Jesus believed that in his work the eschatological time of salvation had begun[3] is sufficient to show that he did think of himself as something much more than a prophet. This indirect evidence is not discussed by Knox at all.

Similarly, in a discussion of the Gospel evidence in the question as to whether or not Jesus thought of his mission in terms of that of the Suffering Servant, only one New Testament text is specifically mentioned.[4] It is felt sufficient to say that the early Church used Isaiah 53 extensively and that this 'places a large burden of proof on any claim that Jesus himself made this same use of the passage; and this burden the meagre Gospel evidence is simply not able to bear'.[5]

Most conspicuously absent from this book is any detailed discussion of the eucharistic words of Jesus, something that one would have thought to be essential in any discussion of Jesus' approach to his own death. Knox refers to them only in the context of his discussion

---

[1] *Death*, pp. 77–107.
[2] *Death*, p. 83.
[3] Summarized above, pp. 74–78. See also pp. 117–27 for the 'indirect Christology' of Bultmann and his school.
[4] Mark 9.12b, Knox, *Death*, p. 105.
[5] *Death*, p. 105.

of the possibility that the sacrificial interpretation could have arisen in the period between the death of Jesus and the establishment of the Eucharist in the Church. But fleeting though this reference to the Last Supper is, in it Knox gives away the whole argument of his book on this point. He concedes[1] 'the possibility that something happened in Jesus' last supper with his disciples—something involving words and actions of Jesus—which provided the basis for the later Eucharist'. If this is so, then the flood-gates are opened for the argument that Jesus interpreted his death in terms of sacrifice, and Knox's position is no longer tenable, since the concept of a prophetic activity culminating in a sacrificial death brings us inevitably to Isaiah 53.

WILDER

Amos N. Wilder argues that the main concern in the teaching of Jesus is with a redemption that would be worked out in the social-historical future of man, and as evidence for the fact that Jesus did think of the future in such non-transcendental terms he offers the following considerations. (i) In his ethical teaching Jesus did not teach an *Interimsethik*, but often spoke as though the world were to continue. (ii) He promised the disciples that they would rule over the twelve tribes of Israel. (iii) In the saying about the Temple, that he would rebuild it after three days, the reference is to the Temple as a figure for Israel itself or the Congregation.[2] But although he sees this as the main element in the teaching of Jesus, Wilder is careful not to eliminate the transcendental eschatological element altogether. He argues that in his eschatological teaching Jesus casts into the form of myth 'the epoch-making, world-transforming significance of his own life, in Jewish terms', and that the purpose of this element in his teaching is to express 'the appeal of the ethical consciousness against things as they are, and the incontrovertible assurance of faith that God will act'.[3] In other words the eschatological teaching of Jesus is the expression in mythological terms of an

[1] In a footnote on p. 48.

[2] *Eschatology*, pp. 50 f. Cf. the three points made by Glasson, and our comments, above, pp. 37 f. Like the similar points made by Glasson, these three actually demonstrate how thoroughly eschatological the teaching of Jesus was. The ethical teaching of Jesus is the eschatological Torah; the promise to the disciples is that they would share the function of the eschatological Son of Man; the figure of the New Temple refers to the eschatological community in its perfect sacral relationship with God (see above, p. 85).

[3] *Eschatology*, pp. 35, 86.

ultimate faith in God, and its purpose is to add point and dynamic to a message that is itself essentially ethical.

In accordance with this central conviction Wilder offers a detailed analysis of the function of the eschatological teaching in relation to the ethical. It is, firstly, a 'sanction of Ethic'. 'The coming event is . . . motive for repentance and for urgency in doing righteousness, and the particular demands are looked on as conditions of entrance to the future Kingdom.'[1] This is the function of the futuristic eschatology of Jesus. But there is also a sense in which the Kingdom is present in the teaching of Jesus, and this gives us the second aspect of the relationship between the eschatology and the ethics. Here the ethical teaching expresses that way of life which is relevant to, and which is made possible by, the Kingdom as a present experience. This is the 'ethic of the time of salvation or new-covenant ethics'.[2] But the coming of the Kingdom in the ministry of Jesus represents a crisis, a period of conflict which calls for devotion, witness and sacrifice, and which lays heavy demands upon the sons and heirs of the Kingdom. 'In particular the most exigent requirements of Jesus have to do with following him in the crisis of the Kingdom. . . .'[3] This is the third aspect of the relationship between the eschatology and the ethics; we may call it 'discipleship ethics'.

The work of Wilder is the most thorough recent discussion in English of the relationship between eschatology and ethics in the teaching of Jesus, and his discussion of the ethics of the time of salvation, and of what we have called 'discipleship ethics', is convincing. The crisis of which Wilder writes is a major element in the teaching of Jesus, and it is 'not one created by the imminence of Judgement but by the conflict of the two eras, the death throes of the one and the birth pangs of the other, a crisis inseparable from the time of salvation'.[4] The fact of this crisis brings with it the demands of the discipleship ethics and the expression of the ethics of the time of salvation.

About the eschatological sanction for ethics we have some reservations, mainly because, as we have made clear above, we do not accept the basic premise that the teaching of Jesus assumes a continuing world order. In so far as the eschatological teaching is a

---

[1] *Eschatology*, p. 145.
[2] *Ibid.*, p. 160.
[3] *Ibid.*, p. 163.
[4] Wilder, *Eschatology*, p. 176.

sanction for ethics we would prefer to speak of the imminent Kingdom as a sanction for the call of repentance to the multitudes, or, better, as the grounds for that call for repentance; and of the in-breaking Kingdom bringing with it the salvation-ethics and the discipleship-ethics for those who have heard and responded to the call for repentance, and who have eyes to see the coming of the Kingdom in the work of Jesus. The coming of the Kingdom brings with it the Law of the Kingdom,[1] and in that Law men find the final expression of the will of God for them in their new situation. They can now experience the eschatological forgiveness of God and the manifestation of his eschatological powers, and in the light of this they are called upon to accept the responsibilities and privileges revealed in the eschatological Law.

In this chapter we have reviewed the work of a group of scholars who accept the basic premise that the eschatology of Jesus may be interpreted in terms of a continuing world order. In many ways this work represents the last stand in the Anglo-American theological world against the movement towards the recognition of the essentially eschatological nature of the Kingdom in the teaching of Jesus which began with the impact of *konsequente Eschatologie*. It represents the last of a number of attempts that have been made to show that Jesus 'transformed' the eschatological concepts that he used. But like the remainder of these attempts it breaks down on the hard fact that it cannot be reconciled with the evidence in the New Testament. According to this evidence Jesus did express his future expectation in terms which involve something more than, and something quite different from, the reformation of a continuing world order, as he also expressed the significance of his own work in terms that imply that he was more than a prophet.

[1] See pp. 76–78 above on the eschatological Torah in the teaching of Jesus.

X

THE KINGDOM OF GOD IN THE TEACHING OF JESUS

THE PRESENT STATE OF THE DISCUSSION

WE HAVE NOW COMPLETED our review of the modern discussion of Kingdom of God in the teaching of Jesus. This review has been by no means complete—no one could pretend to cover completely a discussion as manifold, complex and extensive as this one has been—but it is hoped that it has been sufficient to show what questions have arisen in this context since Schleiermacher gave the concept of the Kingdom of God a central place in his theology and Johannes Weiss offered his historical interpretation of the teaching of Jesus concerning it, and what kinds of answers have been proposed to these questions. The difficulty has been, and is yet, that an answer to one question always tends to raise further questions, so that although certain conclusions may now be said to be established there are still further questions to be answered. It is the purpose of this final chapter to call attention to the conclusions which the discussion has established, and to offer tentative answers to some of the questions that remain; not that these answers may be accepted as final, but that they may serve as focal points for further discussion.

The three major questions that have arisen in the course of the discussion are: (i) is Kingdom of God an apocalyptic concept in the teaching of Jesus? (ii) is the Kingdom present or future, or both, in that teaching? and (iii) what is the relationship between eschatology and ethics in Jesus' teaching? With regard to (i) it may be said to be established that the answer is: Yes. 'Kingdom of God' is an apocalyptic concept in the teaching of Jesus;[1] the many attempts to

---

[1] See above pp. 16–20 (Johannes Weiss), 29 f. (Schweitzer), 53 f. (Burkitt), 113 f. (Bultmann).

deny this have failed,[1] as have the various attempts to interpret the apocalyptic concept in a non-apocalyptic manner.[2] But this raises the further question of the meaning and use of 'Kingdom of God' in apocalyptic, since at this point there is wide disagreement. On the one hand Bultmann can argue that the apocalyptic concept cannot be understood in the context of the world, history or time and must therefore be interpreted existentially,[3] and on the other hand Cullmann can argue that the expectation is concerned with a new era which is the final stage of a continuous time process. Where there is such disagreement we must obviously look once more at our sources. With regard to (ii) it may be said to be established that the Kingdom is both present and future in the teaching of Jesus. The discussion has reached this point;[4] Weiss[5] and Schweitzer[6] were not able to convince the world of scholarship that it was wholly future. Dodd was not able to maintain his original view that it was wholly present and subsequently modified it,[7] and Bultmann's wholly futuristic interpretation was modified at this essential point by his *Schüler*.[8] But to decide that the Kingdom is both present and future raises immediately the question of how we are to understand this tension in the teaching of Jesus. Are we to interpret in terms of the present of Jesus' ministry and of the future of the era of Pentecost and the Christian Church,[9] with or without a reference to a further transcendent realm?[10] Are we to hold to a tension between the present ministry and a future Parousia to be expected in time[11] or should we interpret the tension existentially?[12] With regard to (iii) the relationship between eschatology and ethics, we have seen Weiss' *Interimsethik* accepted,[13] rejected[14] and modified,[15] and we have seen a relationship between

[1] See above, pp. 56 f.
[2] See above, pp. 41–45, 49–52.
[3] See above, pp. 113–17.
[4] See especially chapter V above.
[5] See above, pp. 20–22.
[6] See above, p. 30.
[7] See above, pp. 58–63, 67 f.
[8] Chapter VII above, especially pp. 121–24.
[9] An interpretation very popular in British scholarship. See above, pp. 67 f.
[10] For Dodd's final position on this see above, pp. 61 and 67. For Hunter's similar view, see above, p. 85.
[11] Jeremias, Kümmel, Cullmann, above, pp. 88 f.
[12] Bultmann and his school, chapter VI above.
[13] See above, pp. 30 (Schweitzer), 54 (Burkitt).
[14] See above, pp. 43 f., 55, 94.
[15] Especially by Bultmann, above, p. 117.

the Kingdom as present and the ethical teaching expressed in various ways.[1] This last point is also one that we must discuss further.

QUESTIONS FOR FURTHER DISCUSSION

These then are the questions which we shall attempt to discuss in this chapter: the meaning and usage of 'Kingdom of God' in apocalyptic and the teaching of Jesus; the tension between present and future in the eschatology of Jesus and its interpretation; and the relationship between eschatology and ethics in the teaching of Jesus.

1. *'Kingdom of God' in Apocalyptic and the Teaching of Jesus*

If we recognize 'Kingdom of God' as an apocalyptic concept, then we must go on to ask several further questions about the meaning and usage of that concept in apocalyptic, if we are to attempt to meet the problems posed by the modern discussion. In particular we must ask questions about the concept of time and the nature of the End, and about the particular meaning and usage of 'Kingdom of God' against the general background of the concepts of time and the End. But, of course, we cannot begin with apocalyptic itself; we must begin with the question of time and the End in the Old Testament, and particularly with that aspect of the Old Testament out of which apocalyptic has developed: the prophetic movement.

The question of time and the End in the Old Testament has recently been fully and brilliantly discussed by Gerhard von Rad,[2] who demonstrates that the concept of absolute linear time is foreign to the Old Testament. The modern Western world thinks of linear time and of eschatological linear time, that is, of time moving towards a climax, a fulfilment, an end. Not so the Old Testament. In the Old Testament time is punctiliar; it is conceived of as a series of moments or seasons each one of which is connected with a particular event. There can be no time without an event, and no event without a time, and there is no thought of a climactic future

---

[1] See above, pp. 44 (Wm. Manson), 63 f. (Dodd), 94 f. (T. W. Manson), 127–29 (Bornkamm, Conzelmann, Fuchs).

[2] Gerhard von Rad, *Theologie des Alten Testaments*: I, *Die Theologie der geschicht-lichen Überlieferungen Israels*, [1]1957, [2]1958 (ET, 1962); II, *Die Theologie der prophetischen Überlieferungen Israels*, 1960 (ET in preparation). This work is almost certain to prove itself the authoritative and indeed definitive work on Old Testament theology in our generation and we are heavily indebted to it all through this chapter, as will be evident from the footnotes. We shall quote this work as *Theologie* I and II.

towards which time moves but only of a continuing rhythm of events and their times, of times and their events.[1] Within this context the religious festivals came to be of supreme importance. Originally agricultural festivals, the Israelites 'historicized' them by connecting them with God's salvation activity on their behalf, and in the festivals the salvation activity of God which the festival celebrated, e.g. the Exodus events at Passover, was once more experienced in the present.

So the Israelites continually 'remembered' the saving activity of God on their behalf and in this way began to think 'historically'. But their historical thinking was not concerned with a stretch of linear time, but with a series of time-events in which God had acted to save his people. They thought in a linear manner only in the sense that they put together the sequence of events in which God had acted;[2] history for them was essentially a series of events in which the salvation activity of God had been manifested, a series of events conceived of as a continuity.[3]

With the coming of the prophets something new is added to this conception. The prophets not only see God as active in past salvation events which are remembered and recorded, they claim that his hand is also *and equally* at work in the events of their own day, and they proclaim a future and even climactic salvation activity of God on behalf of his people.[4] It is at this point that we must begin to speak of eschatology, for from Amos and Hosea onwards the message of the prophets is eschatological. Not that they are concerned with the end of time or the end of history, to speak of them in such terms is to ascribe to them a conception of time or history wholly foreign to them; they are concerned with a salvation activity of God in the future which will be analogous to that of the past: Hosea with a new Entry into the Promised Land, Isaiah with a new David and a new Zion, Jeremiah with a new Covenant, and Deutero-Isaiah with a new Exodus. Their hope is eschatological because this future divine activity is the decisive salvation event; the existence of Israel will be determined by that which the prophets foretell rather than by that

---

[1] Gen. 8.22; von Rad, *Theologie* II, p. 115.

[2] Deut. 26.5 ff.; Josh. 24.2 ff.; von Rad, *Theologie* II, p. 119.

[3] According to von Rad the major Old Testament 'historical' traditions conceive of this continuity as reaching backward and forward to different points: the Yahwistic and Priestly works from Creation to the Conquest, the Deuteronomic from Moses to the catastrophe of 587, and that of the Chronicler from the first man to post-exilic times. *Theologie* II, p. 120.

[4] von Rad, *Theologie* II, p. 126. Cf. John Marsh, *The Fullness of Time*, 1952, pp. 53–74.

which is remembered at the Festivals or recorded in the salvation history.[1]

Here then we have an understanding of the essential element in prophetic eschatology; prophetic eschatology is concerned with an event in the future wherein God will manifest his salvation activity in a manner analogous to the salvation events of the past, but different from them in that the eschatological event will be the truly and finally decisive event. It will be a matter of life and death for Israel in that her existence possibilities will be wholly determined by it; her salvation will depend upon the eschatological event which will supersede in this regard all previous acts of God in her history.

With this understanding of eschatology we have reached the heart of the matter so far as the Kingdom of God concept is concerned, for, as Dalman taught us, *malkuth shamayim* and its equivalents refer to the kingly rule, the kingly activity of God; they are used specifically of that final intervention of God in history and human experience which is determinative for the salvation of men. It is no accident that the first occurrences of this concept are in connection with this prophetic expectation of a future, or perhaps better *further and final* salvation event (Micah 2.12 f.; 4.1–7; Isa. 24.21–23; 33.22; 52.7–10; Zeph. 3.14–20; Obad. 21); nor is it accidental that with development and changes in the Jewish expectation the concept tends to be used less and to be replaced by others, although where it is used it always retains its particular reference, as we shall see.

Now this expectation of a further and final salvation event in which God would manifest himself as King is naturally rooted and grounded in the conviction that God is eternally King: Ex. 15.18; Ps. 145.11 ff. The conviction that God is eternally King makes possible the hope that he will manifest himself as King in the decisive salvation event, and this is expressed in one of the rare occurrences of 'Kingdom of God' in apocalyptic—Ps. Sol. 17.3:

> But we hope in God, our Saviour
> For the might of our God is forever with mercy,
> And the Kingdom of our God is forever
> over the nations in judgment.

The prophetic proclamation of a further and final salvation event is the true background to the usage of 'Kingdom of God' in Jewish apocalyptic and in the teaching of Jesus, for it is in

[1] von Rad, *Theologie* II, p. 131.

this conception that we have the unique element in Jewish eschatology. In recent years we have learned to recognize elements
in Jewish eschatology that are not unique but shared by Israel
with her ancient neighbours, and these elements have been
hailed as the true origin of the Kingdom of God expectation.
S. Mowinckel[1] has argued for the existence in Israel of an annual
New Year Festival like that in Babylon and elsewhere at which
Yahweh was ritually enthroned as King and in connection with
which many of the Psalms were used, especially Pss. 47; 93; 95–100,
the so-called 'Enthronement Psalms'. In this cultic festival was
celebrated Yahweh's cosmic conflict, victory and enthronement, and
out of this developed the concept of the kingly rule of Yahweh, the
Kingdom of God, as the central religious idea in the Jewish future
hope. Mowinckel will not call this hope 'eschatological', for to him
'eschatology' must be restricted in usage to references to a complex of
ideas about the last things which are markedly dualistic and which
necessarily involve the sudden and catastrophic end of the present
order and its being superseded by another order of an essentially
different kind,[2] but it is none the less out of this hope that the true
eschatology of later Judaism developed.[3] H. J. Kraus[4] would trace
the Kingdom of God concept back to a yearly festival in which the
Davidic King was enthroned in Zion (II Sam. 6; II Sam. 7; Pss. 132;
78.65–72; 24.7–10; 2; 72; 89.4–5, 20–38, etc.) rather than to a
festival in which Yahweh was enthroned. J. Gray[5] traces the conception back through the Enthronement Psalms to the Ugaritic
myths of Baal's conflict with Mot found at Ras Shamra. These and
the many similar attempts to illuminate the eschatology of Judaism
by means of comparative studies from Babylon, Ras Shamra and
elsewhere are important as contributing to our general understanding
of this immensely complicated subject, but von Rad is surely right in
calling attention to that which is new and original in the Jewish
concept, the salvation activity of God experienced in a series of
'historical' events, and the prophetic proclamation of a further and

---

[1] S. Mowinckel, *Psalmenstudien* II, *Das Thronbesteigungsfest Jahwähs und der
Ursprung der Eschatologie*, 1922. Cf. also his *He that Cometh*, 1956, pp. 139–54.
[2] *He that Cometh*, pp. 125 f.
[3] *Ibid.*, pp. 261–79. Cf. A. Bentzen, *King and Messiah* (ET by the author of
Messias-Moses redivivus-Menschensohn, 1948), 1955, pp. 37 f.
[4] H. J. Kraus, *Die Konigsherrschaft Gottes*, 1951.
[5] John Gray, 'The Hebrew Conception of the Kingship of God; its Origin and
Development', *VT* 6, 1956, pp. 268–85.

decisive salvation event, and in insisting that here is the *distinctive* element in Jewish eschatology. However much the eschatology may have developed, and in developing have been influenced by ideas originating elsewhere, the key element is always the expectation of this further and decisive event in which God will manifest himself as King to the salvation of his people.

That Jewish eschatology did develop through the centuries that separated the prophets from the coming of Christ is clear, for the eschatology of late Judaism, i.e. the eschatology which we find in the apocalyptic literature, is very different from the prophetic pro-clamation of the coming eschatological event. That eschatological event is still there, indeed all apocalyptic is built around this expected event, but the form in which it is expressed has become immensely complicated through the centuries of experience and speculation, and under the influence of Persian ideas.

Characteristic for apocalyptic is an eschatological dualism, the sharp distinction between the present age and the age to come;[1] the prophetic view of a further and decisive salvation event has become an immensely elaborate conception of the end of this present age and the beginning of a new and wholly different one. The circumstances which accompany this change of the aeons are so manifold and various that it is impossible to reduce them to a systematic picture, indeed any attempt to do this is itself a fundamental misrepresenta-tion of the apocalyptic hope, for manifold variety and plasticity belong to its very nature. We read of the 'Messianic woes',[2] the last bitter time of conflict, oppression and catastrophe immediately before the End; of the 'day' which marks the turning-point from the old to the new and which has a hundred names;[3] of the 'last days', 'last

---

[1] The 'age to come' occurs regularly in the apocalyptic literature as a designa-tion of the end time, e.g. Enoch 71.15; Slav. Enoch 65.8; Syr. Bar. 14.13; 15.8; II (4) Ezra 4.27; 7.13; 7.47; 8.1. The term is characteristic of the later apocalyptic rather than the earlier and has not yet been found in the Qumran texts. In the New Testament it is found at Matt. 12.32, where it has been introduced by Matthew for Mark's *eis ton aiōna* (Mark 3.29), and at Mark 10.30 = Luke 18.30 (Matt. 19.29 omits it). This one occurrence does not warrant the assumption that the expression formed part of the characteristic vocabulary of the historical Jesus.

[2] Although this term is found only in the rabbinical literature the ideas expressed by it are a commonplace of apocalyptic, and of the synoptic apocalypses in the New Testament. In Mark 13.8 = Matt. 24.8 the word 'woes' (*ōdines*) is actually found.

[3] To give one example each of some of those found:' that day', Enoch 45.3 f.; 'that great day', Enoch 54.6; 'the day of judgment', II (4) Ezra 7.38; 'the day of the great judgment', Enoch 19.1; 'the great day of judgment', Enoch 22.11; 'the day of consummation', Enoch 16.1; 'the consummation of the end of days', Ass. Mos.

times', 'end of the days' and the like.[1] With the coming of the End
the 'glory' of God is revealed in judgment and salvation,[2] all that has
life and breath will praise him.[3] God will be honoured as the God of
all the world.[4] We find an almost bewildering variety of figures
appearing in connection with the events of the End-time: the
Messiah,[5] who is a Son of David,[6] holy prince,[7] king,[8] a blessed man
with a sceptre in his hand[9] or a transcendental figure from the sea;[10]
the Son of Man;[11] an eschatological priest;[12] an eschatological priest
and a Messianic king together;[13] a prophet like unto Moses,[14] or
Elijah;[15] Enoch;[16] Enoch and Elijah together;[17] Ezra;[18] Baruch;[19]
an angel[20] or the archangel Michael.[21] Sometimes it is God himself

---

[1] 1.18; 'the consummation of the time', 1QpHab. 7.2; 'the day of God', Syr. Bar.
48.47; 'the day of the Mighty One', Syr. Bar. 55.6; 'the great day of the Lord', Slav.
Enoch 18.6; 'the day of thy wrath', 1QH 15.17; 'the day of wrath and indignation',
Jub. 24.28; 'the day of visitation', 1QS 4.18; 'the day of vengeance', 1QM 15.6.
The list could be extended almost indefinitely (cf. Volz, Eschatologie, pp. 163–65).
The word 'day' is not to be pressed, since it is used to translate a variety of terms
which could be translated 'season', 'predetermined time' and the like, and with
this concept we have come to the end of time; we are dealing with the end of the
world (Volz, op. cit., p. 164).

[1] E.g. Enoch 27.3; Noah Fragment 108.1; Ass. Mos. 1.18; Test. Naph. 8.1;
Syr. Bar. 6.8; 25.1; II (4) Ezra 3.14; 6.34; 1QpHab. 2.5; 7.7; 7.12; 9.6; 1QS
4.16, 17; CD 4.4; 6.11; 1QSa 1.1.
[2] E.g. Enoch 102.3, cf. 104.1; II (4) Ezra 7.42 (the brightness of the Most High);
Syr. Bar. 21.23, 25; 1QSb 3.4.
[3] E.g. Enoch 48.5; 61.9–12.
[4] E.g. Enoch 91.13 f.; 63.1 ff.; 10.21; Sib. Orac. 3.710 ff.
[5] E.g. II (4) Ezra 7.28 ff.; Syr. Bar. 29.3; 39.7; 72.2.
[6] E.g. Ps. Sol. 17.21; II (4) Ezra 12.32.
[7] Sib. Orac. 3.49.
[8] Sib. Orac. 3.652; 5.108.
[9] Sib. Orac. 5.414 f.
[10] II (4) Ezra 13.6.
[11] Similitudes of Enoch.
[12] Test. Levi 18.
[13] In the Qumran texts e.g. 1QS 9.11; CD 12.23 f. On this expectation see
especially K. G. Kuhn, 'The Two Messsiahs of Aaron and Israel', in The Scrolls
and the New Testament, ed. K. Stendahl, 1957, pp. 54–64 and A. S. van der
Woude, Die Messianische Vorstellungen der Gemeinde von Qumran, 1957.
[14] An expectation dervied from Deut. 18.15, 18. See Jeremias in TWNT IV,
pp. 862–7.
[15] An expectation derived from Mal. 3.1. See Jeremias in TWNT II, pp. 930–6.
[16] Jub. 10.17; Slav. Enoch 64.5.
[17] II (4) Ezra 6.26.
[18] II (4) Ezra 14.9, cf. 14.49 and 14.14.
[19] Syr. Bar. 76.2; 13.3; 25.1.
[20] Ass. Mos. 10.2.
[21] Dan. 12.1.

who acts directly with no intermediary figure.[1] Just as complex as the picture of the various figures who play their part in the End-time is the series of events which can be connected with it: Resurrection of the righteous[2] or of all men;[3] Judgment;[4] the destruction of Satan, Beliar/Belial and his minions,[5] of the heathen kingdoms and rulers,[6] of all sinners and godless men;[7] the transformation of heaven and earth;[8] the end of the world[9] and its times and seasons,[10] all to be destroyed[11] by fire[12] or water[13] and re-created by God[14] or the eschatological community of Israel.[15] Equally complex is the apocalyptic picture of the life of the salvation time. In the Qumran texts, for example, we read of eschatological healing,[16] great peace and long life, an abundance of children, everlasting blessing, endless joy, everlasting life and eternal light (1QS 4.6–8). The final state of the blessed is to be for ever with God (IQH 4.21), to have eternal peace and long life (1QH 13.17 f.), to know eternal salvation and everlasting peace (1QH 18.29 f.), to enjoy peace, blessing for ever, joy and long life (1QM 1.9). The End-time is pictured as a return to the Paradise conditions,[17] and at the same time it is viewed in a markedly nationalistic and materialistic manner (1QM 12.11 ff.). It is pictured under the imagery of 'glory',[18] and under that of the Temple,[19] and the men of that time will be like the angels.[20] As in the Beatitudes, an eschato-

---

[1] Sib. Orac. 4.40 ff., 181 f.

[2] Ps. Sol. 3.11 ff.; Enoch 91 f.; Test. Judah 25; Test. Benj. 10 f.

[3] Dan. 12.2; Enoch 22; 51.1; II (4) Ezra 7.32.

[4] For a collection of details concerning this most popular apocalyptic theme see Volz, Eschatologie, pp. 272–309.

[5] Ass. Mos. 10.1; 1QH 3.25–36; 1QM passim.

[6] Dan. 7.11; II (4) Ezra 11 f.; Ps. Sol. 17.22; Syr. Bar. 72.6.

[7] Syr. Bar. 85.15; Enoch 80.2–8; 94 ff.; 1QS 2.15 ff.; 4.12 ff.; 5.13 and frequently throughout the Qumran texts.

[8] Enoch 45.4 f.; Syr. Bar. 49.3; II (4) Ezra 6.16.

[9] Syr. Bar. 44.9; 31.5; 85.14; Jub. 23.18.

[10] Slav. Enoch 33; 65.6 f.

[11] Sib. Orac. 5.477–482; Test. Levi 4.1; Ass. Mos. 10.4 ff.; 1QH 3.12–18.

[12] Sib. Orac. 3.80–90; 4.173 ff.; 5.528 ff.; Enoch 1.6 f.; 1QH 3.29; 17.13.

[13] 1QH 8.16–20.

[14] Sib. Orac. 5.212; Jub. 1.29; Enoch 72.1; 91.16; 1QS 4.25; 1QH 11.13 f.; 1QH 13.11 f.

[15] Jub. 19.25.

[16] Cf. Enoch 10.7; 95.4; 96.3; Jub. 1.29.

[17] 1QS 4.20; CD 3.20; 1QH 17.15. Cf. Syr. Bar. 4.3; 73.7.

[18] 1QS 4.7 f. Cf. Test. Benj. 4.1; Enoch 62.15; Syr. Bar. 15.8; 54.15; 48.49; 54.21; 66.7; II (4) Ezra 8.51; 9.31; 7.95; 7.98.

[19] CD 3.19 f.; 1QSb 4.25–27; 4QFlor. 3–7.

[20] 1QS 11.8. Cf. Syr. Bar. 51.5.

logical interpretation is given to Psalm 37 and in the End-time 'the Poor' will inherit the earth.[1] Elsewhere in apocalyptic the idea of having an inheritance in the End-time occurs frequently[2] and it is obvious that expressions such as 'to inherit the age to come', 'to inherit life', 'to inherit eternal life', 'to inherit everlasting life', 'to inherit endless time', 'to have the lot of eternal life', 'to receive the promised world', 'to be given the world to come', 'to acquire and receive the world that does not die' are synonymous with 'to inherit the earth', and for that matter synonymous with 'to share the lot of the angels' (1QS 11.8).

The important point for our purpose is to note that this bewildering complex of expectation does, in fact, revolve around two central themes: God's decisive intervention in history and human experience, and the final state of the redeemed to which the intervention leads. Everything in it has its function in connection with one or the other of these themes. Working upon the basic concept of God's decisive intervention in history and human experience apocalyptic imagination has run wild in depicting the circumstances that will accompany it and the form that it will take. Concerned to depict the final blessed state of the redeemed, the apocalyptic writers run the whole gamut of conceivable joys, from a life of luxury and ease with their former oppressors as their slaves to an eternal sharing of the glory of God in an angelic state. The very variety of imagery used, and the fact that the most varied imagery can be found in the same document, does not indicate that we many different seers each with his own particular expectation, and the work of different seers woven together in one document, but rather that each and every seer is concerned to express the essentially inexpressible and turns restlessly from image to image in the attempt to do so. The imagery is never consistent; it is doubtful if it ever was in the case of any single seer, and it is certainly not so in the case of any document that we possess. The Qumran texts, for example, may offer us a measure of consistency with regard to the intervention of God through the two Messiahs of

---

[1] 4QpPs 37 1.8 f. The interpretation of the 'humble' of Ps. 37.10 in terms of the 'poor' is exactly parallel to the first Beatitude, and this would seem to imply a relationship between the two. See above, p. 83, and below, pp. 182 f. In Enoch 5.7 it is the 'elect' who inherit the earth.

[2] Syr. Bar. 44.13; II (4) Ezra 7.96 (to inherit the age to come); Ps. Sol. 14.10 (to inherit life); Enoch 40.9 (to inherit eternal life); Slav. Enoch 50.2; 66.6 (to inherit everlasting life); Enoch 37.4 (to have the lot of eternal life); Syr. Bar. 14.13 (to receive the promised world); Syr. Bar. 44.15 (to be given the world to come); Syr. Bar. 51.3 (to acquire and receive the world that does not die).

Aaron and Israel,[1] but they certainly offer us the most infinite variety with regard to the depiction of the final state of the blessed, running the whole gamut from crass materialism (1QM 12.11 ff.) to being at one with the angels (1QS 11.8). No: we may not assume a variety of self-consistent types of apocalyptic expectation; what we must do is recognize the two major themes of the intervention of God and the final state of the redeemed and the infinite variety of imagery used in connection with these themes.

In order to relate this to the teaching of Jesus we must ask the question: What is the place of the Kingdom of God in this expectation? The answer is that the phrase or its equivalent is found both in connection with the intervention of God and in connection with the final state of the redeemed. It occurs only rarely—some 7(?9) times in the whole range of the apocalyptic literature.[2] But it does occur in both connections and in these connections only. This matter is so important to the discussion of the teaching of Jesus that we will review each occurrence of the phrase in the apocalyptic literature.

A. '*Kingdom of God*' *in reference to God's decisive intervention in history and human experience*

(i) Ps. Sol. 17.3

> But we hope in God, our Saviour
> For the might of our God is forever with mercy,
> And the Kingdom of our God is forever
>   over the nations in judgment.

We have already called attention to this passage as illustrating the relationship between the conviction that God is eternally King and the hope that he will manifest himself as King in the decisive salvation event.[3]

The psalmist depicts the parlous state of the people of God who have known conquest and captivity (vv. 13 ff.), and this as a consequence of their own shortcomings: 'The king was a transgressor, and the judge disobedient, and the people sinful' (v. 20). The

---

[1] Although it should be noted that this imagery is not found in 1QH, nor in 1QpHab. On this point, and on the variety of Messianic expectation in apocalyptic in general and its significance, see further Morton Smith, 'What is implied by the variety of Messianic figures?', *JBL* 78, 1959, pp. 66–72.

[2] The references are: Ps. Sol. 5.18; 17.3; Sib. Orac. 3.46 f.; 3.767; Ass. Mos. 10.1; 1QM 6.6; 12.7. Two further possible references are: 1QSb 3.5; 4.26. These will all be discussed below.

[3] See above p. 162.

psalmist's hope is that God may raise up for them a new Messianic King, who will destroy their enemies (vv. 21 ff.) and establish them in a state of blessing in which they and their city will be the glory of the world, and the heathen nations their servants. The ground for this hope is simply that 'the Lord himself is our King forever and ever' (v. 46).

Here in this psalm we have then very clearly expressed the eternal relationship between God as King and the people as his subjects and the expectation that he will exercise his kingly power *in the future* in a decisive intervention in history on their behalf, and in v. 3 this future kingly activity is described as the Kingdom of God and depicted as hanging like a Damoclean sword over the nations of the world.

(ii) Sib. Orac. 3.46 f.

> But when Rome shall rule over Egypt as well, as she still hesitates to do, then the mightiest Kingdom of the immortal King over us shall appear. And a holy prince shall come to wield the sceptre over all the world unto all the ages of hurrying time.

The writer goes on to exult in the terrible destruction that will descend upon all Israel's enemies. We read of 'universal wrath on Latin men', 'ruin on Rome', 'cities in which men are to suffer woe', and so on.

Here the Kingdom of God is essentially his kingly activity in bringing destruction on the enemies of his people, the whole visualized in crudely nationalistic terms, but none the less expressing the writer's hope in connection with God's decisive, eschatological intervention in history.

(iii) Ass. Mos. 10.1

> And then his kingdom shall appear throughout all his creation,
> And then Satan shall be no more,
> And sorrow shall depart with him.

The fact that 'his Kingdom' here refers to the kingly activity of God in intervening in history to destroy the enemies of his people and to secure their blessedness is clear, for the writer repeats the same thought twice again, in different words.

> For the Heavenly One will arise from his royal throne,
> And he will go forth from his holy habitations
> With indignation and wrath on account of his sons. (v. 3)

> For the Most High will arise, the eternal God alone
> And he will appear to punish the Gentiles,
> And he will destroy all their idols,
> Then thou, Israel, shalt be happy.   (vv. 7 f.)

(iv) 1QM 6.6

> And to the God of Israel shall be the Kingdom, and among his
> people will he display might.

(v) 1QM 12.7

> Thou, O God, resplendent in the glory of thy Kingdom and the
> congregation of thy holy ones are in our midst as a perpetual help.

These two passages from the Qumran War Scroll both envisage the
intervention of God in the eschatological conflict between the
Children of Light and the Children of Darkness. In this conflict
the Children of Light will be led by the two Messiahs of Aaron and
Israel and the result of it will be the complete destruction of the
Prince of Darkness (Belial) and his minions. In the first passage the
intervention of God is referred to in terms of the Kingdom which is
manifested as God displays his might on behalf of his people, and in
the second the glory of the Kingdom is manifest in the activity of God
and his angels in the course of the war. In both instances the
reference is clearly to God's decisive intervention in history, here
envisaged in the imagery of a holy war.

Thus we have five instances in apocalyptic of 'Kingdom of God'
being used to express the expectation of God's decisive, eschatological
intervention in history and human experience, and the question now
is: Do we find the same reference in the teaching of Jesus? The
question is no sooner asked than answered, for we most certainly do
find this reference, and especially in the sayings recorded at
Mark 1.15; Luke 10.9–11; Matt. 10.7; Matt. 12.28 = Luke 11.20;
Matt. 11.12 (cf. Luke 16.16); and Luke 17.20 f.

In Mark 1.15 the people are challenged by a proclamation of the
fact that the decisive intervention of God in their history, for which
they prayed in their synagogues (the Kaddish prayer) and which was
the central theme of the apocalyptic hope, is at hand; God's answer
to these prayers, his fulfilment of this hope, is now imminent. The
same message is committed to the disciples, Matt. 10.7; Luke
10.9–11. It makes no difference here that the actual formulation

of this saying may well be secondary, the use of 'Kingdom of God' in this way is certainly characteristic of the teaching of Jesus.[1]

Matt. 12.28 = Luke 11.20 is a text that we have already discussed in connection with the meaning of the verb *ephthasen*, and we have argued that the saying is to be understood as meaning that the Kingdom of God has come in Jesus' exorcisms.[2] These exorcisms are the signs of victory in the decisive battle against the power of Satan, as the exorcisms of the disciples are also a sign of the overthrow of the arch-enemy (Luke 10.18). This is markedly parallel to the situation envisaged in the Qumran War Scroll, except that what is there expressed in the imagery of a holy war is here to be found in terms of demon possession and exorcism. The use of Kingdom of God in 1QM 6.6 and 12.7 to express the expectation of God's intervention in the holy war is paralleled by the use of the same concept in the teaching of Jesus to express God's intervention in the situation of the individual sufferer. The markedly new note is the fact that what for the Qumran sect is future is now present in the experience of the individual in contact with God's kingly activity manifest in the ministry of Jesus and his disciples. *The experience of the individual has become the arena of the eschatological conflict.* Within this arena the Kingdom has come in the sense that the sovereign power of God is now being manifested in this aspect of the decisive battle against the arch-enemy. The exorcisms are evidence for the fact that Satan is being rendered powerless and his Kingdom 'plundered' (Matt.12.29 *harpasai* = Mark 3.27 *diarpasai*).[3]

This brings us to the most difficult saying in this group: Matt. 11.12 f. (cf. Luke 16.16).

> From the days of John the Baptist until now the Kingdom of heaven *biazetai* and *biastai harpazousin* it. For all the prophets and the law prophesied until John.

> (Luke 16.16: The law and the prophets were until John: since then the good news of the Kingdom of God is proclaimed, and every one enters it violently.)

A recent careful discussion of this saying by W. G. Kümmel has summarized the previous discussion and indicated the points at

---

[1] The difficulty in this saying is the note of imminence. This will be discussed in detail below, pp. 199 ff.

[2] See above, pp. 64–66, 76.

[3] See above, p. 76.

issue.[1] There is general agreement that the saying is now set in contexts that are plainly editorial; it originally must have been handed down as an independent logion, and an interpretation may not therefore depend upon either the Matthaean or the Lucan context. Further, Kümmel argues that on grounds of redactional probability the first half of the saying in the Matthaean form is the more authentic, and the reference to the law and the prophets is to be preferred in the Lucan form. So we are concerned to interpret Matt. 11.12 and Luke 16.16a leaving Matt. 11.13 and Luke 16.16b out of account as secondary modifications of this more original form.

The actual interpretation of the saying turns upon three points:

  (i) *biazetai*: is it middle or passive?
  (ii) the meaning and reference of *biastai*.
  (iii) the meaning of *harpazousin*.

Now Schrenk has shown[2] that *biazetai* must be taken as a passive and *harpazousin* must be taken with it in a bad sense. So interpretations such as that of T. W. Manson,[3] who renders the saying 'The Law and the prophets were until John: from that time the Kingdom of God exercises its power and men of violence snatch at it,' and who interprets 'men of violence' as 'men who will take every risk and make every sacrifice to have their share in the Kingdom', must be rejected. We must render the saying: '. . . the Kingdom of Heaven suffers violence and men of violence plunder it', and seek further to deter-

---

[1] Kümmel, *Promise and Fulfilment*, 1956, pp. 121–4. Still more recent discussions cannot be said to have added much to Kümmel's work, although they have added still further suggestions to the long list of proposed interpretations of the saying. D. Daube, *The New Testament and Rabbinic Judaism*, 1956, pp. 285–300, has shown that consideration of Jewish background and retranslation into Hebrew or Aramaic is of no particular help here, since almost any interpretation suggested can find support in this way. F. W. Danker, 'Luke 16.16—an opposition logion', *JBL* 77, 1958, pp. 231–43, sees the Lucan form as the more original and argues that it is a quotation of Pharisaic criticism of Jesus' Kingdom proclamation. G. Braumann, 'Dem Himmelreich wird Gewalt angetan', *ZNW* 52, 1961, pp. 104–9, argues for a connection between the *harpazousin* of Matt. 11.12 and the *harpagmon* of Phil. 2.6 and interprets the saying as reflecting a taunt against the early Church to the effect that Jesus had attempted to seize the Kingdom, as Phil 2.6 reflects the taunt that Jesus had sought to make himself equal with God. To the latter taunt the Church retorted that on the contrary, Jesus had taken the form of a servant (Phil 2.6 ff.), and to the former that it was not Jesus but his opponents, not the early Church but their opponents, who sought to seize the Kingdom (Matt. 11.12, in which the *harpazousin* now has an ironical overtone).

[2] G. Schrenk in *TWNT* I, pp. 609 f.

[3] Manson, *Sayings*, p. 133, following R. Otto.

mine to whom the 'men of violence' refers, and how the Kingdom is 'plundered'.

Kümmel argues,[1] with Schrenk, that the 'plundering' refers to men being robbed of the Kingdom, and that the 'men of violence' may be either the world rulers in the spiritual world or Jesus' Jewish opponents, no certainty being possible at this point. What is certain is that with the coming of John the Baptist a new era has dawned in which the Kingdom of God can already be attacked as being present.

With this last point we are wholly in agreement; the 'men of violence' and 'plundering' references remain, however, for further discussion, especially in light of the Qumran texts.

In the discussion of Matt. 12.28 par. immediately above it was argued that here we have a parallelism between Jesus and the Qumran sect in respect of a holy war theology. Now it should further be pointed out that in 1QM the victory of the Children of Light is by no means won without a struggle, even with the intervention of God. On the contrary 'it will be, indeed, a time of [   ] tribulation for the people redeemed of God, but, unlike all their previous tribulations, this one will come to a speedy end in a redemption which shall last forever' (1QM 1.12, Gaster's translation). Matt. 12.28 par. interprets the exorcisms of Jesus as a victory for the Kingdom of God in the eschatological struggle; Matt. 11.12 may surely be interpreted in the same context and as referring therefore to a temporary victory *against* the Kingdom of God in that same struggle.

This suggestion is supported by the use of *harpazousin* in Matt. 11.12. At the end of our discussion of Matt. 12.28 we referred to Matt. 12.29, where the exorcisms of Jesus are interpreted as a plundering of the house of the Strong One, i.e. Satan, and are part therefore of the eschatological conflict. It is worthy of careful note that Matthew here uses precisely the same verb as in 11.12, changing the first occurrence of *diarpasai* in Mark 3.27 to *harpasai*. Whatever may be the reason for this change it is evidence for the fact that the verb in 11.12 can be interpreted as referring to a 'plundering' of the Kingdom of God in the eschatological struggle, and its use in both Matt. 11.12 and 12.29 supports our contention that both sayings have reference to the same eschatological conflict, 11.12 referring to a defeat for the Kingdom of God and 12.29 to a victory.

The Qumran texts also help us in the interpretation of the *biastai*

[1] *Promise*, p. 123.

in our saying. It has been pointed out by O. Betz[1] that a parallel to this expression is to be found in 1QH, where the Qumran psalmist reflects upon his fate as being subject to the attack of 'men of violence' who have sought his life.[2] He moves naturally and smoothly in thought from his past and present experience to the eschatological future; indeed in 1QH 4.22 he dreams of the day when he will rise against his enemies, and the verses which follow make it clear that the reference is to the eschatological conflict. This expression 'men of violence' is also used of the opponents of the Qumran sect in 1QpHab 2.6 which speaks of their fate 'at the End of Days'. In 4QpPs 37 it occurs three times; once (2.12) referring to the sect's opponents and the coming destruction, and twice (3.4 and 4.5) to 'terrible ones of the Gentiles' (Allegro) and the part that they will play in the eschatological visitation. It is clear therefore that such an expression could be used of adversaries of the Kingdom of God in the eschatological conflict, and we are surely justified in so interpreting it in Matt. 11.12.

If we are to translate and interpret Matt. 11.12 as we have suggested then we may ask if there is any indication at all of the actual defeat which the Kingdom of God has suffered and to which reference is here being made. Neither the Matthaean nor the Lucan context may be used here, since both are editorial, but there is a possible clue in the fact that the saying does refer to John the Baptist. With John the era of the Kingdom of God begins; 'Jesus did in fact see in the coming of the Baptist the shift of the aeons';[3] with him begin also the acts of violence against the Kingdom. So much is clear from the saying, and it would be a natural and attractive step further to assume that the reference is in fact to the imprisonment and death of the Baptist. Such may indeed be the case, but we have no means of proving it.

So much for Matt. 11.12. We turn now to the last of the sayings in this group: Luke 17.20 f.

> The Kingdom of God does not come *meta paratērēseōs*; neither shall they say, Lo here, or there; for the Kingdom of God is *entos hymōn*.

The possibilities here can be well seen in the translation offered by the NEB, which has in the text:

[1] O. Betz, 'Jesu heiliger Krieg', *NT* 2, 1957–8, pp. 116–37.
[2] *'riṣim* 1QH 2.21. Literally 'terrible ones'. Gaster, *Scriptures*, p. 137, translates 'fierce men', and Mansoor, *Thanksgiving Hymns*, p. 107, 'tyrants'.
[3] J. M. Robinson, *New Quest*, p. 118. See further above, pp. 122 f.

> You cannot tell by observation when the Kingdom of God comes. There will be no saying, 'Look, here it is!' or 'there it is!'; for in fact the Kingdom of God is among you,

and then adds in the margin, presumably in descending order of probability: '*Or* for in fact the Kingdom of God is within you, *or* in fact the Kingdom of God is within your grasp, *or* for suddenly the Kingdom of God will be among you.'

The version preferred in the NEB text is in fact the version to be preferred. It turns upon four points.

(i) 'Kingdom of God' is understood as God's decisive intervention in history, for which we now have ample evidence in the sayings discussed immediately above.

(ii) *meta paratērēseōs* is interpreted as referring to the pastime, extremely popular in Jewish apocalyptic circles, of watching for and calculating signs that the End was at hand.[1] Jesus emphatically rejects all such calculation because, as we shall argue further below, he rejects the understanding of history upon which it is based.

(iii) 'Lo here, Lo there' recalls the warning about men who will say 'Lo, here is the Christ; or Lo, there', Mark 13.21 par. What is here being negated is the concept that the intervention of God will be such as to be bound up with the appearance of some eschatological figure whose credentials can be checked in accordance with current Jewish expectation.[2]

(iv) *entos hymōn* is translated 'among you'. This is one of the two possibilities here, the other being to translate 'within you'. A choice between these two is not possible on the basis of the New Testament usage of *entos*, since this word occurs again only at Matt. 23.26, where it means 'inside'; nor does general Greek usage help us because the Greek word can have both meanings.[3] So we must turn to more general considerations, and here the decisive observation is that, if the word is to be translated 'within', then we have here an understanding of Kingdom of God without further parallel in the recorded

---

[1] For illustrations see Billerbeck, *Kommentar* IV, pp. 977 ff. *paratērēsis* does not occur elsewhere in the Greek Bible but Moulton and Milligan, *Vocabulary of the Greek Testament*, p. 490, show that the verb could be used of the close observation of an illness. A word that could be used of searching for the symptoms of an illness could certainly be used of searching for the signs of the coming of God's decisive intervention.

[2] The fact that Mark 13.21 is secondary material is here irrelevant; it is an illustration of the kind of searching for a Messiah that is being rejected in Luke 17.20 f.

[3] Kümmel, *Promise*, p. 33, with full references.

teaching of Jesus.[1] It is not the fact that the saying is, according to Luke, addressed to Pharisees that rules out this interpretation since the context is most probably editorial, but the fact that nowhere else does Jesus speak of the Kingdom in this particular manner. There is one apocryphal saying in which Luke 17.21 is recast to make the *entos hymōn* mean unambiguously 'within you', Oxyrhynchus Pap. 654.3, and it is significant that in this saying we have an understanding of 'Kingdom' wholly foreign to the teaching of Jesus.[2]

It can be seen that a consideration of *entos hymōn* establishes the NEB text translation against the first marginal possibility 'within you'. The second marginal possibility, 'within your grasp', is less likely than the text both because it involves a very free translation of *entos hymōn* and also because it loses the sharp antithesis between what is being asserted and what is being negated in this saying. The third marginal possibility 'for suddenly the Kingdom of God will be among you' preserves the antithesis in the saying, but is less likely than the text because it requires the introduction of 'suddenly', for which there is no warrant in the original, and because it puts the whole emphasis upon the future coming of the Kingdom, which is unlikely in view of the evidence for the Kingdom as present in the teaching of Jesus. The NEB text translation therefore stands and this leads naturally to the interpretation we have suggested above. One aspect of this interpretation which warrants further discussion is, as we have suggested under (ii) above, the interpretation of history that is being rejected in this saying, and to this we now turn.

One of the points at which apocalyptic differs most radically from prophecy is in its understanding of history.[3] The prophets had anchored their hopes for the future in the certainty that God had acted in certain historical events, was acting and would act.[4] This activity was a challenge to Israel to repent; where they faced catastrophe this was because God was acting in history, and they could hope for salvation because God was entering and would enter history on their behalf. In all of this it was not the history in itself that was important but the fact that God was active in it, that he was entering

---

[1] So, in effect, T. W. Manson, *Sayings*, p. 304; Kümmel, *Promise*, pp. 33 f.

[2] Jeremias, *Unknown Sayings of Jesus*, 1958 (ET by R. H. Fuller of *Unbekannte Jesusworte*, 1951), pp. 15 f. Another version of this saying, to which the same comments apply, has been found in the Coptic Gospel of Thomas (Logion 3).

[3] In what follows we are heavily indebted to von Rad, *Theologie* II, pp .314–21, and Rössler, *Gesetz und Geschichte*, 1961, pp. 55–60.

[4] See above, pp. 162 ff.

into it and challenging them within it. In the apocalyptic understanding of history all this has changed and instead of a history as a
series of events within which the activity of God may be known we
have the conception of history as a universal whole, a unified process
which begins with Adam[1] or with the world empires arising out of
the primeval chaos,[2] and which ends with the eschatological climax.[3]
Each part of this process is important as it relates to the whole, and
although each part is what it is because of the activity of God[4] none
the less these parts are not important because in them the activity
of God may be known, they are important because they fulfil the
divine plan. The important thing about history, for apocalyptic, is
that it is running a predetermined course to a predetermined climax,
all in accordance with the divine plan.[5] This is why apocalyptic can
portray history in mythological terms; the individual events have
ceased to be important as events in which God is active and through
which he may be known, what matters is the sequence of events
leading up to its preordained climax and it is in this climax that God
will be known as he brings salvation to his people.[6] So the interest of
apocalyptic is directed entirely towards this end, and a major
preoccupation of the apocalyptic seers is in the calculation of this
end[7] and in the delineation of the signs of its coming,[8] something that
is possible for them because the predetermined plan is 'written in the
book of truth' and the seers have access to this.[9]

The apocalyptic understanding of history is presupposed in
searching for signs of the end or calculating its coming, and in
rejecting this approach in Luke 17.20 f. Jesus is rejecting the understanding of history which it presupposes. The coming of the Kingdom
cannot be calculated in advance, nor will it be accompanied by signs
such as apocalyptic sought, because the Kingdom is the sovereign
power of God breaking into history and human experience in a

[1] Enoch 85.3; Syr. Bar. 56.5.
[2] Dan. 7.2.
[3] Enoch 90.20, 29; Test. Levi 18.2; Syr. Bar. 70.7; Ass. Mos. 10.3; etc.
[4] Enoch 89.20, 59; Syr. Bar. 63.6; Ass. Mos. 4.5.
[5] Enoch 39.11; 92.2; II (4) Ezra 14.11; Syr. Bar. 69.2; Ass. Mos. 12.5.
[6] Enoch 58.6; Syr. Bar. 74; II (4) Ezra 7.98; Dan. 7.27.
[7] II (4) Ezra 14.11 f.; Syr. Bar. 53–74; Enoch 93.1–14; 91.12–17. Billerbeck,
Kommentar IV, pp. 986 ff.
[8] Enoch 99.4 ff.; Jub. 23.23 ff.; II (4) Ezra 4.51–5.13; Syr. Bar. 25.1–29.2.
Billerbeck, *Kommentar* IV, pp. 977 ff.
[9] Dan. 10.21; Similarly Enoch 103.2; 106.19–107.1; Test. Levi 5.4. Billerbeck,
Kommentar II, pp. 175 f.

manner to be determined by God, it is not history moving inevitably to a climax predetermined in accordance with a divine plan to which apocalyptic seers have had access. In effect, we have in this saying a rejection of the apocalyptic understanding of history and a return to the prophetic understanding.

The contention that Jesus rejected the apocalyptic conception of history and returned to that of Old Testament prophecy can be supported by other factors in his teaching. For example, we have the deliberate choice of the expression 'Kingdom of God', with its emphasis upon the kingly activity of God, rather than one of the several more favoured by apocalyptic: 'the consummation', 'the end of days', 'the age to come', or the like. Then we have the complete absence from the teaching of Jesus of any of the elements which characterize the apocalyptic seers and grew out of their under-standing of history: the signs and calculations, the periods and epochs of world history, the visions and readings of the heavenly books, the portrayal of events in mythological terms, and so on. Finally we have the genuine teaching of Jesus underlying the synoptic apocalypses and probably preserved in Luke 17.22–37; 21.34–36; Mark 13.32–37.[1] This puts the emphasis upon the sudden and unexpected manner of God's in-breaking into history and human experience and upon the responsibility of men to be prepared to respond to this crisis, thus reiterating the prophetic rather than the apocalyptic emphases.

We have now completed our discussion of the use of 'Kingdom of God' in apocalyptic and in the teaching of Jesus, where the reference is to God's decisive intervention in history and human experience, and we proceed therefore to:

B. *'Kingdom of God' in reference to the final state of the redeemed to which God's intervention in history and human experience is designed to lead*

The use of the term 'Kingdom of God' in this connection is very rare in apocalyptic; there are two certain instances of it (Sib. Orac. 3.767 and 1QSb 4.25 f.), one probable instance (Ps. Sol. 5.18 f.), and one further possible instance (1QSb 3.5).

The rarity of this use should not surprise us; apocalyptic was concerned to stress this final stage of things as the inevitable fulfilment of the divine plan and to depict its glories, and tended therefore to choose terms other than Kingdom of God. Jesus, on the other hand,

[1] T. W. Manson, *Teaching*, pp. 260 ff.; *Sayings*, pp. 141–7, 334–7.

used 'Kingdom of God' almost exclusively in the same connection, and this can only be because his concern was to stress the kingly activity of God here, and to maintain the dynamic continuity of concern with God breaking into history and human experience and continuing to act in the establishment of the final blessed state. Gone is the inevitable fulfilment of the divine plan; in its place we have the challenge to recognize and to respond to the sovereign authority of God in the establishment of the final blessed state no less than in the initial in-breaking into history and human experience.

(i) Sib. Orac. 3.767

Sib. Orac. 3.652–795 describes a series of eschatological events[1] which culminate in God's setting up of his eternal Kingdom over all men.

> And then indeed he will raise up his Kingdom for all ages over men, he who once gave a holy law to godly men, to all of whom he promised to open out the earth and the world, and the portals of the blessed, and all joys, and everlasting sense and eternal gladness (767–71).

We can see at once why 'Kingdom' should be used here, for the emphasis is all upon the initiative and activity of God and 'Kingdom' is therefore the appropriate expression.

(ii) Ps. Sol. 5.18 f.

> They that fear the Lord rejoice in good gifts
> And thy goodness (is/will be) upon Israel in thy Kingdom
> Blessed be the glory of the Lord, for he is our King.

The difficulty with this reference is the fact that there is no verb 'to be' in the crucial sentence, undoubtedly due to Semitic influence,[2] and a verb must be supplied. If we supply 'is' then the reference is to the present experience of Israel; if we supply 'will be' then the reference is eschatological, the psalmist is looking forward to the final blessed state.[3] Most commentators have supplied 'is' and given

---

[1] God sends a King from the East and, with God's supernatural help, he fights against and destroys the Gentiles and their enmity (652–97). Then the children of God live in peace and quietness protected by the hand of the Holy One (698–709), the Gentiles now acknowledge God (710–40).

[2] J. Viteau, *Les Psaumes de Salomon*, 1911, p. 115.

[3] A further possibility is to omit the *en* before *tē basileia sou* and so make the Kingdom refer to Israel. So Viteau, *op. cit.*, pp. 284 f., who reads: 'et ta bonté se répand sur Israel, son royaume'. But this is a most unlikely reading and most commentators have included the *en* in their text. So Rahlfs, *Septuaginta* II, 1935,

the sentence a present reference,[1] but this would seem the less likely of the two alternatives, for the reason that the only other reference to Kingdom of God in the Psalms of Solomon is a reference to the eschatological Kingdom,[2] and that the construction of the psalm is such as to make an eschatological reference here very likely. It is a prayer based on the psalmist's perfect trust in God, the King; in v. 16 ff. the prayer is being answered, both in terms of what may be expected of the present (vv. 16, 18a) and also of what may be hoped for in the eschatological future. If this reasoning is correct, then we have here a reference to Kingdom of God as the final blessed state of his people.

The third and fourth references to be considered under this heading are both from 1QSb, the 'Formulary of Blessings'. This is one of the two 'appendices' to 1QS, the Manual of Discipline, the other being 1QSa, the 'Rule of the Congregation'. Both of these appendices are eschatological in character, i.e. they are concerned with the community as it will exist in the End-time, after the destruction of Belial and his minions in the eschatological war. 1QSb consists of a series of blessings in which are expressed the hopes of the community for the End-time: for the laymen of the community, for the Messianic High Priest, for the priests, and for the Messianic King.

(iii) 1QSb 3.5

In connection with the blessing for the Messianic High Priest there is found the line:

> May he grant thee grace and peace everlasting and *malkuth*. . . .

The manuscript is defective and the word, or words, following *malkuth* are missing. This makes certainty of interpretation impossible, and two possibilities have been suggested. The original editor of the text, J. T. Milik, translated '*et le royaume* . . .' and added a note:

---

p. 447; Ryle and James, *Psalms of Solomon*, 1891, p. 62; Rendel Harris, *Odes and Psalms of Solomon* (Syriac Version), 1909, p. 144 (translation of the Syriac text); Gray, *Apocr. and Pseud.* (ed. Charles) II, 1913, p. 638.

[1] Ryle and James, *op. cit.*, p. 63, understand 'thy Kingdom' as a reference to Israel, the true Israel being coextensive with the divine Kingdom, but admit the possibility of an eschatological reference. Rendel Harris, *op. cit.*, p. 144, translates the Syriac 'thy grace is on Israel in thy Kingdom', but offers no commentary; Gray, *op. cit.*, p. 638, translates the Greek 'thy goodness is upon Israel in thy kingdom', but does not discuss the verse.

[2] Ps. Sol. 17.3, discussed above, pp. 168 f.

'*cf*. "*le royaume des cieux*" *dans le Nouveau Testament et dans les textes talmudiques*'.[1] T. H. Gaster follows this, translating: 'grant thee grace [and peace everlast]ing, and [an inheritance in] the kingdom of [heaven].'[2] A. S. van der Woude, on the other hand, calls attention to 1Q21 1.2 where *malkuth* occurs followed by 'priestly', and argues that this is the reference here,[3] in which argument he is supported by J. Maier,[4] in which case we must translate 'priestly dominion' or the like. So, although this text certainly refers to the final blessed state we cannot be certain that it is using *malkuth* as 'Kingdom' in reference to it.

(iv) 1QSb 4.25 f.

In the Formulary of Blessing addressed to the priests we find the following:

> Thou art as an angel of the Presence in the dwelling of sanctity [mayest thou serve forever] to the glory of the God of Hosts; mayest thou be surrounding as one who serves in the palace of the Kingdom.

This is a reference to the function of the priests in the final blessed state, when they will serve in the temple of the New Jerusalem. In Qumran the final blessed state was envisaged in terms of the imagery of an eschatological temple[5] and the use of 'Kingdom' here is then certainly a use of this term in reference to the final state of the redeemed.

Such, then, are the instances of this usage in apocalyptic; that the same usage is to be found in the teaching of Jesus is, of course, clear and needs no particular exegetical demonstration. We will content ourselves with listing, and discussing briefly, some of the characteristic examples.

(i) Matt. 5.3–12; Luke 6.20–23: the Beatitudes[6]

In their present form these are undoubtedly editorial in arrangement, but that Jesus did teach something very like this there can be

[1] *DJD* I, pp. 124 f.
[2] *Scriptures*, p. 98.
[3] *Messianische Vorstellungen*, p. 110.
[4] *Die Texte vom Toten Meer* II, 1960, p. 160.
[5] E.g. 1QH 3.19–23 where the psalmist envisages his final destiny in terms of a perfect sacral relationship between himself, the host of the holy ones, the congregation of the sons of heaven, and God; and 4QFlor. 1.1–7 which envisages the blessed state of the community at 'the end of days' in the imagery of a sanctuary.
[6] See above, p. 83.

no doubt. There is general agreement that the Lucan form is the more original of the two, although some scholars prefer the third person formulation of Matthew.[1] Parallels to the Beatitudes have been found in the Coptic Gospel of Thomas as follows:

> Logion 54: Jesus said: Blessed are the poor, for
> yours is the Kingdom of Heaven.
> Logion 69b: Blessed are the hungry, for the belly
> of him who desires will be filled.

It should be noted that these two are not found together in Thomas, an indication that the individual Beatitudes could and did circulate in the tradition as separate units. The Beatitude as a saying form is well known to us from the Old Testament and from apocalyptic, Hellenistic Jewish and rabbinical literature;[2] and a particularly interesting passage as background to the Beatitudes in the teaching of Jesus is to be found in the Qumran texts 4QpPs37 1.8 f.:

> And the humble shall inherit the earth and they shall delight in the abundance of peace. The interpretation of this concerns [the congregation of the] Poor who accept the time of affliction; they will be delivered from all the snares. . . .[3]

Here we have Ps. 37.11 being interpreted eschatologically, just as it is in Matt. 5.5, and applied to the Qumran sect as 'the poor', so interpreting '*nwym* as '*bywnym*, and inevitably recalling Luke 6.20.[4] 'The Poor' is a favourite self-designation of the Qumran group;[5] does Luke 6.20 quote this Qumran self-designation and re-apply it to those who accept the challenge of Jesus' proclamation? This is certainly possible, but whether it be the case or not certainly the Beatitudes of Jesus have the same eschatological orientation as has 4QpPs37. They look forward to the future blessed state, and they teach something about it; they teach that in it the values of the world may well be reversed, for it will be the establishment of the values of God. This theme of the reversal of existing values in the future blessed state is found elsewhere in the synoptic record of the teaching of Jesus. In Mark 10.31, 'The last shall be first and the first

---

[1] E.g. Bultmann, *Tradition*, p. 114 (ET, pp. 109 f.).

[2] Art. *makarios* in *TWNT* IV, pp. 367–9 (Bertram).

[3] Following the text as edited and reconstructed by J. M. Allegro, *PEQ*, 1954, pp. 69–75.

[4] Cross, *Ancient Library*, pp. 61 f., already referred to above, p. 83, n. 1.

[5] E.g. 1QpHab 12.3, 6, 10; 1QM 11.9, 13; 13.14; 1QH 2.32; 4QpPs37 2.10 of the sect as a whole; 1QH 3.25; 5.16–18 of an individual member of the sect.

last' follows a reference to 'life eternal in the age to come'.[1] Matt. 10.26 par. speaks of the hidden that will be revealed, and Matt. 18.4 refers to the one who humbles himself becoming great in the Kingdom of Heaven (cf. Matt. 23.12; Luke 14.11; 18.14). So we can see that Jesus did use 'Kingdom of God' in reference to the final state of the redeemed, and that he taught that it would be a state of things in which the present order of life would be reversed.

Frank M. Cross, Jr.,[2] sees in the second Lucan Beatitude a reference to the eschatologcal banquet, a parallel to which he finds in 4QpPs37 2.10 f. where Ps. 37.21 f. is interpreted of 'the congregation of the Poor . . . (who) will inherit the mount of the height of Is[rael; in his] holy [mountain] they will delight'.[3] This is an attractive suggestion and would strengthen the case for a relationship between the Beatitudes and the Qumran sect. Certainly Luke 6.21 can be interpreted in terms of the eschatological banquet, and that this is a concept used in the teaching of Jesus can be seen from the passage to which we now turn.

(ii) Matt. 8.11 cf. Luke 13.28

This verse has been fully and clearly interpreted by J. Jeremias,[4] who points out that in biblical symbolism the act of eating and drinking mediates the vision of God. From its origin in Isa. 25.6–8 the concept of an eschatological banquet as a symbol of participation in the final blessed communion with God is used in apocalyptic[5] and it plays a real part of the teaching of Jesus. Not only is it found here in Matt. 8.11, but it also lies behind Mark 14.25 par.; Luke 22.16; and, as we have already noted, Luke 6.21 par. It should also be noted that it lies behind the symbol of the marriage feast in Mark 2.19, where the joy is a fact of present experience, an indication of the tension between present and future in the teaching of Jesus.

(iii) Matt. 5.20; Mark 10.14 f. par.; Matt. 7.21; Mark 10.23–25 par.; Matt. 21.31 (cf. v. 43); Mark 9.47 par. Entering and receiving the Kingdom of God

All exegetes of these sayings are heavily indebted to Hans

---

[1] Matt. 19.30 has this following a reference to inheriting eternal life, and Luke 13.30 has it following a reference to the Kingdom of God.
[2] *Ancient Library*, p. 67 n. 81. See above, p. 83 n. 1.
[3] 4QpPs37 2.10 f. Cross's reconstruction.
[4] J. Jeremias, *Promise*, pp. 59–65.
[5] E.g. Enoch 62.14.

Windisch,[1] who pointed out that the concept of conditions for entry into the final blessed state has a long history in Israel. It has roots in Deut. 4.1; 6.17 f.; 16.20, where obedience to the commandments is a condition for entry into the promised land; it is found in Old Testament apocalyptic, Isa. 26.2 f. (entry into the holy city); and it plays a part in the temple liturgy, where Pss. 15 and 24 are concerned with conditions for entry into the temple.[2] The prophets reflect the same concept, e.g. Isa. 33.13 ff. and 58.13 f., and it has its place in apocalyptic: II (4) Ezra 7.14; Ps. Sol. 14.10. In the teaching of Jesus it is used specifically in connection with the Kingdom of God, which in these sayings is certainly the final state of the redeemed, and it is here most probably a development of the Old Testament 'Torah of entry' into the Temple. The truly remarkable thing about the teaching of Jesus at this point is not that he uses this concept in connection with the future kingdom, but that he applies it in such a way as to include those people whom his contemporaries would have rejected, and to exclude those of whose place in the Kingdom his contemporaries would have been most certain. In this respect, as in others, he deliberately flies in the face of the traditions and conventions of first-century Judaism.

This brief discussion of some characteristic passages from the teaching of Jesus indicates that Jesus did use Kingdom of God in this second apocalyptic sense, i.e. in reference to the final state of the redeemed with God. We need labour this point no further, since it is not a point at issue in the modern discussion; no competent scholar would deny that this is a characteristic usage in the teaching of Jesus. The point that we would emphasize is the one we made earlier in this section: although 'Kingdom of God' is found with this reference in apocalyptic it is rare there, but in the teaching of Jesus it is the characteristic term used in this connection.

This concludes our discussion of the use of 'Kingdom of God' as a technical term in apocalyptic and in the teaching of Jesus. We believe that we have shown that the term is rare in apocalyptic, but that it does occur there in reference (a) to God's decisive intervention in history and human experience, and (b) to the final state of the redeemed to which this intervention is designed to lead. In precisely these same ways it is used in the teaching of Jesus, with the significant

---

[1] 'Die Sprüche vom Eingehen in das Reich Gottes', *ZNW* 27, 1928, pp. 163–92. See above, p. 80 n.3.

[2] S. Mowinckel, '*toroth d'entrée*', quoted by Windisch, *op. cit.*, p. 181.

difference that what is rare in apocalyptic is normative in the teaching of Jesus. This difference indicates a difference in emphasis and a difference in the understanding of history. By his use of the term Jesus puts all the emphasis upon the activity of God, and he implies that history is the sphere in which the activity is manifest, rather than a process working towards an inevitable conclusion. We may not interpret the eschatological teaching of Jesus in terms of a linear concept of time, for this is foreign to the prophetic understanding to which he returns; we may not necessarily understand it in terms of the end of history or of time, for the one emphasis is upon the activity of God as decisive for man's salvation and as securing for man the perfect relationship with God envisaged in the imagery of the perfect blessed state. Whether this latter point necessarily *involves* the end of history or time will depend upon our understanding of the tension between present and future in the teaching of Jesus, to the discussion of which we now turn.

2. *The Tension between Present and Future in the Teaching of Jesus concerning the Kingdom of God*

This tension can be recognized in two ways: (*a*) it can be shown that there are aspects of the teaching of Jesus in which the Kingdom is present and further aspects in which it is future; and (*b*) it can be shown that there are individual sayings or sections of teaching in which a tension between present and future is reflected. In order to approach the question of the nature of this tension we will look more carefully at the teaching of Jesus from both of these viewpoints.

A. *The Kingdom of God as present and as future*

We have no need now further to labour the point that the Kingdom of God is both present and future in the teaching of Jesus. This has been one of the points firmly established by the modern discussion and we have already summarized the evidence from the teaching of Jesus itself.[1] Our problem is not the establishment of these aspects of the teaching of Jesus but their interpretation.

In this respect the Kingdom as present is much the easier of the two. The Kingdom is God's kingly activity manifested in a breaking into history and human experience to visit and redeem his people in

---

[1] See above, pp. 74 ff. (the Kingdom as Present) and pp. 83 f. (the Kingdom as Future).

a manner decisive for their salvation,[1] and the claim of the teaching of Jesus is simply that this is happening in his ministry. As to *how* this is happening we have three interrelated points that occur and re-occur in the teaching: (i) the exorcisms are interpreted in terms of an eschatological conflict situation (Matt. 12.28 par.; Mark 3.27), which same situation is envisaged in Matt. 11.12. With the coming of Jesus the eschatological conflict begins, the arena for which is the situation and experience of the individual challenged by Jesus, or by his disciples (Luke 10.18). (ii) Jesus confronts his hearers with the challenge that in his ministry prophecy and imagery traditionally associated with the Messianic times are being fulfilled, and they must now make the ultimate decision once and for all in response to this.[2] (iii) More particularly Jesus offers to his hearers the challenge of the eschatological forgiveness of sins, and accepts into eschato-logical fellowship with himself the repentant sinner, doing this as a direct exhibition of the will of God.[3] The common factor in all of these points is that they are directly related to the experience of the individual. Whatever reservations one may have about the thorough-going existentialism of Bultmann and his school, there can be no doubt but that they have done us an invaluable service in directing our attention to the sphere of individual human existence as the sphere in which the Kingdom of God is manifested. There is in the teaching of Jesus an explicit rejection of the sphere of external—one is tempted to say 'photographable'—events as the medium in which the Kingdom is manifest, and a concentration upon the experience of the individual that is nothing short of remarkable, especially in view of the very different teaching of apocalyptic at this point.[4] There is no single element in the teaching of Jesus concerning the Kingdom as present which does not explicitly or implicitly relate directly and solely to the experience of the individual. The only 'external' factor is Jesus himself, his message and his ministry, and the Kingdom is not manifest in him except to those who come to him with faith, i.e. to those who are prepared to relate this challenge to their own existence

---

[1] We shall not concern ourselves here with the question of the place of the Gentiles in Jesus' Kingdom of God teaching. Jeremias, *Promise*, has shown that the Gentiles are included in the ultimate prospect even though Jesus may, in fact, have restricted his own ministry to the Jews.

[2] Points 1–3, pp. 74 f. above.

[3] Point 6, p. 76 above; and the emphases in the work of the Bultmann school, especially Fuchs, p. 126 above.

[4] The synoptic apocalypses which reflect the general teaching of Jewish apocalyptic at this point are, of course, secondary. See chapter VIII above.

that the Kingdom may become for them a matter of personal experience. It is for this reason that we have been careful to speak of the Kingdom as 'God's kingly activity manifested in a breaking into history *and human experience*'.

In this connection we should say a last word about Luke 17.20 f., and especially about the significance of the 'among you' in that saying. What is here being taught is that God is acting as King in and through the ministry of Jesus and his disciples, and it is up to the contemporaries of Jesus to recognize this and to respond to it. The Kingdom is now present in history; not in that the stars are falling from the heavens, or that the Jews are successfully driving the Romans into the sea, or that the dry stream beds are now flowing with water twenty-four hours a day and 365 days a year; but in that the power of demons is broken, sins are forgiven, sinners are gathering into an eschatological fellowship around Jesus. These are truly historical events in that they are present to human experience, and they are so present whether or not any given human being recognizes them. In this sense they are 'external' events, but they are not 'photographable' events, they are not 'signs' as apocalyptic understands this word. One could have photographed an exorcism, one could have recorded the proclamation of the forgiveness of sins, but the kingly activity of God would not be manifest on the photograph or in the recording—the exorcism *could* be due to the power of Beelzebub, the proclamation of the forgiveness of sins *could* be blasphemy.[1] To experience the kingly activity of God one must have *faith*, i.e. one must interpret the event aright and commit oneself without reservation to the God revealed in the event *properly interpreted*. Then, and only then, does the Kingdom become a matter of personal experience. But it *does* become present as personal experience, and so the Kingdom as present in the teaching of Jesus means, in effect, the Kingdom as potentially-actually present in the personal experience of the believer.

What, then, is to be expected of the future? Here we must begin with the so-called 'apocalyptic Son of Man sayings', for the authenticity of this particular aspect of the teaching of Jesus can no longer be seriously doubted.[2] The most recent research on this subject, that of H. E. Tödt,[3] has shown that the authentic core of this teaching

---

[1] See above, pp. 139 f.
[2] See chapter VI above.
[3] See above, pp. 109 f.

lies in those sayings which most clearly exhibit a tension between present and future, which teach the future consummation of that which has begun in the ministry of Jesus (Matt. 24.27 par.; 24.37, 39 par.; Luke 17.30; 11.30; Matt. 24.44 par.; Luke 12.3 ff. par.). These sayings make it clear beyond any shadow of doubt that Jesus looked for such a future consummation, but they do not tell us anything about the form that such a consummation would take. The 'coming' or 'days of the Son of Man' is simply an image used in speaking of the consummation, and as such no more implies the literal descent of a figure from the other side of the stars than the image of the Messianic Banquet implies the setting up of trestle-tables all over the slopes of Mount Zion. The one thing these sayings teach us about this coming consummation is that it will include the element of judgment, a message also to be found in the twin parables of the Tares Among the Wheat and the Dragnet (Matt. 13.24–30; 13.47 f.).

The same tension between present and future is to be found in the 'parables of contrast',[1] where the emphasis is upon the hope generated for the community of Jesus' followers by the certainty of the consummation; in Mark 9.1, where the emphasis is upon the difference between the hidden (debatable) present and the manifest future;[2] and in Mark 14.62, where the emphasis is upon the consummation as vindicating Jesus and his ministry.[3] None of these elements in the teaching of Jesus tell us anything more about the consummation (or Parousia) than that it will include judgment, that it holds out hope, and that it will vindicate Jesus; the exact nature of the consummation/Parousia remains a mystery.

Other elements in the teaching of Jesus indicate further things to be expected of this consummation, without thereby elucidating the mystery of its exact nature. The Beatitudes imply that it will involve the establishment of the values of God, which may well involve the reversal of existing values; a theme also be found in Mark 10.31; Matt. 10.26 and Matt. 18.4.[4] The imagery of the Messianic Banquet, which is used in Matt. 8.11 (cf. Luke 13.28) and which lies behind the Eschatological Prospect at the Lord's Supper (Mark 14.25 par.; Luke 22.16) and the Beatitude Luke 6.21 par.,[5] teaches that it will

---

[1] Mustard Seed, Leaven, Patient Husbandman, Sower. See above, p. 139.
[2] See above, pp .138 ff.
[3] See above, p. 143.
[4] See above, pp. 83, 181 ff.
[5] See above, pp. 182 f.

mean a perfect participation in the ultimate blessings of God; and the imagery of the New Temple (Mark 14.58 par.; 15.29 par.) which, as we saw earlier in this chapter,[1] is a regular apocalyptic symbol for the final blessed state, describes the community of the redeemed as enjoying a perfect sacral relationship with God.[2]

A final aspect of the teaching of Jesus which remains for consideration at this point is that which has direct reference to a crisis subsequent to that of his own ministry. Here we find the commands to watchfulness on the part of the disciples,[3] the warnings addressed to Israel,[4] and the warnings apparently addressed to various groups in Israel.[5] This is the nearest approach in the teaching of Jesus to the cosmic End of apocalyptic, and it is undoubtedly this element in the teaching that gave rise to the synoptic apocalypses. But what is here being taught is surely nothing more nor less than the reality of judgment as an aspect of the consummation. The disciples are caught up in the tension between present and future and may not rest upon the laurels of their first decision; the Sadducees, scribes and Pharisees who are blind to the challenge of Jesus and his ministry must face the consequences in terms of the ultimate judgment of God. In other words we have here the same theme that we found in the Son of Man sayings, and neither here nor there do we have any details about the exact nature of that judgment and its coming. If the reality of judgment was to be proclaimed to the contemporaries of Jesus then there was no choice but to use this kind of imagery; the very difference between these sayings and parables on the one hand and the synoptic apocalypses and Jewish apocalyptic in general on the other must warn us not to read into this teaching more than it actually contains, just as the extent and vigour of this teaching must warn us not to ignore its message.

The conclusion to be drawn from this discussion of the teaching of

---

[1] P. 181.

[2] See above, p. 83.

[3] Luke 12.35–46 par.; 12.49–53 par.; 13.22–30 par. ;17.22–30. See above, p. 83.

[4] Mark 11.12–14 par.; Matt. 7.19; Luke 23.29–31; 21.34; Luke 13.6–9; Mark 9.50 par. Jeremias, *Parables*, pp. 122, 125 f.

[5] Luke 12.16–20, the Rich Fool, addressed to the rich (?Sadducees); Matt. 24.45–51a, the Servant entrusted with authority; Matt. 25.14–30 par., Pounds and Talents; Mark 13.33–37 par., all addressed to the leaders of the people, especially the scribes; Matt. 15.14 cf. Luke 6.39; Matt. 7.3–5 par.; Matt. 12.33 cf. Matt. 7.16–20 par. addressed to the Pharisees; and Matt. 23.37 par. addressed to the capital city. Jeremias, *Parables*, pp. 123–5.

Jesus concerning the future is, we believe, that Jesus did look toward a consummation of that which had begun in his own ministry, and that he did indicate various aspects of that consummation. But he did not offer any specific instruction as to its exact nature. We may not therefore resolve the tension between present and future for us as individuals by externalizing the future teaching in terms of cosmic catastrophe and the descent of a heavenly being, nor may we refer it to a heavenly realm or to a life beyond death. There is no warrant for any of this in the teaching of Jesus. To do justice to this teaching we must hold fast to the conviction that the consummation of that which has begun in the ministry of Jesus *will be*, and that it will be just as much a reality to be experienced as was the beginning in the ministry of Jesus and in the experience of those who first believed in him. How? When? Where? may be natural questions but they are illegitimate questions in view of the fact that the teaching of Jesus seems deliberately to avoid anything that could be construed as an answer to them (Mark 13.32). This teaching puts the emphasis where it belongs: on the state of tension between present and future in which the believer must live and move and have his being.

B. *Direct reflection of the tension between present and future in the teaching of Jesus*

The division we are here making is obviously an artificial one, since all the eschatological teaching of Jesus reflects this tension to a greater or lesser extent, and under (*a*) above we have discussed sayings which reflect it directly, e.g. the apocalyptic Son of Man sayings, the contrast-parables and Mark 14.62. But it is none the less a convenient division because in all the teaching we discussed above the emphasis is upon either the present or the future, whereas there are elements in the teaching of Jesus which reflect the tension between present and future without putting the emphasis upon either.

The first thing to be considered here is the use of the imagery of the Messianic Banquet which, as we noted earlier[1] is used both in connection with the present experience of the disciples and in connection with the future consummation. The references to the future consummation were discussed under (*a*) above, and it is clear that this imagery was so used by Jesus with a future reference. But in Mark 2.19a[2] the reference is certainly to the present experience of the

---

[1] See above, p. 183.

[2] Mark 2.19b–20 is secondary. Jeremias, *Parables*, p. 42 n. 82; Bultmann, *Tradition*, p. 96 (ET, p. 92).

disciples[1] and we have therefore to recognize that the experience of the blessings of God to which this imagery refers is a sphere in which the tension between present and future is manifest. The forgiveness of sins *is* and *will be* a matter of personal experience: the blessings of the end time *are* and are *to be* known.[2]

The second thing to be considered in this connection is the work of James M. Robinson on the formal structure of sayings of Jesus relating to the Kingdom.[3] He is able to show that the tension between present and future is directly evident in the formal structure of many sayings, and he makes the point that present and future are thereby directly and explicitly related to one another and have reference to the existential experience of the individual. We have nothing to add to this, we refer to it simply as a major point to be recognized in the teaching of Jesus: the tension between present and future is a matter of personal experience and this emphasis must be maintained in any exegesis of the eschatological teaching of Jesus.

Lastly, in this connection we must consider the Lord's Prayer, for this is a place at which the tension between present and future is most clearly seen and most directly related to experience of the individual.[4] Now the Lord's Prayer is obviously one of the most important sections of teaching that we possess, if it is not indeed *the* most important, and it is particularly relevant to our study in that it was taught to disciples of Jesus and must therefore be held to reflect those aspects of their experience which Jesus himself held to be most important, those things about which he taught them to pray.[5]

[1] Jeremias, *Parables*, p. 94.

[2] It would seem therefore that here we have reached a point of direct comparison between the preaching of Jesus and the proclamation of the kerygma; one that we may set beside the conclusions reached by the post-Bultmannians with regard to the relationship between Jesus' understanding of himself and the kerygma's understanding of him.

[3] Already reviewed above, pp. 123 f.

[4] In what follows we are indebted above all to J. Jeremias, 'The Lord's Prayer in Modern Research', *ExpT* 71, 1959–60, pp. 141–6, and also to E. Lohmeyer, *Das Vater-Unser*, ⁶1960; K. Stendahl, 'Introduction and Perspective' in *The Scrolls and the New Testament* (ed. Stendahl), 1957 (= *Scrolls*) pp. 1–17; K. G. Kuhn, 'Temptation, Sin and Flesh' in *Scrolls*, pp. 94–113; and P. Fiebig, *Jesu Bergpredigt*, 1924 (for texts of Jewish parallels).

[5] We do not feel a need to defend the authenticity of the Lord's Prayer as Jeremias reconstructs the probable original form. In view of the current Jewish practice in this regard it would have been most unusual if Jesus had not taught his disciples a prayer. The ease with which it can be translated back into Aramaic and its obvious Aramaisms (e.g. debt/sin = *ḥoba*) show that it has been well preserved in the tradition, which indeed we would expect with a prayer that would

The first thing to be noted about the teaching implicit in the Lord's Prayer is the address: the disciples are taught to address God as *abba*, father. Jeremias[1] has shown that this is a unique feature of Jesus' own practice, and that it is totally without parallel in first-century Judaism. The disciples are being taught to use the child's word of God, a practice specifically avoided by the Jews, and this can only be an indication of the new relationship with God which they enjoy as a result of their response to his kingly activity manifest in Jesus and his ministry. So at the beginning of the prayer we are face to face with a major point: proper response to the kingly activity of God results in a new relationship with him characterized by the privilege of addressing him as *abba* with all that that implies.[2] The same point is made negatively in the saying recorded at Mark 10.15 par.: 'Whoever does not receive the Kingdom of God like a child shall not enter it', and this must be described as a highly characteristic emphasis in the teaching of Jesus. We should note that Mark 10.15 par. most probably has a future reference,[3] whereas the *abba* of the Lord's Prayer certainly has a present reference; an indication of the characteristic tension between present and future in the teaching of Jesus. But the point implicit in both is the same: the experience of the Kingdom of God is the experience of new relationship with God; the manifestation of the kingly activity of God in history and human experience is to lead to this new relationship with God. This is to be enjoyed now (*abba*) and it will in some way be consummated in the future (Mark 10.15 par.).

The next thing to concern us in the Lord's Prayer is the petition: 'Thy Kingdom come'. In close connection with 'Hallowed be thy name' it parallels the Kaddish prayer: 'Magnified and sanctified be his great name in the world that he has created according to his

---

certainly be learnt by heart and carefully transmitted. The changes that have been introduced into the text are all readily understandable as liturgical expansions, and the two different settings in Luke and Matthew are readily explicable in terms of catechetical instruction in a predominantly Gentile and a predominantly Jewish-Christian community respectively (Jeremias). In view of all this the occasional scepticism about the Lord's Prayer that one meets (e.g. in the work of Grässer, above, p. 147) is not to be taken seriously.

[1] *ExpT* 71, p. 144.
[2] Cf. Paul in Rom. 8.15; Gal. 4.6. It would seem that this is another point to direct relationship between the preaching of Jesus and the proclamation of the kerygma, in this instance the Pauline interpretation of the kerygma.
[3] See above, pp. 183 f.

purpose. May he establish his Kingdom in your lifetime and in your days and in the lifetime of all the house of Israel, even speedily and at a near time', and so the petition is clearly eschatological.[1] But we must remember that those who are being taught to use this petition are those for whom the Kingdom is already a matter of personal experience. They are therefore either being taught to pray that others may share this experience; or, more probably, they are being taught to pray for the consummation of that which has begun within their experience. In this case we have here another example of this highly characteristic tension between present and future; caught up in this tension the disciples are to direct their prayer to the future in which it will be resolved. Later the early Church was to express this same understanding of the tension between present and future in its prayer 'Our Lord, come' (I Cor. 16.22); in the tension between the first and second coming of the Lord we have precisely the same eschatological orientation as in the case of the disciples, for whom the Kingdom has already come, being taught to pray 'Thy Kingdom come'.[2]

We turn now to the next petition: the prayer for 'daily' bread. Already a problem for Origen, who could find no equivalent for the adjective *epiousion* in the Greek literature known to him,[3] intensive discussion of this petition among modern scholars has produced two possible interpretations. The first is to interpret it as a prayer for the necessities of life: 'The disciples are God's servants, and what they ask is a sufficient provision from day to day to enable them to perform the tasks that God appoints them to do: enough today for tomorrow's duties.'[4] The second is to interpret it eschatologically; to understand it as referring to the 'bread of Life', i.e. to the gifts of the end time which for the disciples may be known here and now: 'Jesus gives to the children of God the privilege of stretching out their hands, to grasp the glory of the consummation, to fetch it down, to believe it down, to pray it down—right into their poor life; now already, here already, this day already.'[5]

Of these two possibilities the second is to be preferred. The first is after all no more than a version of something that was a common-

[1] So already Weiss and Dalman, above, pp. 19, 26.

[2] Another parallel, and a very important one, between the message of Jesus and the understanding of the early Church.

[3] Origen, *De Orat.* 27.15, quoted by J. M. Creed, *The Gospel According to St Luke*, 1950, p. 157.

[4] T. W. Manson, *Sayings*, p. 169.

[5] Jeremias, *ExpT* 71, p. 145.

place of Jewish piety, the trust in God for one's daily needs,[1] and if it were to be accepted here then we would have the sudden interjection of this commonplace in a prayer that is otherwise wholly eschatological. Again we have the fact that Jerome found in the Gospel according to the Hebrews the Aramaic *mahar* which clearly has an eschatological reference.[2] Finally, the imagery of the Messianic Banquet in the teaching of Jesus makes it natural to understand 'bread of the morrow, that is, of the future' in terms of participation in the blessings symbolized by the Messianic Banquet. So this petition also exhibits the characteristic tension between present and future and this time the reference is to those End-time blessings of God that are already known in the experience of the disciples. They are being taught to pray for a continuing experience of those things that have become theirs in their eschatological fellowship with one another and with Jesus. They know them 'here already, now already' (Jeremias) as they will know them fully at the consummation.

Supreme among the blessings of the End time was the forgiveness of sins,[3] and so the Lord's Prayer moves naturally from the general to the specific: 'Forgive us our sins, as we ourselves forgive everyone who is indebted to us', i.e. 'who has sinned against us'. The forgiveness of sins was the basis upon which those who responded to the challenge of God's eschatological forgiveness in the ministry of Jesus entered into the fellowship of his disciples. But here again the tension between present and future is maintained. The disciples may not rest content with the initial forgiveness of sins, real though their experience of this forgiveness was, and valid though it was as the foundation-stone of their new relationship with God. No: in the tension of their relationship with God between the Now of their first response and the Then of the consummation the forgiveness of sins is a continuing experience and must find a continual place in their prayers.

The second part of this petition, 'as we ourselves forgive everyone who has sinned against us', is, in fact, the really unique thing in the Lord's Prayer and as such deserves very special attention. Together

---

[1] Examples in Billerbeck, *Kommentar* I, pp. 420 f.

[2] Jerome, *Commentary on Matthew* I 7, on Matt. 6.11 (PL 26.43): 'In the Gospel called according to the Hebrews, for "substantial bread" I found "mahar", which means "of the morrow"; so that the sense is: our bread of the morrow, that is, of the future, give us today.' Jeremias, *ExpT* 71, p. 145, points out that in later Judaism *mahar* means not only the next day but also the future, the final consummation.

[3] See above, p. 75.

with the address *abba* it is that in Jesus' prayer which has absolutely
no parallel in Jewish prayers of the period. The remainder of the
prayer does have some kind of parallel in these prayers,[1] even though
the differences are also marked: the freshness, directness and brevity
of the prayer of Jesus[2] and its characteristic eschatological tension
between present and future are not to be found in the Jewish prayers.
But the 'as we ourselves forgive everyone who has sinned against us',
like the *abba*, has no such parallel. The nearest thing to this in
Judaism is in Ecclus 28.2 'Forgive thy neighbour the injury (done to
thee), and then, when thou prayest, thy sin will be forgiven', but
although this thought lived on in rabbinic Judaism[3] it found no place
in Jewish prayers for forgiveness. Characteristic of these is the sixth of
the 'Eighteen Benedictions':[4] 'Forgive us, our Father, for we have
sinned against thee; wipe away our transgressions from before thine
eyes. Blessed art thou, O Lord, who dost abundantly forgive.'
Indeed Abrahams, a Jewish scholar, can and does contrast the
'unconditional' forgiveness of the Jewish prayers with the 'conditional' forgiveness of the Lord's Prayer.[5] It is not surprising therefore
that in the catechetical instruction for Jewish-Christian converts
represented in Matthew 6 the Lord's Prayer is followed by a saying
current in the synoptic tradition which calls special attention to this
petition and its meaning: 'For if you forgive men their trespasses,
your heavenly Father will also forgive you.' (Matt. 6.14 cf. Mark
11.25). So we have here a most important new element in the
teaching of Jesus, and one that we must consider carefully.

We begin this consideration by noting that the verb in Matt.
6.12b is an aorist (*aphēkamen*) in contrast to Luke's present
(*aphiomen*).[6] It has been argued by Jeremias that this is an Aramaism,
representing the Aramaic perfect which should be translated as a
present since it indicates an action which takes place here and now:

---

[1] I. Abrahams, *Studies in Pharisaism and the Gospels* (= *Studies*) II, 1924, pp. 98 ff.
[2] The best example of this is the 'Hallowed be thy name, Thy Kingdom come'
of the Lord's Prayer as compared with the Kaddish parallel given above, pp. 192 f.
[3] Billerbeck, *Kommentar* I, pp. 424 ff.
[4] Translating the text printed in Fiebig, *Jesu Bergpredigt II*, p. 51.
[5] Abrahams, *Studies* II, pp. 95 ff.
[6] The present (*aphiemen*, an orthographic variant of *aphiomen*) is read by the
textus receptus in Matt. 6.12b, and is also to be found in some ancient manuscripts
(either as *aphiemen* or *aphiomen*). Certainly this present is an ancient variant in the
text here, since Origen knows both the perfect and the present readings. Modern
critical texts are unanimous in preferring the perfect: Tischendorf, von Soden,
Nestle, Merk, Souter and Kilpatrick all read it, and both the RSV and the NEB
represent it in translation.

'Thus the correct translation would be "as we herewith forgive our debtors".'[1] This would seem to be a strong argument, since the Aramaic *perfectum praesens* would explain the *aphēkamen/aphiomen* variant in the textual tradition.

Reading this petition then in the light of the Aramaic perfect, in the 'as we herewith forgive' we have a striking link between the disciple's reception of God's forgiveness and his own willingness to forgive; a link reinforced by the saying Matt. 6.14 cf. Mark 11.25 and quite without parallel in the Jewish prayers of the period. In the teaching of Jesus the willingness to forgive is, as Jeremias puts it,[2] 'the outstretched hand, by which we grasp God's forgiveness': this is a new note; and it is a note paralleled in importance only by the *abba* of address to God in this prayer. Indeed, these two can be brought together as key elements in the teaching of Jesus, and not least in the eschatological teaching, for the *abba* expresses the new relationship with God which ensues on the basis of the Kingdom proclamation of Jesus and the disciples' response to it, as we argued above, and the 'conditional' element in the prayer for forgiveness indicates the essential nature of this response and is therefore the key to the understanding of the relationship between eschatology and ethics in the teaching of Jesus, as we shall argue below. For the moment, however, let us content ourselves with noting the obvious relationship of this whole petition to the experience of the disciples, and the fact that this petition, like all the others in this prayer, is set in the context of the eschatological tension between the Now of the ministry of Jesus—or the first experience by the disciple of the forgiveness offered to him in that ministry—and the Then of the consummation.

The last petition of the Prayer, 'Lead us not into temptation', presents two problems to the exegete: the meaning of 'lead us not', and the reference in 'temptation'. Here there are two ancient Jewish prayers to help us: the Eighteen Benedictions, and the evening prayer in b. Berakhoth 6ob. The sixth and seventh of the Eighteen Benedictions are as follows:[3]

> Forgive us, our Father, for we have sinned against thee;
> Wipe away our transgressions from before thine eyes . . .
> Look thou upon our afflictions, and strive in our strivings;
> Redeem us for thy name's sake. . . .

[1] *ExpT* 71, p. 146.
[2] *Ibid.*
[3] Again translating the text printed in Fiebig, *Jesu Bergpredigt II*, p. 51.

The evening prayer is as follows:[1]

> Do not let me come (causative of the verb 'to
> come') into the hand of sin,
> Nor into the hand of temptation,
> Nor into the hand of shame.

From the first of these prayers we can see that the contemporaries of Jesus[2] moved naturally in prayer from a prayer for forgiveness to a prayer for the help of God in their daily experience, and it is only natural to assume that the prayer of Jesus moves similarly from forgiveness to the idea of God's 'striving in our strivings'. The second offers us help with regard to the 'lead us not into temptation', for there is general agreement that this must reflect a Semitic causative tense which is to be understood as having permissive force, and here we have an example of this from a prayer which Jesus may well have known.[3] So the prayer of Jesus is to be understood as a prayer for the continual help of God in our personal experience: may he so strive in our strivings that we may not be permitted to come into the hand of (i.e. under the power of) 'temptation'.

The concept of 'temptation' in the New Testament has been carefully examined by K. G. Kuhn in his essay, 'Temptation, Sin and Flesh', in *The Scrolls and the New Testament*.[4] He shows that *peirasmos*[5] always comes about through Satan in the New Testament conception, and that the conception is of the believer being constantly subjected to the attacks of Satan as he lives in the world.[6] Now in this respect the New Testament is parallel to the Qumran texts, for these texts exhibit exactly the same dualism and exactly the same concept of the member of the sect being subject to the *peirasmoi* of Satan.[7] In the Qumran texts there is the expectation that this situation will be sharpened as the eschatological war begins: 'It will be a time of *peirasmos* for the people redeemed of God, but, unlike all their

---

[1] Translating the text of the Venice edition printed in Fiebig, *op. cit.*, p. 54.

[2] That the Eighteen Benedictions is the most important of the Jewish prayers, and that it goes back to the first century, is generally accepted. Kuhn, *Achtzehngebet und Vaterunser und der Reim*, 1950, p. 10.

[3] Jeremias, *ExpT* 71, p. 146.

[4] See p. 191 n. 4.

[5] It is impossible to find one English word that can represent the range of meaning in the Greek word *peirasmos*: temptation—trial—tribulation—test. From this point then we will follow the example of Kuhn's essay and use *peirasmos*, rather than the inevitably misleading 'temptation'.

[6] Kuhn, *Scrolls*, p. 100.

[7] 1QS 1.17 ff.; 3.22–25; 4.16–19. Kuhn, *Scrolls*, p. 100.

previous *peirasmoi*, this one will come to a speedy end in a redemption that will last forever' (1QM 1.12). Indeed, in these texts one cannot distinguish between the present *peirasmos* being experienced by the member of the sect and that expected of the eschatological future. Conscious that they are the eschatological people of God their thought moves naturally from the one to the other.[1]

We have argued already that the teaching of Jesus reflects a holy war theology like that of the Qumran texts, with the essential difference that in the ministry of Jesus the eschatological conflict has already begun in human experience.[2] So it is natural, and indeed essential, to recognize that the last petition of the Lord's Prayer has reference to the eschatological conflict. The *peirasmos* here is the attack of Satan in this eschatological conflict, as it is in Mark 14.38 and Rev. 3.10.[3] What is envisaged is, as in Matt. 12.28 par., the experience of the individual as the arena of the eschatological conflict,[4] and the petition is therefore that God may intervene in the disciples' conflict-experience that the conflict may constantly and ever be resolved in victory for the man of God's lot, to paraphrase a favourite Qumran expression. The disciple is caught up in the eschatological conflict-situation, his experience becomes part of the total war between God and Satan; but in this experience he is not left to fight alone, God will 'strive in his strivings' that he may not find himself to have come into the power of the *peirasmos*, to have succumbed to the attack of Satan. Here again we must note the characteristic tension between present and future; the *peirasmoi* of the individual disciple are part of the eschatological struggle, but not yet its climax; the victories gained are real victories, but not yet the final victory.

We are now in a position to draw together some of the points we have made in this discussion of the tension between present and future in the teaching of Jesus concerning the Kingdom of God. We have argued that it is a tension between that which began as God manifested himself as King in the ministry of Jesus, and that which he will consummate in a manner and at a time of his choosing. But the teaching of Jesus gives us no guidance as to this manner and this time; rather it directs attention to what will be involved in the

[1] See above, p. 174, and Kuhn, *Scrolls*, p. 110.
[2] See p. 171, above, in connection with an exegesis of Matt. 12.28 par. Kuhn makes a similar point, *Scrolls*, p. 111.
[3] Kuhn, *Scrolls*, pp. 94 f., 111.
[4] See above, p. 171.

consummation: judgment, the vindication of Jesus himself, the establishment of the values of God, and the enjoyment of all the blessings to be associated with a perfect relationship with God. Far from discussing the manner and time of the consummation in the way so popular in Jewish apocalyptic—and in Mark 13 and its parallels—the teaching of Jesus seems to be concerned much more with the consummation as a certainty of future human experience, as it is concerned also with the present manifestation of the Kingdom in human experience. So the tension between present and future is a tension, above all, within human experience, and this is most evident in the Lord's Prayer. This prayer begins by celebrating the new relationship with God now enjoyed by the disciple as a result of God's kingly activity in his history and his experience, and goes on to concern itself with the key elements making up the totality of a believing existence within this eschatological and experiential tension between present and future: the kingly activity of God which will continue until it reaches its climax in the consummation; the eschatological blessings of God known and to be known; the forgiveness of sins which is supreme among these blessings and which is continually to be experienced ever more deeply as the disciple responds in terms of readiness to forgive; and the eschatological conflict into which the disciple is now caught up and in which he must now play a part. How, when and where this tension will be resolved we cannot say, and the silence of the teaching of Jesus on this point is surely significant. Our concern must not be with the resolving of this tension but with what it itself means to us, and what we must do and look for within it. This last note of 'what we must do within it' brings us naturally to the final point to be discussed in this work: the relationship between eschatology and ethics. But before we move on to that we must say a word about Mark 1.15: 'The time is fulfilled, and the Kingdom of God is at hand: Repent, and believe in the Good News.'

This is an extraordinarily difficult saying to fit into an interpretation of the eschatology of Jesus. It does not belong to that aspect of the teaching of Jesus in which the Kingdom is present, Dodd's attempt to interpret it in such a way as to make it agree with Matt. 12.28 par. having failed.[1] At the same time it does not belong to that aspect of the teaching in which the Kingdom is future. We have seen that the future Kingdom is the consummation of that which has

[1] See above, pp. 64 ff.

begun in the ministry of Jesus and in the experience of his disciples, but Mark 1.15 is set before the ministry of Jesus begins. Now this is not a particularly valid point in itself because the placing of the saying is an editorial matter, but it becomes an important point when we recognize that Mark 1.15 itself plainly refers to the imminence of something that has not yet come and therefore cannot be reconciled with the teaching concerning the consummation of that which has begun. So this saying does not belong either to the teaching of the Kingdom as present or to that of the Kingdom as future; where then does it belong? Well, if it is an authentic saying it must belong prior to both of these elements, and be interpreted therefore as referring to the imminence of that moment when the Kingdom shall be manifest in Jesus and his hearers respond to this. In this case we have three elements in the teaching of Jesus concerning the King-dom: imminent in Mark 1.15; present in, e.g., Matt. 12.28 par.; and future, e.g. in Matt. 6.10 par. If this is indeed the case then Mark 1.15 has been properly set at the beginning of the ministry of Jesus, and Matt. 10.7 (cf. Luke 9.2) equally properly at the beginning of the ministry of the disciples; the sayings announce the imminence of that which will come in those ministries and which God will consummate in his own way and time. But such an interpretation requires the assumption that the tradition has preserved such a sophisticated distinction between the sayings, which in itself is highly unlikely. Far more probable is the assumption that Mark 1.15 and Matt. 10.7 have in fact been produced in the tradition as summaries of the message of Jesus, as Luke 9.2 is clearly a traditional summary (cf. Luke 8.1; Acts 8.12). Indeed, Mark 1.15 can be shown to be a traditional summary, using terms taken from the teaching of Jesus but reflecting early Christian theological conceptions, by the follow-ing arguments. (i) 'The time is fulfilled' is strikingly reminiscent of Gal. 4.4; Eph. 1.9 f., and of the interpretation of the Gospel story by the evangelists, especially Matthew. (ii) Although 'Kingdom of God' and 'repent' are certainly terms used by Jesus, 'believe in the Good News' is equally certainly characteristic of the early Church[1] and to 'repent and believe in the Good News' is the characteristic climax to

---

[1] To believe in (en) occurs elsewhere in the NT only in the B text of John 3.15, but the verb with epi or eis (variants at John 3.15), is the characteristic early Christian formulation for faith in Christ or God. 'Good News' is from the vocabu-lary of the early Church (Mark 1.1!), it is almost certainly a Pauline formulation for the saving message concerning Jesus, and 'to believe in the Good News' is the beginning of Christian faith as Paul understands it: Rom. 10.14.

the apostolic kerygma, Acts 11.17 f.; 20.21. Mark 1.15 is therefore a summary of the message of Jesus formulated in the tradition and as such cannot be held to affect an interpretation of the teaching of the historical Jesus.

3. *The Relationship between Eschatology and Ethics in the Teaching of Jesus*

The preceding discussion will have made it clear that we believe that the eschatological teaching of Jesus is concerned above all with the experience of the individual who responds to the challenge of the kingly activity of God in his ministry, and that the ethical teaching is therefore concerned with what the individual must do as he is then caught up in the eschatological tension between present and future. Our argument is that the ultimate purpose of the intervention of God in history and human experience is to make it possible for man to enter into a new and perfect relationship with himself, and that the ethical teaching is designed to illustrate the kind of response which man must make in order to enter into this relationship. We propose now to argue this point in three ways: (*a*) from the teaching contained in the Lord's Prayer; (*b*) by reference to recent work by Professor Jeremias on the meaning of the Sermon on the Mount; (*c*) through a consideration of the biblical concept of Law.

A. *The teaching contained in the Lord's Prayer*

In the discussion of the Lord's Prayer immediately above it was pointed out that there are two things in this prayer that have no parallels in the prayers of first century Judaism: the address to God as *abba*, and the 'condition' added to the petition for forgiveness: 'as we ourselves herewith forgive those who have sinned against us'. We need now only reiterate what was said above concerning these two supremely important elements in the prayer: the former indicates the new relationship with God which proper response to the Kingdom proclamation of Jesus makes possible; the latter indicates the kind of response that is called for in the case of the central aspect of the Kingdom proclamation, the forgiveness of sins. Since this proclamation is eschatological, and since the command to forgive is certainly ethical, then we are here face to face with the relationship between eschatology and ethics in the teaching of Jesus: the ethical teaching is designed to illustrate the kind of response that must be made to the eschatological teaching in order that man may enter even more fully into that which is offered to him as God manifests himself as King in the ministry of Jesus.

The Lord's Prayer, being necessarily brief, restricts itself to the central aspect of forgiveness of sins, but that the same kind of proclamation-response pattern underlies the whole ethical teaching of Jesus has been argued by Professor Jeremias in his work on the Sermon on the Mount.

B. *Professor Jeremias on the Sermon on the Mount*

In his short but extremely important work *Die Bergpredigt*,[1] Jeremias approaches the question of the meaning of the Sermon on the Mount, reviewing and rejecting in turn: the *perfectionist conception*, that Jesus gave simple commandments and expected his disciples to keep them; the *theory of the impossible ideal*, that the commandments are given to drive men to despair and so to open their eyes to the wonder and mercy of God, the idea of an *Interimsethik*, that the ethical teaching indicates the kind of repentance demanded in the brief interim period between the ministry of Jesus and the coming of the Kingdom.[2] Against these Jeremias sets out his own understanding of the Sermon, which he develops by means of characteristically careful and thorough arguments: in its present form it represents early Christian catechetical instruction and as such it was preceded by the proclamation of the Gospel, it was preceded by conversion. But what is true of the Sermon as a whole is true also of the individual sayings out of which it has been constructed; to understand them we must presuppose that they were preceded by something else: by the proclamation of the Kingdom of God and the new relationship with God which this makes possible for the disciples. Jeremias demonstrates this through five examples: Matt. 5.14, 'You are the light of the world', which presupposes that the disciples had found in Jesus 'the light of the world'; Matt. 6.15, 'If you do not forgive men their trespasses, neither can your heavenly Father forgive your trespasses', which must be read in the light of the conclusion of the parable of the unmerciful servant: 'So also your heavenly Father will do to every one of you, if you do not forgive your brother from your heart' (Matt. 18.35), and which therefore presupposes the great debt-cancellation of which the parable speaks; Matt. 5.32 f., the saying on

---

[1] J. Jeremias, *Die Bergpredigt* (Calver Hefte 27), 1959 (ET by the present writer, *The Sermon on the Mount*, 1961).

[2] The theory of Weiss and Schweitzer. See above pp. 22 f., 30.

divorce, which presupposes the proclamation that the time of the law has run out because the time of salvation is beginning and the pure paradise-will of God is now valid (Mark 10.2–12); Matt. 5.44 f., the command to love one's enemies which presupposes the dynamic of the boundless goodness of God; and Matt. 5.38 f., the turning of the other cheek, which refers not to insults in general but to formal persecution of the followers of Jesus as heretics, and which refers to Isa. 50.6, and therefore puts the disciples in the prophetic succession, i.e. it presupposes their acceptance of responsibility in proclaiming the Kingdom of God. In these sayings we can see specific instances of that which is true of all the sayings of Jesus in the Sermon: they presuppose Jesus' proclamation of the Kingdom and the disciples' acceptance of this. They are therefore given as examples of a 'lived faith'; the gift of God clearly precedes the demands of God.

We may argue then that the ethical teaching of Jesus presupposes the proclamation of the Kingdom as present in his ministry and is designed to guide men in their response to this; it is designed to guide them to that response by means of which they appropriate to themselves that which is offered to them in this proclamation. Since the Kingdom is ultimately to be related to human experience, then the ethical teaching illustrates the response by means of which men enter ever more fully into this experience. Here again we must pay careful attention to the characteristic tension between present and future and recognize once more that this is a personal tension. But now we may add to this the recognition that the personal tension is not only between present and future but also between partial and complete, between beginning and consummation. In the case of the forgiveness of sins, for example, men must respond in terms of forgiveness to others as they move from the first experience of forgiveness towards the perfect sacral relationship with God in the 'temple not made with hands'. Or in the case of the law of love, men must respond in terms of loving one another, including their enemies, as they move from the initial impact of the love of God in their experience towards the perfect fellowship of love 'sitting at table with Abraham, Isaac and Jacob in the Kingdom of God'. In both of these cases, and in all others that could be mentioned, the initial impulse derives from the impact of what God is doing in human experience and the response to this is the dynamic by means of which men move from the beginning towards the consummation. So the eschatology does not stand at the beginning only, as the basis upon which men

must build that better things may be, as would be the case with a
purely realized eschatology; nor does it stand at the end only, as the
end for which men must strenuously prepare themselves as best they
may, as would be the case with a wholly futuristic eschatology and an
interim ethic. Rather eschatology stands both at the beginning and
the end, as the determining dimension of men's existence as believers,
as men who respond to the challenge of the message of Jesus concerning the Kingdom of God; and the ethical teaching indicates the
nature of that dynamic response by means of which men move from
the beginning towards the end.[1]

c. *The biblical concept of Law*

At this point we do not propose to offer any research of our own, so
far as the Old Testament is concerned, but to rely once more upon
the scholar to whose work on Old Testament theology we are greatly
indebted: Gerhard von Rad.

According to von Rad[2] there is already to be found in the Old
Testament something that is, at any rate in form, analagous to what
the New Testament calls Gospel. There is to be found in the Old
Testament a proclamation of the salvation activity of God on behalf
of his people, and far from being in opposition to this the Old Testament Law, properly understood, is essentially a response to it.

Von Rad argues that from the time of entry into Canaan there
was a covenant renewal festival at Shechem in which the *Heilsgeschichte*—the history of God's salvation activity on behalf of his
people—was recited, and that this recitation was followed by a
proclamation of the commandments. The people were faced with a
decision, not as to whether or not they were going to keep the
commandments but as to whether or not they were going to accept
God's salvation activity on their behalf. If they accepted this then they
responded to it by accepting the commandments, the purpose of
which was to further the relationship with God which his salvation
activity on their behalf had made possible. The commandments, so
to speak, put the Israelite in a position to experience further salvation
gifts of God to him.

According to this understanding the Old Testament has at its

---

[1] We do not mean to imply, of course, that the consummation is dependent
upon, or is brought about by, the response of man. Both initial impact and final
consummation are wholly the work of God, as the Kingdom is wholly his activity.
[2] We are now following especially von Rad, *Theologie* II, pp. 402–24.

heart not a law to be fulfilled in order that men may achieve righteousness in the sight of God, but a gospel to which men respond and by responding enter into a dynamic relationship with God their redeemer; this dynamic relationship is 'life' (Deut. 30.15, 19).

A significant element in this understanding of Old Testament Law is the insight that the twin constituent elements of saving activity of God and response of the people are capable of development in accordance with changing circumstances and experience. Von Rad illustrates this point in detail,[1] but we will restrict ourselves to the major change introduced by the prophets.

The prophets proclaim the fact that the people have not kept the Law and that they are therefore under judgment. It is important to note however that the prophets do not reproach the people with having failed to keep the Law in the sense that they have failed to fulfil individual moral commandments. They reproach the people with having failed to respond in the right manner to God's saving will and saving activity on their behalf, e.g. Isa. 1.2–4; the people are under judgment for not having responded as they should to the saving guidance and saving activity of God, e.g. Isa. 28.22. But this judgment will not be the end: the prophets proclaim not only judgment but also an eschatological salvation; the coming of a new and decisive epoch in the *Heilsgeschichte*, a saving activity of God that will make possible a new and this time perfect response which will lead to a new and perfect relationship with God, Jer. 31.33; Ezek. 37.1–6.

Von Rad's point that the conceptions of the salvation activity of God and the response of man could develop can now be further illustrated from the Qumran texts.

1QS 1.18b–2.18 is from the Qumran covenant renewal ceremony and reads in part as follows:

'When they enter into the covenant the priests and the levites bless the God of salvation and all the works of his truth, and all those entering into the covenant say: Amen, Amen. Then the priests enumerate God's righteous deeds together with all his wonderful works, and recount all the merciful acts of grace towards Israel (i.e. they recite the *Heilsgeschichte*). Then the levites enumerate the sins of the children of Israel and all their guilty transgressions and their iniquities under the dominion of Belial.' There follows a general confession and then '. . . . but his loving mercy he has bestowed

[1] *Theologie* II, pp. 406 ff.

upon us from eternity to eternity. And the priests bless all the men of God's lot who walk perfectly in all his ways . . . And then the levites curse all the men of Belial's lot. . . .'

Here we have the classic pattern of proclamation, and response to proclamation, somewhat affected by the characteristic Qumran dualism.

An important point about this covenant renewal ceremony is that the covenant which is regularly renewed in this manner is a 'temporary' covenant: it is valid only so long as Belial shall hold sway. 1QS 2.19: 'Thus they shall do year after year all the days of the dominion of Belial.' We pointed out above[1] that in 1Q34 ii 2.5-8 we have a reference to what will be after Belial has been destroyed. This destruction of Belial will be the eschatological saving activity of God on behalf of his people, the 'show of glory' and 'works of God's right hand' which will lead to a new response, the 'instructions of glory and the heights of eternity'.

So Qumran offers us evidence of the fact that the classic Old Testament conception of Law as response to the saving activity of God by means of which man entered into a relationship with God was current among the contemporaries of Jesus, although mixed with a more 'legalistic' understanding (e.g. CD 3.12–21). Indeed the persistence of this basic Old Testament emphasis is the reason why the Law always remained a joy and a privilege and never a burden, even to the rabbis with their developed 'legalism'. The contemporaries of Jesus could and did look forward to a new and decisive (eschatological) epoch of the *Heilsgeschichte*, and to a new response to this by means of which they would enter into the perfect relationship with God that this would make possible. It is precisely the claim of the teaching of Jesus that this is happening in his ministry; the Kingdom is now present as God manifests his kingly activity, and the new necessary response to this is constantly being illustrated in the ethical teaching that is the eschatological Torah.[2] For this reason Jesus sets his own understanding of the will of God over against the Law of Moses (the antitheses of the Sermon on the Mount) and ventures to declare the paradise-will of God now valid (Mark 10.6 ff.).

[1] Pp. 77 f.
[2] See above, pp. 76–78.

INDEX OF NAMES

INDEX OF REFERENCES

OLD TESTAMENT

QUMRAN TEXTS

NEW TESTAMENT

NEW TESTAMENT APOCRYPHA